LAW IN SPORT
AND PHYSICAL ACTIVITY

Annie Clement, Ph.D., J.D.
Cleveland State University

WCB Brown & Benchmark

Copyright © 1988, by Benchmark Press, Inc.

Library of Congress Cataloging in Publication Data:

CLEMENT, ANNIE 1937-

LAW IN SPORT AND PHYSICAL ACTIVITY

Cover Design: Gary Schmitt

Copy Editor: Lynn Hendershot

Library of Congress Catalog Card number: 87-70299

ISBN: 0-697-14803-3

Printed in the United States of America

10 9 8 7 6 5 4

Contents

Preface... 1

1. The Role of Law In Sport and Physical Activity...................... 3
   Legal Literacy 6
   References 6

2. The Legal System 7
   Sources of Law 7
   Creation of Law.. 8
   The Courts 10
      Federal Courts.. 11
      State Courts 13
   The Legal System: A Changing System 14
      Immunity Statutes.. 15
   Summary 17
   References 18

3. Research Skills for The Study of Law 19
   Law Libraries 19
      Case law 20
      Statutes or Codes 20
      Annotated Reports.. 20
      Legislative History Reports 20
      Administrative Materials 21
      Periodicals 21
   Case Analysis.. 21
      Title 22
      Facts 22
      Issue 24
      Decision or Holding 24
      Reasoning of the Court.. 24
      Importance of Decision 25
      Decree 26
   Summary 26
   References 26

4. Negligence in Physical Activity 27
A Legal Duty of Care 27
Breach of the Legal Duty of Care 29
Breach of the Legal Duty as Proximate Cause of Injury 30
Substantial Damage 30
Degrees of Negligence.. 30
    Negligence 31
    Gross Negligence 31
    Wilful, Wanton and Reckless Misconduct 31
Defenses 31
    Contributory Negligence... 32
    Comparative Negligence 32
    Assumption of Risk 33
Remedies and Damages... 37
Summary 37
References 38

5. Case Analysis in Negligence 39
Educational Malpractice or Faulty Teaching 39
    Early Malpractice Case... 40
    Contemporary Malpractice Cases 41
    Standards for Negligence Influence Malpractice Decisions 45
    Teacher Becomes Class or Team Member 46
    Participation in Pain 47
Failure to Supervise 47
    Play Within Established Rules and Matched Teams 48
    Use of Safety Equipment 49
    Role of Teacher in Extracurricular Activities 50
    Accidents Involving Crossing of Streets 52
    Supervision of Students Excused From Participation 52
Cases in General... 53
Faulty Equipment 54
Duty of Care of Property Owners 56
    Invitee 57
    Licensee.. 57
    Trespasser.. 57
Cases Involving Facilities in General 58
Summary 61
References 61

6. Intentional Torts 63
Intentional Torts to Persons 63
    Battery 64

Assault 67
False Imprisonment 67
Reckless Misconduct 68
Intentional Torts to Property 71
Fraud, Deceit and Misrepresentation 71
Damages 73
Defenses to Intentional Torts..................................... 73
Consent 73
Self-Defense and Defense of Others 74
Necessity 74
Discipline 74
Summary 75
References 76

7. **Product Liability** **77**
Negligence in Product Liability.................................... 78
Breach of Warranty... 81
Express Warranty 81
Implied Warranty: Merchantability and Fitness 82
Case Analysis of Breach of Warranty 83
Disclaimers 84
Strict Liability in Tort 84
Manufacturing Defects 84
Design 85
Instructions and Warnings 85
Defenses 87
Damages 89
Summary 89
References 90

8. **Strict Liability in Physical Activity**............................. **91**
Defamation 91
Status of Person as A Factor in Defamation 92
Defenses and Damages in Defamation 93
Cases in Defamation 93
Employer-Employee and Vicarious Liability 94
Independent Contractor 95
Test to Determine Difference Between Principal-Agent
    and Independent Contractor................................... 96
Worker's Compensation Statutes 99
Cases Under Master-Servant and Worker's Compensation 101
Summary 102
References 103

9. **First and Fourth Amendments to The Constitution** **105**
    First Amendment 106
        Freedom of Speech 107
        Freedom of the Press 118
        Invasion of Privacy 119
    Fourth Amendment 120
        System for Searching 120
        Student Complaints 122
        Drug Screening 125
    Summary 128
    References 128

10. **Fourteenth Amendment to the Constitution** **131**
    Equal Protection 132
    Substantive Due Process 134
    Procedural Due Process 134
    Title IX of The Education Amendments of 1972 135
    Fourteenth Amendment Equal Protection Cases in Athletics ... 136
        Females Requesting Membership on Male Teams 137
        Males Seeking Membership on Female Teams 141
        Females Requesting Equal Financial Aid and Support
            for Separate Teams 142
    Title IX Cases 144
    Equal Protection in Grade Standards 150
    Due Process Cases 150
    Summary 153
    References 153

11. **Contracts** **155**
    Agreements 155
    Breach of Contract 156
    Written Agreements 156
    Cases in Contract 158
        Employment Agreements at School Level 158
        Employment Agreements at the Collegiate Level 161
    Summary 162
    References 162

12. **Handicapped Legislation** **163**
    Section 504 and Public Law 94-142 165
    Free Appropriate Public Education 166
        Related Services 167
    Cases in Handicap Sports Participation 168

Summary 171
References 171

13. Risk Management **173**
   Identification 174
      Facilities 175
      Equipment... 176
      Assessment 177
      Content and Progression of Activity 177
      Officiating 178
      Supervision 178
      Waivers 178
      Emergency-Accident Procedure............................. 180
      Securing Rights of Participants 180
      Personnel... 181
      Fiscal and Contract 181
   System Audit.. 182
   Evaluation 183
   Control 184
      Avoiding or Eliminating the Program or Activity 184
      Accepting the Risk and Agreeing to Assume
        the Responsibility 185
      Transferring the Risk Through Either Insurance or Contract .. 185
      Changing Activity to Reduce Potential Injury 186
   Summary 187
   References 188

Appendix A **189**

Glossary **207**

Index of Cases **211**

Index... **213**

Preface

Law in Sport and Physical Activity is designed to meet the needs of the teacher preparing an introductory course in law and physical activity, at either the undergraduate or graduate level. Sufficient materials are provided to enable the teacher to use the book with or without the use of a law library. However, the use of a law library is encouraged. Law libraries can be located in law schools and in local county courthouses. Resources adequate to guide the graduate student to research also are provided. *Law in Sport and Physical Activity* is an equally suitable handbook for use by teachers, coaches, principals, owners and supervisors of spas, corporate fitness personnel and private consultants in aerobics and other sports.

This book contains a discussion of those legal elements of greatest concern to the specialists in sport and physical activity. Cases used in the text have been selected because of their illustration of specific points or because of their recognized importance in the legal or sport field. No effort has been made to be comprehensive or to report the most recent cases. Sections of the book contain significantly more case examples than other sections as a result of the quantity of litigation existing in some areas.

1

The Role Of Law In Sport And Physical Activity

Professionals engaged in the administration, supervision and teaching of physical activity as sport, athletics, recreation, physical education or fitness have, over the past few years, become increasingly concerned about the possibility of being named in a law suit. Connors (1981) and Appenzeller (1978) note that coaches and physical educators are the persons most often sued in the educational setting. Connors, in *Educational Tort and Malpractice,*

> estimates that one-third of the suits brought against educators are settled out of court in the U.S., because the teachers were so obviously negligent that the insurance companies involved did not want to face juries. I also estimate that approximately one-third of the suits brought against educators are routinely dismissed by trial judges as being trivial, because the teachers were obviously not negligent. That leaves about 33% of the suits resulting in jury trials where the issue of negligence is real. Of that number, about one-half are appealed. There are between 200 and 500 appealed cases reported every year; this means that there are probably between 1,200 and 3,000 suits brought against teachers or administrators every year. (1981, ix)

Although most cases are settled at some point in the procedural process, professionals involved in a suit usually are required to prepare documents as though they might go to court.

As people choose to increase the amount of time they dedicate to physical activity, participate in risk events and strive for superior athletic achievement, injuries will occur. When they do, some will be severe. Personal standards for sport achievement have soared. The person who was once pleased to negotiate an intermediate downhill ski run now expects to be a racing contender. The individual who spent a few evenings a week doing sit-ups while watching the evening news is now engaged in intense aerobic dance workouts three nights a week.

This increased and more intense participation will contribute to an increase in the number of accidents and injuries. As the number of injuries increases, victims look to some one other than themselves to blame. When the extent of the injury is such that medical assistance and rehabilitation expenses become prohibitive, victims also will look to some one else to share the expense.

Today many more people are willing to take substantial risks in physical activity. When injured, these risk takers are less inclined to assume either personal or monetary responsibility for their injuries. Medical science has learned to save many of these seriously injured victims, but only at great financial expense. A law suit serves to determine who is responsible and who, in turn, has the financial obligation for the expenses resulting from the injuries. No person is exempt from a law suit. The administrator, supervisor and teacher of physical activity should anticipate that they could be held responsible for a student's or client's injury.

Physical activity is a risk profession. It provides one of the few environments in which people can experience risks in a controlled setting. School physical education classes provide a system where young people test themselves in a risk taking manner. Students acquire confidence as they take risks, succeed, and then try a more difficult task. As in all other endeavors, most people succeed; but, some people fail.

A student fails English and receives an "F". A student who fails to move across a balance beam could fall and break an ankle. Failure in physical education can mean an injury. If the injury is serious, the student may look to the teacher, the school and the school's insurance carriers for responsibility.

Professionals need to communicate to participants that certain activities involve risk. At the same time, these professionals should control the environment so only those risks inherent in the activity remain. Activities such as diving, vaulting, skiing, skating and dance involve a high level of cognitive understanding of how one's body will react under certain conditions. Performers capable of focused concentration and who possess competent skills in balance and timing are not necessarily at risk in all activities. Performers not able or willing to think and concentrate, and who possess weak balance and timing skills need to recognize the possible risk in executing advanced activities.

Because of the wide range of physical skill capacity among the population, those sports considered inherently dangerous for some people will be a challenge enabling others to reach their maximum potential. As a primary example, the forward, backward and sideward roll, which possess no risk for most of the population, can provide a risk for severly overweight, poorly coordinated or ill-conditioned persons.

Risks need not, and should not, be eliminated simply because they are risks. If the elimination of risks were to become practice, most people would not drive to work every day. Driving to work is a risk of a life-threatening accident occurring. We know traffic accidents happen daily in our community; however, most people continue to drive to work. Certain risk-taking activities are essential to any well-rounded program of physical activity.

Professionals need to realize the possibility they may be sued. They should prepare themselves with information to assist them in planning a safe environment, thus decreasing the chance for injury and the probability of suit. They also can gain insight into how to protect themselves should a suit occur. Professionals should prepare for suit in the same manner they prepared themselves for an accident.

First aid and safety education is an integral part of the preparation for nearly all persons working in physical activity. These courses provide facts and information as to what could happen, advice on how to avoid accidents and detailed instruction on what to do in the event of an accident. Students and professionals simulate accident situations and practice first aid techniques. Fortunately, many professionals seldom need to use their first aid and safety knowledge, yet they pride themselves on the ability to respond positively should an accident occur.

Physical activity specialists need to take this same interest in acquiring knowledge of the law, and in examining situations in which litigation might be anticipated. They should learn to design risk management programs that will prevent injuries, and acquire skills essential to demonstrating the high quality of their administration, supervision and teaching. Should they be sued, professionals need to be able to clearly guide their attorney in presenting all facts of the case related to physical activity.

Physical activity professionals will not be expected to become attorneys nor be able to dispense legal advice. They should be able to explain their role in physical activity to an attorney. In doing this, physical educators should be legally literate.

LEGAL LITERACY

Legal literacy will be acquired by understanding the elements of those legal concepts relating specifically to the management, supervision or teaching of physical skills. You, as a physical activity professional, will be expected to know a series of legal concepts, just as you are expected to understand the physiological concepts of strength, endurance and flexibility. Additionally, knowledge of these concepts will enable any physical activity professional to become familiar with standard legal terminology.

The legal concepts deliberated in this book will be followed by a discussion of the concepts in hypothetical fact patterns related to human movement. The legal concepts will then be examined in the context of relevant court cases. Examination of case law will enable you to become better acquainted with actual legal situations. Equally important to the learning of law is to develop a capacity to view legal principles as they operate in a daily work routine. For example, the method of measurement used in a classroom may focus on size or strength rather than physical ability, thus triggering a civil rights risk.

The first aid course did not make you a doctor. In fact, it cautioned you against assuming the role of a physician. Legal literacy will not make you a lawyer. It will impress upon you the need for professional legal guidance and the complexity of legal issues that may be part of any one case. Knowledge of the law will help you design a sound risk management program and a quality learning and performing environment. It also will enable you to communicate effectively with members of the legal profession.

The primary legal area to be examined in physical activity is tort. Tort is essentially the law of physical injury. Tort, by definition, is a civil wrong (other than contract) for which the court will provide a remedy in the form of an action for damages (Keeton, 2). Torts covered in this text are Negligence (Chapters Four and Five), Intentional Torts (Chapter Six), Product Liability (Chapter Seven) and Strict Liability (Chapter Eight).

Scholastic, intercollegiate and recreational sports at all levels have taken on new dimensions of importance. Various management techniques such as employing personnel and negotiating agreements with vendors have become the responsibility of the physical activity professional. To meet these needs, legal principles of contract and employment will be considered. Civil rights issues also will be addressed, as they serve to be an extremely important part of future litigation in school environments.

References

Appenzeller, Herb. (1978). Physical Education and The Law. Charlottesville, VA: The Michie Company.
Connors, Eugene T. (1981). Educational Tort Liability and Malpractice. Bloomington, ID: Phi Delta Kappa.
Keeton, W. Page (Ed.). (1984). Prosser and Keeton on the Law of Torts. St. Paul, MN: West Publishing Co.

2

The Legal System

To work effectively with legal concepts one must learn how law is created and the role of the courts in the interpretation of law. Understanding sources of law and the structure and function of federal and state courts will provide such information.

SOURCES OF LAW

Law in the United States is derived from federal and state constitutions, legislative enactment and the results of decisions rendered by federal and state courts. The United States Constitution and the constitutions of each state create the federal and state judicial systems. Federal government powers are limited to those powers identified in the Constitution. The Tenth Amendment to the Constitution provides that all powers not specifically granted to the federal government in the Constitution be made available to the states.

Federal and state statutes, executive orders and city ordinances form the basis for statutory law. Congress, state legislatures, city councils and county boards of commission have authority to enact laws dealing with a wide range of concerns. Their powers are limited only by federal and state constitutions. For example, states, communities and local municipalities have the power to regulate, within their jurisdiction, resources and human activity for the promotion of health, safety and welfare.

Administrative law covers the rules, regulations and directives issued by the executive branch of government within the scope of the acts of Congress. Specific administrative agencies such as the Office of Civil Rights are charged with the responsibility of overseeing the execution of the rules, regulations and directives.

Court decisions form the basis for common law in the United States. Under common or case law, court results—precedents established in local, state or federal courts—will be considered in future litigation. As a result of the use of precedent, law may differ from one state to another, from one local court to another, or from one federal jurisdiction to another. It means a particular legal decision may be used in Minnesota, while a slightly different precedent or decision may be used in Ohio. These differences, in relation to physical activity, are not extreme. Laws discussed throughout the text will relate to the general principles of law and will avoid unique regional decisions.

Professionals in sport, recreation, fitness, exercise science and physical education should develop a legal system appropriate to their needs. This means acquiring knowledge of the United States Constitution; the constitution of the state in which they are employed; federal, state and local statutes; executive orders; and city ordinances that pertain to their role in the delivery of human movement and sport services.

CREATION OF LAW

Article I of the Constitution vested all legislative power in Congress, and dictated that Congress would consist of a Senate and a House of Representatives. The passage of a bill through Congress (the creation of a law) is a complex endeavor that involves an understanding of a set of procedures (Goehlert 1979), as well as a comprehension of the informal influences of lobbying and networking. Steps in processing a bill through Congress are:

1. The President of the United States, a private person or an organized group of people prepares a draft of the legislation and submits it to a member of Congress.
2. The bill is introduced in either the House or the Senate; often, a slightly different version of the bill is introduced in the House and in the Senate. The bill's first reading formality is fulfilled by printing the title of the bill in the *Congressional Record*, a daily legislative news publication found in most libraries.
3. Bills are assigned a number and referred to committees having jurisdiction over the legislation. A list of the current standing committees of Congress appears in Table 2-1.
4. The bill may be considered by the committee or the committee may refuse to study the bill. The bill may receive treatment ranging from a cursory examination to lengthy periods of public hearings. Persons who ultimately will be responsible for the administration of the proposed law, technical experts and members of

Table 2-1. *Standing Committees of The Congress of The United States*

House	Senate
Agriculture	Agriculture, Nutrition and
Appropriations	Forestry
Armed Services	Appropriations
Banking, Finance and	Armed Services
Urban Affairs	Banking, Housing and Urban
Budget	Affairs
District of Columbia	Budget
Education and Labor	Commerce, Science and
Government Operations	Transportation
House Administration	Energy and Natural Resources
Interior and Insular	Environment and Public Works
Affairs	Finance
International Relations	Foreign Relations
Interstate and Foreign	Governmental Affairs
Commerce	Human Resources
Judiciary	Judiciary
Merchant Marine and	Rules and Administration
Fisheries	Veterans' Affairs
Post Office and Civil	
Service	
Public Works and	
Transportation	
Rules	
Science and Technology	
Small Business	
Standards of Official	
Conduct	
Veterans' Affairs	
Ways and Means	

the public are called upon to testify. These hearings enable members of Congress to assess the potential impact or ramification of the legislation and to clarify the contents of the bill. While in committee, the bill may be changed, amended or entirely rewritten. Bills favorably recommended by a committee are accompanied by a report from the committee.

5. After deliberation by the committee, the Senate submits the bill to the full chamber. The House of Representatives requires the bill pass through a second stage of review by a committee on rules. That committee can either amend or offer a substitute for the bill.

6. The bill is debated on the floor of the Senate or the House of Representatives.

7. If the bill is passed by the Senate or the House of Representatives, it is then sent to the other chamber for consideration. It undergoes the previously described process (steps 2 through 6).

8. If the House and Senate versions of the bill differ, the bill is sent to a conference committee composed of members of both houses. There, a compromise is arranged.
9. A bill that passes Congress is sent to the president. The president has 10 days to sign or veto the bill. If the president fails to act in 10 days, the bill becomes law without his signature. If Congress adjourns or is not in session at the end of the 10 day limit, the bill does not become law. It is referred to as a pocket veto. The president has, in effect, vetoed the bill.

Bills take varying lengths of time to pass through Congress — often more than one year. After the bill becomes law, Congress is responsible for evaluating the implementation and impact of the law. Congressional committees are charged with watching over the agencies and programs within their jurisdiction.

State statutes are created in a similar manner, with variations unique to individual states. Committee structure may differ significantly from those identified at the federal level. Industry and the unique needs of each state often dictate the make-up of the committees. State professional organizations can provide you with an outline of the steps needed to submit legislation.

The value of knowing how a bill is created is twofold. First, it enables the professional to better understand how statutory law is created. Secondly, this understanding provides the professional wishing to advance a statute through legislation accurate reference to carry out the task. Professional organizations as well as private citizens often submit statutes. As United States citizens, we are privileged to advance a statute. As professionals in physical activity, we need to exercise our rights on behalf of our profession. We need to submit statutes requisite to the successful licensing and monitoring of the field.

THE COURTS

The United States has two judicial systems: one at the national, or federal level, and one in each state. Through certain aspects of their responsibilities interrelate, these systems are largely independent. Each state is governed by both its own state constitution and the United States Constitution. Jurisdiction of the federal court system extends to all cases and controversies arising under the United States Constitution and all statutes and treaties pursuant to the constitution. State and local courts are responsible for controversies arising under the state constitution and the laws of cities and counties.

Local courts also hear the cases of citizens, unless the issue relates to a citizen's right that has been prescribed or limited by the United States Constitution. When such rights have been affected, the cases are under the federal courts. Should the laws of a county, city or state be in conflict with the United States Constitution, the controversy also will be brought to the federal courts. In some situations, the state court will be the court of last resort. With other circumstances, the federal court will be the final court. Sometimes the state and federal court systems will have concurrent jurisdiction or joint responsibility for law enforcement.

Federal Courts

The federal courts are structured in three tiers: the District Courts at the lowest level, the Courts of Appeals at the intermediate level and the Supreme Court at the top level (Figure 2-1). Other courts established by the Constitution include the Court of Claims, Court of Military Appeals and Customs Court. The national judiciary also includes legislative and administrative agencies created by Congress, which perform judicial functions subject to review by the courts. (Review refers to the power of a court to examine decisions made by administrative units. The examinations ascertain the validity of the rulings in light of applicable statutes, regulations, previous opinions and finding of fact.)

Federal courts deal with certain kinds of cases often referred to as federal questions, and with certain parties to a dispute referred to as diversity of citizenship. Federal question means the case involves an interpretation and application of the Constitution of the United States, Acts of Congress or treaties. Diversity of citizenship refers to a case between two parties, each residing or doing business in a different state; a case between a citizen of the United States and an alien; or a case between a

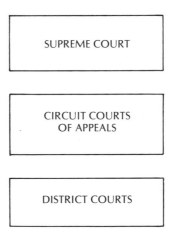

Figure 2-1. *Federal Courts.*

United States citizen and a foreign government. The amount in controversy in the latter situations must exceed $10,000.

Article III of the United States Constitution extends federal jurisdiction to all cases involving the United States Constitution and all statutes and treaties which may be made in persuance of the Constitution. Admiralty and maritime law, statutory and international in character, fall under the exclusive jurisdiction of the federal courts. Controversies involving persons such as ambassadors, public ministers and consuls also fall under the jurisdiction of the national judiciary, as do controversies involving two or more states.

District Courts: The district courts are the basic civil and criminal trial courts in the federal system. Most cases in federal law originate here, and no case is appealed to a district court. There are 92 district courts in the 50 states, the District of Columbia, Puerto Rico, the Virgin Islands, the Canal Zone and Guam. Each court is presided over by a single judge who has been appointed by the President of the United States.

District courts usually establish the record used to determine the guilt or innocence of the defendant in criminal matters and the determination of responsibility in civil issues. The report of the facts of the controversy are usually established in the district court. For example, the fact that one student hit another with a golf club, or that the exercise machine came apart or that the instructor prohibited the aerobic class from resting for 20 minutes would be established at the district level. Juries often are used in these courts.

Courts of Appeals: The courts of appeal are the intermediate courts. They take cases only on appeal from a federal district court or from a regulatory commission, such as the Securities and Exchange Commission or the Civil Aeronautics Board. The United States is presently divided into 11 courts of appeals districts, each having a group of three to nine judges. Cases are heard and decisions rendered by as few as two judges; however, three is a more standard number. The appeals court reviews the proceedings of the original trial court to ascertain whether the substantive and procedural rights of the parties involved have been honored. The court also decides whether the statute or regulation under which the indictment was brought is constitutional.

Supreme Court: The Supreme Court, the highest court of the United States, is presided over by one chief justice and eight associate justices, all appointed by the president for life. The Constitution gives the Supreme Court original jurisdiction or the capacity to create the record only for cases involving ambassadors, public ministers, consuls and for those proceedings in which a state is a party. Its appellate jurisdiction is more flexible, as it can be altered by an act of Congress. (Appellate jurisdiction means the record is reviewed to ascertain that the substantive and procedural rights of the parties involved have been honored, and that the statute or regulation under consideration is constitutional.)

At present, the Supreme Court may review cases which originate in the state courts, the lower federal courts or in the federal regulatory boards and commissions. The Supreme Court is required to take an appeal from the highest state court, from a United States court of appeals in a case in which a federal statute or treaty has been declared invalid, or when a state constitutional provision or statute appears to violate the United States Constitution or an Act of Congress. (Note: the route of appeal from the highest state court is directly to the Supreme Court and not through the lower federal structures.)

Many of the cases that go to the Supreme Court are by a writ of certiorari, not by the appeals route. A writ is an order issued by the court calling up an important case for review because the case is constitutionally significant. The Supreme Court makes its decision to take cases on certiorari and on appeal; they are required to take only those cases mentioned earlier. The refusal of the Supreme Court to hear an appeal or to accept a petition for certiorari generally means the members have decided to accept the decision of the highest state court, or the lower federal court, as valid.

State Courts

Court systems differ from state to state. (Effort will be made to generalize with reference to the state courts, therefore the discussion may not mirror the exact judicial form in a particular state.) State judges are either appointed by the governor or elected by popular ballot.

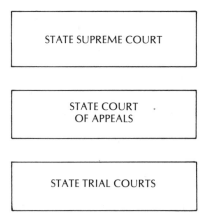

Figure 2-2. *State Court System.*

In large urban communities, courts are classified by the types of cases presented: juvenile courts meeting the needs of youth, criminal courts hearing offenses against society and civil courts adjudicating issues involving the rights of the private sector. In smaller cities, the same court may provide services to all three groups. Although courts may differ from state to state, all states have trial and supreme courts. A minority of states have courts of appeals (Figure 2-2). All states have administrative agencies that perform judicial functions and are subject to judicial review.

State Trial Courts: When parties decide to resort to the judicial system to settle a dispute, their initial contact will be with a trial court. Civil and criminal cases usually are tried in different courts at this level. Trial courts decide disputes of fact. Detailed findings of fact based upon the evidence provided are then subjected to rules of law; thus, the judge and jury, or a judge standing alone, renders a decision.

State Courts of Appeals: A party wishing to appeal a judgment made by the trial court can take the case to a court of appeals. With the exception of a few states, both civil and criminal cases go to the same court of appeals. Courts of appeals use the record of facts obtained in the trial court, but review the questions of law before making a decision. If one of the parties is not satisfied with the decision of the state court of appeals, the issue may be taken to the state supreme court.

State Supreme Court: The state supreme court is the highest appellate court and the court of last resort in the state. A case initiated in a state court will remain in the state system. State supreme courts are the courts of last resort on matters of state law. As a court of appeals, the state supreme court will examine the record to be sure the substantive and procedural rights of the parties have been properly adjudicated and that the constitution, statutes and regulations of the state have been adequately interpreted. When appropriate, a state supreme court decision can be appealed directly to the United States Supreme Court.

THE LEGAL SYSTEM: A CHANGING SYSTEM

The legal system is known as a system based on the Constitution, statutes and case law. Although the Constitution can be changed only by an amendment, statutes and case law change over time. As a result of this slow progression of changes, you will observe some differences in the 1980 case decisions from those rendered in the 1940s or 1960s. One example of the change is found in the immunity system of this country.

Before beginning to work with the theory of tort, it is necessary to trace the history of government statutes, with reference to the responsibilities and liabilities of public servants at the federal, state and local levels. Many sport and physical activity professionals are in public service positions and will be governed by these statutes. Cases used throughout the text have been taken from states and the federal government when they were under various immunity statutes. Therefore, decisions have been rendered on whether the person or agency could be sued, rather than on the facts of the case. In an effort to understand these decisions, we will examine the concept of immunity, governmental immunity and sovereign immunity.

Immunity Statutes

Immunity, by definition, means freedom from suit. Most immunities are special statuses awarded to areas of the government. At one time, agencies and employees of federal, state and local government were immune from liabilities for which a private person would have been held liable. Historically, these immunities were broad and shielded tortious acts.

State and national level immunity has been called sovereign immunity, with some historians noting "you cannot sue the king," and others asserting that a suit against the government is in essence a suit against all tax payers. Although most immunity no longer exists, there are some employees and agencies remaining under immunity. Physical activity personnel, on occasion, continue to be governed by immunity.

Federal Tort Claims Act: The Federal Tort Claims Act of 1946 provided the basis for major changes observed in today's immunity laws. The act declared that when the government engaged in activities in which private persons were also engaging, the government could then be sued. The Federal Tort Claims Act gave the masses consent to sue the federal government in tort. The act provides "monetary recovery from the federal government where damages, loss of property, personal injury or death are caused by the negligence or wrongful acts of federal employees acting within the scope of their employment, and where the United States, if a private person, would be liable in accordance with the law of the place where the tort occurred." (28 U.S.C.A. §2675 [1976])

Under governmental immunity, teachers and others working for federal, state or municipal agencies could not be sued. However, as the states and federal government abolished such immunities, injured persons were enabled to file claims and to receive damages.

The Federal Tort Claims Act has a number of specific exceptions, including activities of the military, the postal service and the federal treasury. An exception having a profound impact on physical activity professionals is the exemption for all claims arising out of intentional torts. (28 U.S.C. A. §2680 (h) [1976]) This means a professional, immune from liability as a result of their employer's immunity, will be found personally liable for any tort judged to be an intentional tort. For example, a member of the park service commits a tort, but is immune under sovereign immunity. However, if found to have committed an intentional tort, that individual will be found personally liable. So if the claim is intentional — arising out of assault, battery, false imprisonment, libel, slander, misrepresentation or interference with contract rights — employees will not be immune.

Immunity is also retained for discretionary functions or duties, though specific definition of a discretionary function or duty is difficult to obtain. However, examination of decisions suggests immunity generally covers policy judgment and planning. This means an employee will not be held liable for the act of planning an event or setting up a system which could result in harm to others. Though an employee's plans and policies may be immune, should the results of carrying out the plans and policies create a risk to society, the persons carrying out the plans and policies must warn of the risk. Immunity does not justify the government's failure to warn of a risk or to supply information sufficient to permit those affected to take safety measures.

Immunity for State Government: State governments have had the same immunity as the federal government. Nearly all states, with the exception of Maryland and Mississippi, have consented to at least some liability for torts. Some have waived tort immunity in cases in which the state or its agencies can procure liability insurance; others have abolished immunity entirely.

Immunity for Municipal Agencies: Municipal agencies also hold immunity in tort, but different in scope from federal and state sovereign immunity. Local governments are not sovereigns, therefore their immunity is called governmental immunity. Most municipalities are immune only for injuries resulting from their discretionary acts (policy judgment and planning). Local government officials often are covered by immunity, and public recreation workers' discretionary decisions are usually covered; however, their interactions with people often are not covered. Teachers are least often covered.

As you examine cases, you need to decide whether the decision was made on immunity, or on the merits of the case. When immunity has influenced the decision, you should also note the date of the case and determine whether immunity would influence the decision if made today.

An Example of a Court Interpretation of Immunity: A recent case illustrating immunity and the type of immunity — discretionary (decisional) or ministerial (operational) — is *Webber v. Yeo* (1985). Webber, a student in a beginning swimming class dove from the edge of the pool, and never surfaced. Efforts to revive him failed. The issue in the wrongful death action was whether the instructor failed to properly administer mouth-to-mouth resuscitation prior to removing the boy from the water. The trial court dismissed the case. The Court of Appeals of Michigan looked at the case from an immunity doctrine. Using *Ross v. Consumers Power Co.* (1984), another Michigan case, they stated that individual government employees are immune from court liability only when they are:

   a) Acting during the course of their employment, and are acting or reasonably believe they are acting within the scope of their authority;
   b) Acting in good faith; and
   c) Performing discretionary — decisional, as opposed to ministerial — operational, acts.

The court held that the system of rescue constituted a discretionary act for which the instructor was immune from tort liability. The court also held that the resuscitative efforts, the allegedly negligent instruction and supervision and the failure to warn parents of potential harm in a swimming class were ministerial acts. For these ministerial acts, the defendant did not have immunity from tort liability. Therefore, the instructor was liable for each of the above acts. The court stated:

Based on the above analysis we conclude that the trial court properly granted summary judgment with respect to the discretionary acts of defendant class instructors. The trial court, however, improperly granted summary judgment as to the ministerial acts of defendant class instructors and defendant school administrators. (233)

The case was remanded for trial on these questions.

SUMMARY

The Constitution, statutes, administrative decisions and the results of court cases constitute the law used in the United States. Congress, through the Senate and House of Representatives, has the power to create new law. Citizens may exercise their rights to create new law by processing a request through the appropriate channels of Congress. Court systems are organized for the federal government and within each state. Each system consists of a lower court in which the facts are ascertained for the record prior to judicial decision, and a series of higher order or courts of appeals in which the record is examined for procedural or substantive error.

Legal systems are changing systems, as statutes and case law overturn existing precedent. Immunity is one example of how change in statutory law can have a profound impact on the liability of specific persons employed in certain positions.

Professionals should identify immunity statutes in their localities and understand the interpretations that would be made, and how they would be affected should a lawsuit occur.

References

28 United States Code Annotated §2671-2680.
Goehlert, Robert. (1979). *Congress and Law-Making*. Santa Barbara, CA: Clio Books.
Kaiser, Ronald A. (1986). *Liability and Law in Recreation, Parks, and Sports*. Englewood Cliffs, NJ: Prentice-Hall.
Keeton, W. Page (Ed). (1984). *Prosser and Keeton on the Law of Torts*. St. Paul, MN: West Publishing Co.
Ross v. Consumers Power Co., 420 Mich. 567, 363 N.W. 2d 641 (1984).
Webber v. Yeo, 383 N.W. 2d 230 (1985).

3

Research Skills For
The Study Of Law

Once major concepts of a content area are clear, specific research skills are needed. Most courses provide a brief overview of a subject and an opportunity for the student to practice the research tools. This chapter will guide the entry level sport law student to articles, cases and books on law applicable to sport, recreation and physical activity. It will enable the beginner to locate statute and case law cited in the text and in periodicals. This chapter also will assist graduate students and faculty members in preparing presentations and articles for publication. Legal publications can be found in courthouses, public libraries, public and private institutions that offer pre-law courses and university and college law schools. Numerous private and law firm libraries also exist; however, they may be difficult to access.

LAW LIBRARIES

Law library sources can be separated into two distinct categories: primary, and secondary. Primary sources are legislative statutes, court decisions, executive decrees and orders and administrative regulations and rulings. Federal and state statutes and appellate court decisions are the primary documents most often used in legal research. Secondary sources include textbooks, treatises, practice manuals, commentaries, restatements and periodicals that explain and describe the law.

Law libraries, typically smaller than standard public libraries, are easy to learn. Reference materials are usually centrally located. When possible, attend a guided tour prior to initiating research.

Library holdings fall into the following categories: case, statutes or codes, annotated reports, reports containing legislative history, administrative materials, periodicals, treatises and casebooks. Treatises and casebooks most closely represent what psychologists or historians would refer to as textbook or subject matter presentations. Hereafter, these sources will be referred to as textbooks.

Case Law

Case law plays an important role in sport, recreation, and physical activity, as many legal theories have evolved as a result of case decisions. Cases are located through topical areas in case digests, and by citations from textbooks and periodicals. Results of case law are published according to the organization of the courts with reporters for the U.S. Supreme Court, for the federal appellate courts, for all state appellate and supreme courts. They are available in most law libraries. Reports and summaries of local trial law also may be available.

State appellate court decisions will be used most often in examining tort and personal injury litigation, and federal appellate decisions will play the same role in Constitutional and civil rights issues. If the tort law discussions do not specify a specific court, you are to assume that the case is in a state appellate court. If the Constitutional and civil rights discussions do not identify a specific court, you are to assume that the case is in a federal appellate court. Refer to Figures 2-1, 2-2 and the discussion of the Supreme Court to trace the sequence of movement of a particular case.

Statutes or Codes

A systematic compilation of statutes and regulations is usually identified as a Code. The regulations of federal agencies are first published in the Federal Register and later codified into the Code of Federal Regulations. The United States Code Annotated (U.S.C.A.) contains federal, legislative and congressional statutes. Each state has a similar code.

Annotated Reports

Annotated reports are legal references reported according to subject matter. For example, *American Law Reports* includes past developments and current laws in most states and future trends.

Legislative History Reports

Researchers often will trace the history of a law to locate documents which will reveal the intent of Congress or a state legislature. Statutory research will include pre-enactment history of earlier statutes and the current status of law under consideration. Legislative historical documents include presidential messages, congressional bills, reports of hearings, committee reports, debates, house and senate hearings and senate executive reports.

Administrative Materials

Administrative materials are located under the title of the agency. Therefore, knowledge of the agency is very important to the researcher. Such information also can be located in the *United States Government Manual, Federal Register, Code of Federal Regulations* and *Administrative Rules and Decisions.*

Periodicals

The following sport and law periodicals will assist professionals in maintaining knowledge of the law. Each publication is followed by an address where you could obtain this information.

- *The Exercise Standards and Malpractice Reporter* and *The Sport, Parks and Recreation Law Reporter*
  Professional and Executive Reports
  4571 Stephen Circle, N.W.
  Canton, Ohio 44718
- *The Entertainment and Sports Lawyer*
  Publication of the American Bar Association Forum Committee on the Entertainment and Sports Industry
  The American Bar Association
  750 N. Lake Shore Drive
  Chicago, Illinois 60611
- *Sport and The Courts*
  P.O. Box 2836
  Winston-Salem, North Carolina 27102

Many other periodicals deal with issues of law in sport and physical activity on a single article basis. Intramurals, collegiate athletics and commercial fitness also are covered. The indexes of legal periodicals will identify these articles. Card catalogue, organized by author, subject and title, also will guide the researcher to books and treatises.

A legal dictionary will be helpful to any person working with a legal case or problem. Legal dictionaries can be found in any library.

CASE ANALYSIS

After a judge renders a decision in a case, an explanation of the reasoning behind the decision usually is written. The explanation and a summary of the presentation to the court is published as an opinion.

When several judges have participated in the decision and agreement does not exist among the judges, one judge writes the decision (the opinion of the majority of the judges). Disagreeing judges are then free to write their dissenting opinions. A case opinion appearing in a reporter will usually contain the following general categories: title, facts, issue, decision or holding, the reasoning of the court and decree. The complete case for *Larson*, located in Appendix A, is used in the following analysis.

Title

The case title is *Larson v. Independent School District No. 314, Braham.* The title includes the names of the litigants, the reporter citation, the court, the attorneys involved and the status of the case. The litigants are Larson, the plaintiff and Independent School District No. 314, Braham, the defendant. The plaintiff is the party bringing the cause of action against the person or agency believed to be responsible or at fault for the injury. Injury in the courts may be physical, psychological or economic. The defendant is the party against whom the action has been brought.

A case in a court of appeals also may refer to one party as the appellant, the person or party appealing the case, and to the other party as the appellee or respondent, the party against whom the case is appealed.

The reporter citation is 289 N.W. 2d 112 (1979) which means the case can be located in Volume 289 of the *North Western Reporter*, second series on page 112. The case was decided November 9, 1979. The court deciding the case was the Supreme Court of Minnesota (See Figure 2-2, Chapter Two).

The names of the attorneys for the case are located in Appendix A.

Facts

Though facts are the actual events that take place, each party may present a different rendition of the occurrence. Usually, the court notes whether the facts are in dispute or in agreement. Published facts are those that have been determined in the hearing or trial. Facts for *Larson* included the following:

On April 12, 1971, Steven was severely injured while performing a gymnastic exercise known as a "headspring over a rolled mat", a required activity in his eighth grade physical education class. As a result of landing on his head, and from the force of running and diving onto the rolled mat, Steven broke his neck. The injury resulted in quadraplegic paralysis.

At the time of the accident, Steven was a student at Braham Junior-Senior High School. He was participating in a compulsory physical education class being taught by Lundquist, a first-year teacher with a teaching certificate in physical education. Lundquist had commenced teaching physical education classes at the school on March 10, 1971, when the former physical education teacher, Mark Embretson, was required to report for military duty. The accident occurred nine class periods after Lundquist had replaced Embretson. Lamont was the superintendent of the school district, and Peterson was the principal of Braham Junior-Senior High School. (115-116)

The District Court (Isanto County, Judge Thomas G. Forsberg), awarded Larson, the injured student, a judgment against the teacher and principal and found the school district jointly and severally liable in a certain sum. The court also entered a directed verdict in favor of the principal.

	Trial Court Decision
First-Year Teacher	90 percent negligent
Principal	10 percent negligent
Injured student	0 percent negligent

The joint and several liability award against the teacher, the principal and the school district is in the amount of $1,013,639.75 to the boy, and $142,937.89 to his father. The trial court also ruled that procurement of liability insurance waived the school districts absolute defense of governmental immunity.

This tells us that Larson and his parents, the people who brought the action as a result of the injury, have been successful in the trial court against the teacher, the principal and the school district jointly and severally for the reported sum of money. The percentages identified in the table tells us that Minnesota is a comparative negligence state. In a comparative negligence state, fault is allocated by percentage to each party responsible for the injury (see Chapter Four). Jointly and severally, as used in this case, indicate that the school could pay the amount available in its insurance policy, and that the other parties would pay the balance of the judgment according to the comparative negligence decision of the trial court.

Joint and several usually means that when a money judgment has been awarded against more than one person, each person is held for the total balance of the money judgment. For example, if three persons were held liable for $45,000, each person is liable for the entire $45,000. In the event that one person is not able or does not pay his or her share, the other two people become liable for the first person's share.

The directed verdict for the superintendent means that Larson, the party with the responsibility of proving that he was damaged as a result of the superintendent's actions, has failed to present a prima facie case for consideration by a jury. Therefore, the trial judge has ordered a verdict without sending the matter to the jury. Burden of proof will be discussed throughout the text; it represents the system that the moving party, or plaintiff, uses to gather evidence to demonstrate the defendant was in fact liable for the injury. The prima facie case means that the court (the judge or the judge and the jury) believes the plaintiff's evidence is sufficient to enable the plaintiff to take the next step and go to the jury, or that the court believes the plaintiff's conclusion is reasonable.

Issue

The issue is the disputed questions of fact and law to which the parties are seeking answers. In this case, the major issues are whether the teacher was negligent in the teaching and spotting of the headspring, and whether the principal, the superintendent and the school district were negligent in supervising the teacher.

Decision or Holding

The decision or holding is the answer to the questions raised in court. In *Larson*:

1. The superintendent "was not sufficiently involved in the action or inaction upon which plaintiffs based their cause of action. There was, therefore, insufficient evidence that a negligent act by Lamont caused Steven's accident." (119)
2. The teacher was not entitled to immunity (freedom from suit), and the evidence established that he was negligent. Therefore, the teacher was liable for the negligent spotting and teaching of the exercise.
3. The principal was found personally negligent; his liability to the plaintiff was vicarious.

Reasoning of the Court

The reasoning of the court is the basis upon which the judge and/or the jury reach their decision.

Reasoning includes the following:

1. . . . there is sufficient evidence in the record that Lundquist was negligent in teaching the headspring at the time and that Steven's accident occurred because Lundquist was negligent in spotting the headspring. (116)
2. As principal, Peterson had a duty to exercise reasonable care

in supervising the development, planning, and administration of the physical education curriculum within the school; in supervising and evaluating the work of teachers within the school; and in maintaining conditions conducive to the safety and welfare of students during the school day. In effect, the jury found that Peterson's actions as an administrator were unreasonable and that his failure to reasonably administer the curriculum and supervise the teaching of an inexperienced instructor created the opportunity for Steven's accident to occur. (116)

3.   Superintendent Lamont was a level removed from these responsibilities. There is no showing in the record that Lamont had or should have had knowledge that Peterson had allowed an unsafe physical education curriculum to develop, that Peterson had improperly carried out the transition from Embretson to Lundquist, or that Peterson had failed to provide Lundquist with adequate supervision. There is no showing that Lamont was inadequately supervising Peterson's performance, or that Lamont had special knowledge of problems in the physical education curriculum or of Lundquist's teaching methods which would have put him on notice that the safety of students was being threatened.

Lamont was not sufficiently involved in the actions or inactions upon which plaintiffs based their cause of action. There was, therefore, insufficient evidence that a negligent act by Lamont caused Steven's accident. The trial court's directed verdict in favor of Lamont was proper. (119)

Evidence from which the jury decided the defendant principal was negligent came from various teaching professionals: a former principal, (who later became a superintendent), a university professor of physical education curriculum and a high school gymnastics coach and director of physical education. Their testimonies were that gymnastics was a dangerous activity requiring careful planning, that a new teacher should receive more supervision in curricular planning than an experienced teacher and that a principal should consult with a new teacher as to the level of skill and previous experience of the class.

Importance of Decision

Decisions of higher courts of the same jurisdiction (see Figures 2-1 and 2-2 for federal and state jurisdictions) and previous decisions of the same appellate court are binding when the facts and the issues are the same. Binding means that the holding of this case must be applied in cases where the issues of law and facts are the same. This is known as applying precedent.

Decree

A decree is the resolution of the litigation which determines the rights of all parties. There are two kinds of decrees: one that is final, and one that recommends some other action, such as a retrial or a remand. Retrial means to send back for a new trial; remand means to return the case to the court from which it came for further action on one or more issues. The *Larson* decree is final.

SUMMARY

Case analysis should be used to learn details of litigation. That knowledge can be used to create and implement risk management programs or to prepare research reports. Whether the results of the case establish new law or utilize existing law from other jurisdictions (states or regions) is important and should be studied.

Library research also can identify patterns of litigation: where the litigation is occurring, and what activities appear to have been called into court. A clear understanding of court decisions, with reference to class size, curricular planning and progression, needs to be applied by curriculum planners and independent fitness consultants.

References

Kunz, Christina (1986). *The Process of Legal Researching.* Boston, MA: Little, Brown and Company.
Nemeth, Charles P. (1987). *Legal Research.* Englewood Cliffs, NJ: Prentice-Hall.
Price, Miles O., Harry Bitner, and Shirley R. Bysiewicz (1979). *Effective Legal Research.* Boston, MA: Little, Brown and Company.
Statsky, William P. (1983). *Case Analysis and Fundamentals of Legal Writing,* 2nd Ed. St. Paul, MN: West Publishing Company.
Statsky, William P. (1985). *Legal Research and Writing: Some Starting Points,* 3rd Ed. St. Paul, MN: West Publishing Company.
The Living Law: A Guide to Modern Legal Research. (1987). Rochester, NY: The Lawyers Co-operative Publishing Company.
Uberstine, Gary A. (1985). *Covering All the Bases: A Comprehensive Research Guide to Sports Law.* Buffalo: William S. Hein Company.
West's Law Finder. (1985). St. Paul, MN: West Publishing Company.

4

Negligence In Physical Activity

Negligence is "the omission to do something which a reasonable [person], guided by those ordinary considerations which ordinarily regulate human affairs, would do, or the doing of something which a reasonable and prudent [person] would not do." (*Black's Law Dictionary*)

Negligence is conduct which falls below the standards established by law for the protection of others against unreasonable harm. Unreasonable harm exists when danger is apparent or should be apparent. The elements of negligence are:

1. a legal duty of care,
2. breach of the legal duty,
3. the breach of the legal duty as the proximate cause of the injury, and
4. substantial damage.

Negligence is described in degrees with negligence, gross negligence, and wilful, wanton and reckless misconduct identified as the measures of negligence. Defenses to negligence include contributory negligence, comparative negligence and assumption of risk. Remedies in negligence tend to be compensatory and punitive.

A LEGAL DUTY OF CARE

The key in negligence is legal duty. Legal duty means that one was responsible or obligated to behave in a certain manner, or the "defendant owed a duty to conform to a standard of conduct established by law for the protection of plaintiff." (Karns 1986) A relationship sufficient to create a legal duty may arise by statute, ordinance, administrative rule, contract, voluntary assumption or judicial decision. Relationships such as teacher-pupil, coach-athlete, fitness specialist-client, employer-employee and principal-agent establish a legal duty.

Within each sport, or specific area of human movement, there exists a hypothetical standard at which a trained professional is expected to teach, inspect and use equipment and supervise. The legal duty, or standard of care, is either the standard established for the professional with specific expertise or that expected of a reasonable person under similar circumstances. A legal duty of care may exist even though one is not on the payroll. Job status is often not the factor; technical expertise is the basis upon which one is judged. Experts in physical activity often are surprised to learn that the same duty of care exists when they serve as volunteers for their school or church as when they are paid professionals.

There is no general duty to act affirmatively on behalf of others. For example, if a recreation director is walking past a playground in a strange city and notices a child has been injured, that director has no obligation or responsibility to provide first aid for the injured child. A duty exists only because of a special relationship, or because one volunteered to help. By volunteering to help, a special relationship is created.

If the recreation director decided to provide help to the child on the playground, they would be obligated to continue the help until professional assistance was obtained. Once one begins to provide assistance to an injured person, that assistance must continue until professional help arrives. Also, a special relationship is created when it is perceived that one's decision to help may have stopped others from providing assistance. The volunteer also must be careful not to injure others or to create further injury to the person receiving assistance.

The legal duty of care to another is satisfied when all unreasonable risks of harm are eliminated. To successfully eliminate the unreasonable risk, the professional must recognize and know the danger. When courts determine negligent conduct they analyze the recognition and knowledge of unreasonable conduct in light of:

1. the magnitude and type of risk involved,
2. the utility of the interest advanced, and
3. possible alternatives.

The magnitude and type of risk necessitates an examination of the incident and the actions taken to determine what the parameters, or types of potential risk, are and to establish a continuum of risk — from a sprained toe to death. Magnitude of risk also includes the number of people involved or the property loss that may occur as a result of the incident. As the *probability for injury increases, the need to take precautions also increases. As the probability for injury decreases, so does the need to take precautions.* When the risk is death, the court may continue to expect a high level of precaution in a low probability risk situation.

In examining the utility of the interest involved, the court will consider the social and other societal values of continuing the activity despite the injury potential. When an activity is continued because of its social value, society seems to create elaborate rules to ensure the safest environment possible. For example, some people justify maintaining football because of its value to society, in spite of the fact that it may cause catastrophic injury. Others feel trampolines and diving boards are two pieces of equipment of great value in the teaching of human movement, and should be retained despite the number of injuries that occur.

The court also will note if the best alternative for accomplishing a particular goal has been selected. Which alternative would a reasonable person have selected in that situation? When there are choices of activities, all that meet a specific goal, which one is safest? Which one is most cost-effective? These questions will be the test. The professional does not guarantee safety against any and all harm, but protects against harm which is unreasonable.

We have seen legal duty described as a need to perform in a certain way. Not performing or not doing a particular task may breach a legal duty. Failure to administer first aid to an injured athlete may be a breach of the coach or trainer's legal duty to the athlete.

Standard of care or level of legal duty is the most difficult element to ascertain in the area of physical activity. Very few specific standards have been created by professionals in sport, recreation, sport management, corporate fitness or physical education. Therefore, experts are employed by both plaintiff's and defendant's attorneys to establish standards for the judge and jury in each case. Professionals, aware of the use of expert testimony to ascertain a standard, should maintain comprehensive files documenting procedures used in supervision, instruction and care of equipment. In addition to such documentation, professionals should know authorities who would substantiate the high quality of their selected systems.

BREACH OF THE LEGAL DUTY OF CARE

First, it must be established that legal duty, an element of negligence, existed in the case. Then, proof must be provided by the plaintiff or injured person that the duty was breached.

Teachers, recreation directors and fitness supervisors have specific duties of care. Among those duties is the provision of first aid or immediate and temporary care at the scene of an accident. Although the supervisors need not personally provide the first aid, they are obligated to make provisions for such care. Failure to make provisions for first aid is a breach of legal duty.

Persons engaged in instruction are obligated to provide learning experiences which are challenging, but not so far beyond the capacity of the learner that injury is likely. When students are injured as a result of being allowed to participate in such risk activities, professionals could be in breach of their duty of care.

BREACH OF LEGAL DUTY AS THE PROXIMATE CAUSE OF INJURY

It must be proved that the breach of the duty was the real or actual cause of the injury. For example, was the defendant's negligent act the cause of the injury? Would the same harm have resulted had the negligent act never occurred? After establishing actual cause, proximate cause must be ascertained. Proximate cause is assessed by determining whether or not the harm to plaintiff was a reasonably foreseeable consequence of the defendant's act.

SUBSTANTIAL DAMAGE

The injury resulting from the breach of the legal duty must involve substantial damage. Substantial damage means the individual has sustained physical damage which has incapacitated him or her (fractures or back injuries, for example). The person must be more than "physically stiff" the day following the injury for substantial damage to exist. If a question exists as to whether the damage is substantial, the question will go to the jury. An injury had to occur before a negligent act is found by the court, and that act had to have resulted in substantial damage.

DEGREES OF NEGLIGENCE

Another factor in the standard of care selected by the courts is the level of negligence. Courts apply negligence according to statutes identifying negligence as viewed by the state in which the action is tried. Some states use degrees to describe various levels of negligence: negligence, gross negligence and wilful and wanton neglect. Gross negligence is more serious than negligence; wilful and wanton neglect is the most serious. In some states, the professional in physical activity will be expected to meet the standards of general negligence. In others, Illinois for example, they will not be found negligent in tort unless wilful and wanton neglect exists.

Negligence

An absence of that degree of care and vigilance which persons of extraordinary prudence and foresight are accustomed to use or . . . a failure to exercise great care. (Keeton, 211)

An example of negligence would be failure to make a routine inspection of the physical activity setting or of the equipment used by students or clients.

Gross Negligence

. . . very great negligence or the want of even slight or scant care . . . failure to exercise even that care that a careless person would use. (Keeton, 211-212)

Examples of gross negligence would be (1) failure to inspect the facility or the equipment when the professional knows that certain unsafe conditions began to appear after a specified period of time, and (2) failure to provide appropriate activities for beginners in a lesson plan in which a number of students are novice performers.

Wilful, Wanton and Reckless Misconduct

An intentional act of an unreasonable character in total disregard of human safety. (*Restatement of the Law of Torts (Second)* § 500)(587)

Examples of this degree of negligence would be (1) failure, after knowledge of impending danger, to exercise ordinary care to prevent the danger; (2) failure to discover a danger which could have easily been discovered by the exercise of ordinary care; and (3) failure to inspect the installation of new equipment to determine that it has been properly installed or that persons qualified to install the equipment have certified that it is properly installed.

DEFENSES

The defenses against negligence most often encountered in physical activity situations include contributory negligence, comparative negligence and assumption of risk.

Contributory Negligence

Contributory negligence means the plaintiff, or injured person, is responsible in part for his or her injuries. The plaintiff's conduct has somehow contributed as a legal cause to the harm the plaintiff has suffered. The conduct of the injured person has fallen below a standard to which the injured person is required to conform for their own protection. (*Restatement of The Law of Torts, (Second). (507). §463.*)

In contributory negligence the defendant is not relieved of any duty toward the plaintiff. "Although the defendant has violated his duty, has been negligent, and would otherwise be liable, the plaintiff is denied recovery because his own conduct disentitles him to maintain the action. In the eyes of the law both parties are at fault; and the defense is one of the plaintiff's disability, rather than the defendant's innocence." (Keeton, 451 and 452)

If an adult fitness client who has been told to warm up before working on the machines, decides not to warm up and sustains a torn muscle, the client will be considered contributarily negligent for failing to warm up. The client is sufficiently responsible for the injury to relieve the consultant, or teacher, from responsibility. Also, the child who took his jump rope to the top of the gymnastics equipment when he knew he was not to be on the equipment, tied the rope to the equipment with a faulty knot, and swung from the rope, sustaining injuries as a result of his fall, was contributarily negligent. The standard of conduct used in negligence, that of a reasonable person under ordinary circumstances, is also the standard applied in contributory negligence.

Contributory negligence on the part of the plaintiff is a bar to recovery. If it can be established that the plaintiff's own negligence was a factor in the plaintiff's injury, the court will not hold the defendant liable for the injury. Contributory negligence is a defense to negligence. At times, it is a defense to gross negligence, but it is not a defense to wilful, wanton and reckless misconduct, nor to an intentional tort. Note that contributory negligence may change the recovery, but it does not affect the duty of care that must be provided.

Comparative Negligence

Comparative negligence is a system in which the plaintiff's contributory negligence reduces the plaintiff's recovery from the defendant, in proportion to his or her relative fault. For example, the defendant may be found to be 30 percent at fault (contributarily negligent), and the plaintiff 70 percent at fault. On a $10,000 judgment, the breakdown would be:

Party	Fault	*Judgment Sum Paid*
Plaintiff	30 percent	Assumed balance
Defendant	70 percent	$7,000 owed to plaintiff

The majority of the states have adopted some form of comparative negligence; however, not all have adopted the "pure" form previously described. A popular approach to apportioning fault is the modified, or 50 percent system in which the plaintiff's contributory negligence will not bar recovery if it remains below a specified portion of the total fault. There are two categories within the modified form: the equal fault bar, and the greater fault bar. Under the equal fault bar, the plaintiff will not recover if the plaintiff's fault is equal to or greater than that of the defendant. To recover, the plaintiff's negligence must be less than the defendant's. Under the greater fault bar, the plaintiff is denied recovery only if the plaintiff's fault is greater than the defendant's. Recovery can occur if the plaintiff's negligence is equal to or less than the defendant's.

Assumption of Risk

Assumption of risk is a defense to negligence and strict liability. Keeton (1984) explained assumption of risk from three different perspectives: express consent, duty and misconduct defense. Express consent is when the plaintiff, in advance, has given express consent to relieve defendant of an obligation and has agreed to take chances of injury from risks known to be involved in the activity. Duty means that plaintiff voluntarily entered into an agreement, such as an employment contract, knowing that risks were involved in the activity. In the misconduct defense, plaintiff is aware of a risk in the task, yet voluntarily takes on the responsibility or continues to work or play in an unsafe environment. (Keeton 1984, 480-481)

Express consent is generally in the form of a signed statement executed between the physical activity specialist, or the agency employing the specialist, and the performer or learner. Implied consent is often attributed to the purchase of a ticket. For example, these consents may be found on the reverse side of a ski lift ticket or a hot air balloon ride ticket. These agreements will be analyzed under contract law; however, characteristics of these contracts which have an impact on assumption of risk are the following.

When the bargaining between the parties or the elements of the contract reveal that one party was at a tremendous disadvantage, the courts have refused to uphold the agreement. These agreements will not be allowed to cover wilful, wanton misconduct or gross negligence.

The defense of assumption of risk can be used only when the parties:

1. know the risk exists,
2. understand the nature of the risk, and
3. freely choose to incur the risk.

Age, experience and knowledge of pertinent information are vital factors in determining a plaintiff's ability to comprehend and appreciate a risk.

Though minors will be held to a lower level of comprehension and appreciation of the risk involved, they may not be completely absolved from having assumed a risk. A 14-year-old Red Cross certified life saver sustaining severe injuries as a result of jumping into a pond in a national forest preserve without checking the bottom, may be found by a court to have assumed a level of responsibility for his or her actions. However, a six-year-old with no Red Cross training who engaged in the same activity, would be unable to understand the danger.

When an individual encounters a dangerous situation, it is often assumed that he or she has learned to appreciate it and has assumed the risk. Knowledge and appreciation of risk is not based on a reasonable person's standard but on a standard tailored specifically for the individual involved. Students routinely performing on gymnastic equipment and clients routinely engaged in advanced level swimming are expected to know and appreciate the risk involved. However, persons using equipment or taking instructions for the first time are not expected to possess the same level of knowledge and appreciation.

In many court cases, knowledge and appreciation of a danger is a question for the jury. Only in those situations where it is obvious the plaintiff understood the danger is the issue resolved by the judge. How professionals prepare to demonstrate that their students or clients had knowledge and appreciation of the risks involved in the activity in which they participated will be thoroughly studied under Risk Management in Chapter Thirteen.

The decision to assume the risk must be free and voluntary; some sign or manifestation of consent must be present to relieve the defendant of their obligation. Should the plaintiff be placed in a position where the consent was forced, the plaintiff can not be said to have assumed the risk.

When the defendant's negligence is also a violation of a statute, the plaintiff may or may not be held to an assumption of the risk. Many states have held that plaintiffs continue to assume the risk under these circumstances, while a number of states have held that a plaintiff may not assume the risk of the defendant's violation of a safety statute enacted explicitly for the protection of the public.

Since the late 1950s, a number of states have abolished assumption of risk. New Jersey took the lead in 1959, with a number of states following the pattern each year.

Rutter v. Northeastern Beaver County School District (1981) presents a number of issues unique to sport and athletic competition in reference to the assumption of risk doctrine. Two important issues revolve around the student's knowledge and appreciation of the danger and whether he voluntarily agreed to participate in the activity: Howard Rutter, a 16-year-old high school student, was severely injured while participating in a summer football practice. Engaged in a supervised game of "jungle football," Rutter was struck in the right eye by an opponent. Blindness, or loss of an eye, was caused as a result of a detached retina.

Rutter and his parents filed suit against the school district, the two coaches who conducted the practice and the opposing player. The case went to trial. At the close of the appellant's case, the appellees were granted a compulsory nonsuit. A nonsuit means that the appellant was not able to maintain the cause of action or to prove the case. Failure to maintain a cause of action means that inadequate factual support was presented to prove the legal theory presented. A motion to strike the nonsuit was denied. However, the Superior Court of Pennsylvania affirmed the denial. The Supreme Court of Pennsylvania reversed and remanded.

With reference to the student's knowledge and appreciation of the danger involved, the Supreme Court of Pennsylvania noted that Rutter's testimony was: "I never imagined that I would lose an eye." (1204) The court went on to say:

> Since appellant's knowledge is assessed on a subjective basis, and since appellant was a young person of limited experience, it was improper for the court to grant a compulsory nonsuit as a matter of law based on appellant's supposed assumption of risk. (1204)

This decision establishes that an athlete, or any participating student, needs to clearly understand what dangers exist in order to be able to assume a risk.

The next issue was the voluntariness of Rutter's assumption of the risk: Was he forced to choose between two evils? He volunteered to play football; therefore had he also volunteered to play "jungle football," a game in which no protective or safety gear is used? In addition, evidence in court attested to the fact that the football coach had implied that boys failing to participate in the pre-season football conditioning program — which included the "jungle football" — would have little chance of making the team. Whether Rutter voluntarily agreed to participate in the "jungle football" was perceived by the court to be a question for the jury.

As comparative negligence becomes universal, states will no longer place as much emphasis on assumption of risk. This case has served as one of Pennsylvania's cases in which assumption of risk has been abolished. (Joseph 1983)

Participants often are asked to sign releases prior to participation in activities. This is important for the value the release may fulfill under contract law, and because the release documents imply that the participant was aware of the dangers involved in participating in the activity. In signing the statement, the participants state that they have read the statement and are aware of the risks involved.

Such signed statements often are misinterpreted to mean that the participant has agreed not to sue. A person cannot sign away his or her right to sue, in the event that he or she is involved in a situation where wilful, wanton or reckless misconduct occurs. Parents cannot sign away the rights of their minor children. (Minor, as used in this text, identifies persons below the age of majority according to the statutes of the state in which they reside. Adult refers to persons above the age of majority.) What the parent signs on behalf of the child, or what the adult participant agrees to, is the knowledge of a full disclosure of the risks including probability, extent and magnitude of the harm that could occur while participating in the activity. In the event of a suit, such an agreement will be examined by the court to determine its validity as a defense.

Spectator injuries often provide an area for the examination of assumption of risk doctrine. In *Clark v. Goshen Sunday Morning Softball League* (1985), a father brought his adult son to the baseball park to meet the players. As he was talking to people, Mr. Clark was hit by a ball thrown by the players in warm-up which missed the receiver. Clark brought suit for his injuries against the player involved and the league. The court noted that:

(1) risk assumed by spectator at softball or baseball game is the same during warmup as during game itself; (2) spectator, who had accompanied adult son to softball field to introduce him to other players, was a "spectator" as a matter of law, notwithstanding his subjective motive or intent; and (3) neither league nor player who threw "wild pitch" which struck spectator had duty to warn spectator of danger, and they were therefore not liable for injuries. (263)

The court also looked to Prosser's term of implied acceptance of risk:

By entering freely and voluntarily into a relation or situation where the negligence of the defendant is obvious, the plaintiff may be found to accept and consent to it, and to undertake to look out for himself and relieve the defendant of the duty. Those who participate or sit as spectators at sports . . . may be taken to assume all the known risks of being hurt by . . . flying baseballs. *** However, the fact that the risk may be assumed is by no means conclusive as to whether it has been assumed. *** The plaintiff must know and understand the risk he is incurring and . . . his choice to incur it must be entirely free and voluntary! (270)

The court ruled that the defendant did not have a duty to warn the plaintiff of the hazards of baseball and that the facts provided no evidence that the baseball league or the player engaged in reckless or intentional misconduct.

REMEDIES AND DAMAGES

Remedies can be compensatory, restoring the person to the position they were in prior to the event, or punitive, deterring the wrongdoer from acting in the same manner again. Both of these awards are usually monetary. Injunctive relief, another remedy, is a court order demanding that the activity be stopped.

In torts the damages are compensatory, and occasionally punitive. Compensatory damages are those fees paid for medical expenses; lost wages; emotional suffering, such as humiliation or indignity and any other bills directly related to the incident. Compensatory damage is to make the injured person whole, or to pay for the damage done. Should the injury have caused the person to become a paraplegic, it may be necessary to include the permanent cost of special care to maintain the individual.

Punitive damages are assessed in an effort to punish a party for the damage done to society in general, and to the plaintiff in particular. They are not in response to the bills the plaintiff has obtained as a result of the incident. A punitive damage award might be made in a situation where there was wilful, wanton and reckless misconduct in a negligence action, or when an entire community has been subjected to a hazard in a strict liability action. The purpose of a punitive damage award is to deter the person from acting again in a similar manner.

SUMMARY

Negligence is the doing of an act or the failure to do an act which a reasonable person would be expected to do. It is conduct which falls below the standard established by law to protect persons against unreasonable harm. For negligence to exist there must be a legal duty of care. The duty must have been breached, and the breach must be the proximate cause of the injury. Substantial damage must have occurred.

Degrees of negligence are negligence, gross negligence and wilful, wanton and reckless misconduct. Defenses to negligence include contributory negligence, comparative negligence and assumption of risk. Remedies usually are compensatory and, when applicable, punitive.

References

Black, Henry Campbell (1979). *Black's Law Dictionary*, 5th Ed. St. Paul, MN: West Publishing Company.
Clark v. Goshen Sunday Morning Softball League, 493 N.Y. Supp. 2d 262 (1985).
Joseph, Kenneth. (1983). Tort Law - Negligence - Assumption of Risk - Sport Injuries. *Duquesne Law Review. 21*, 815-833.
Karns, Jack E. (1986). Negligence and Secondary School Sports Injuries in North Dakota: Who Bears the Legal Liability? *North Dakota Law Review 62*, p. 455.
Keeton, W. Page, Dan B. Dobbs, Robert E. Keeton, and David G. Owen. (1984). *Prosser and Keeton On Torts*, 5th Ed. St. Paul, MN: West Publishing Co.
Restatement of The Law of Torts (Second), (1965).
Rutter v. Northeastern Beaver County School District, 496 Pa. 590, 437 A. 2d 1198 (1981).

5

Case Analysis In Negligence

Negligence is found in most physical activities in the form of malpractice or faulty teaching, inadequate supervision or faulty equipment. Within this chapter, each of these areas will be discussed, applicable cases will be reviewed and suggestions for the professional will be noted. (Note that the cases discussed have been taken from state court of appeals decisions unless specific reference is made to some other court.

EDUCATIONAL MALPRACTICE OR FAULTY TEACHING

Among the negligent actions is faulty teaching, or educational malpractice. This tort has received considerable attention in recent years. In educational malpractice, the injury which may or may not be physical, is failure to learn or failure to be able to demonstrate that something has been learned. For example, failure may be not passing a test in a class room, or not swimming a length of a swimming pool.

Educational malpractice shares the characteristics familiar to medical and legal malpractice, mainly, negligence on the part of the professional. Such negligence is directly related to the teacher's specialty (the teaching of physical skills). Under educational malpractice, courts have asked questions about what was being taught and whether course outlines and acceptable progressions were being followed.

In general, faulty teaching or the use of faulty tests may result in injury. The injury (damage to the student, client or learner) is failure to learn, or failure to be able to obtain a job or meet some other designated requirement. In the teaching of physical activity, failure to learn a skill may also result in a physical injury. For example, if a teacher failed to provide adequate instruction to a student preparing to use the diving board, the student may sustain a physical injury when entering the water. Such an injury could be a result of malpractice, or the failure to properly instruct.

Early Malpractice Case

Examination of educational malpractice cases find the teaching of physical skills creating the history of this tort. From 1938 to 1981 nearly all educational malpractice torts were in the teaching of physical skills. In *Bellman v. San Francisco High School District* (1938), a sophomore sustained a head injury while executing a gymnastics stunt of a brief run, a flat dive over two people and a roll. The student failed to support her body with her arms as her body moved into the roll, denying her the opportunity to tuck her head prior to rolling. The student alleged that the instructor should have known that not all students could perform the exercise safely, that the plaintiff's mental and physical condition did not make her a proper subject for tumbling instruction and that the teacher's instructions were improper. She won a jury trial, which later was affirmed on appeal. The statement that the teacher's instructions were improper and that the student may not have been an appropriate candidate for instruction introduced to the world the concept of educational malpractice.

Bellman also represented a case in which the jury was allowed to decide if the exercise was inherently dangerous, if the student should have been required to take the course and if it was an appropriate activity for a girl. Witnesses for the defendant were denied the opportunity to place books containing pictures of the activity and curriculum guides identifying the stunt as part of the junior high school program, into evidence. Justice Shenk's dissenting opinion clearly illustrated the problem in the following:

> . . . the majority has totally disregarded the rights of boards of education and trustees of school districts to provide courses in physical education in accordance with the power vested in them by law of the state and has placed within the power of the jury to say whether such courses should be offered. (900)

In this case, the jury had enormous discretion and the teacher had little opportunity to demonstrate, through experts and curricular materials, that her duty of care to the student had, in fact, been maintained.

A reading of *Bellman* is valuable because it confirms the feelings most professionals have about what will happen to them in a court of law. It clearly demonstrates the helplessness which many feel. Note: such extreme lack of support for the teacher does not exist in recent decisions.

Contemporary Malpractice Cases

The results in contemporary physical education cases have changed considerably from the results of Bellman. In *Lueck v. City of Janesville* (1973) the court found no evidence that the teacher had failed to use ordinary care in furnishing adequate equipment or in the instruction, supervision or assistance given to the student. The plaintiff, a 17-year-old high school student, was attempting to do a forward roll on still rings when he slipped and fell, sustaining serious injuries. A summary of how the teacher in this situation testified follows:

1. Provided student's grades for the past two years and the criteria upon which they were derived.
2. Identified the progression used in teaching gymnastics and the level of difficulty of the stunt the student was performing at the time of the accident.
3. Verified that sufficient instruction had been provided to enable the student to describe the skill level of the stunt and precautions requisite to its successful performance. Other members of the class were also able to take the stand and attest to the details of the instruction.
4. The teacher clearly articulated his personal approach to individualized instruction.
5. Student and teacher provided detailed descriptions of the safety procedures used in progressions, in determining student's capacity to perform, and in assessing the need for a spotter. Further, the student knew, and related to the court, that he was not to execute a new stunt without going over it with the instructor.
6. Competent expert witnesses explained individualized instruction in gymnastics and the value of its use in the classroom. They also addressed the topic of spotting and its relationship to the acquisition of self-confidence.
7. In response to the alleged negligence of the teacher to fail to assign a spotter to a performing student, the expert and the defendant demonstrated that there were no facts to support negligence but that the idea of the need for a spotter at all times was speculative.

The standard of care in this situation was the standard of a reasonable physical educator. (Although professionals might have a higher personal standard, when they choose to serve as an expert witness they must work with a standard that is reasonable.) It appears that Lueck was upheld because he proved his planning was thorough, he engaged counsel who believed in the capability of the plaintiff and he articulated his goals and demonstrated that he was, in fact, a competent teacher.

In *Larson v. Independent School District No. 314, Brahan* (1979), (the case used in the Case Analysis in Chapter Three) an eighth-grade student became a quadraplegic after breaking his neck while performing a hand spring over a rolled mat. This case provides a number of points that should be noted by teachers, principals and others who are responsible for instruction:

1. Curriculum bulletins used by the Minnesota district as a standard for planning and teaching were considered relevant in the jury determination of whether defendant had breached his duty of care. Such bulletins were not considered mandatory affirmative requirements; however, in situations where the bulletins were not used, the teacher was expected to identify the conceptual plan to which he or she was committed.
2. The principal had responsibility for informing a new teacher of his or her duties.
3. The principal was responsible for an examination of the progression of the gymnastics class, and a determination of whether the teacher was executing the steps in an acceptable manner. One specific question asked was whether an advanced skill had been introduced to the student before it was ascertained that the student knew the elementary skills.
4. Proper spotting or adequate safety devices unique to the activity were documented as used in the classroom.
5. Unit plans were produced. The expert witness stressed the need for detailed units and lesson planning for beginning teachers. Unit planning was considered essential to ensure proper progression and safety.
6. It was deemed essential that substitutes and new teachers become aware of each student's capacity, with reference to baseline skills.

Although the physical educator was found liable, this case established that when a well-planned physical education program exists and can be documented, the courts are eager to support the teacher. In situations where planning is inadequate, courts find it difficult to support the professional. Professionals should note that competent planning and skillful execution of instruction is the framework upon which a successful defense is built and documented.

In *Dibortolo v. Metropolitan School District of Washington Township* (1982), a student obtained a verdict for damage to her mouth. The damage was a result of an injury sustained when taught a preliminary run as part of the jump and reach test. Expert testimony verified that instruction for the jump and reach test requires a student to begin in a standing, not a running position. The court said,

> the evidence that [the teacher] did not demonstrate the exercise, that she specifically directed the student to run during a structured physical activity such as the vertical jump, when juxtaposed with the expert testimony, that such an instruction is not only erroneous, but is also unsafe, would have entitled a jury to reasonably infer that the teacher's conduct exposed the student to an unreasonable risk. Furthermore, there was sufficient evidence from which a jury could have justifiably concluded that [the teacher's] instructions were the proximate cause of the plaintiff's injury. A proximate cause of plaintiff's injury is one which sets in motion the chain of circumstances leading to the injury. (511)

A teacher's instruction was upheld in the recent case, *Smith v. Vernon Parish School Board* (1983). A 15-year-old, straight "A" student was injured when she joined four other students in jumping on a trampoline while the teacher had briefly left the room. Student testimony established that the students had been instructed not to jump in a group, or to jump without supervision. Also, while executing the feat, one member of the group was to hide in the curtains of the stage and report the whereabouts of the teacher.

This case not only reinforced the need to provide proper instruction to students, but gave support to the principle that when the instruction was adequate, the teacher's presence may not be necessary. In this case, the instruction had been given, each student who testified knew of the instruction and was able to repeat the instruction while on the stand.

Most teachers have a distinct fear of what one of their students might decide to do on a moment's notice. *Clark v. Furch* (1978) provided a situation no teacher could anticipate. The plaintiff was a six-year-old kindergartener. A physical education class of 22 students was engaged in rope-jumping activities on a typical elementary school playground. The physical education teacher allowed the children to engage in free play for a few minutes near the end of the class period.

"Plaintiff, still in possession of a jumping rope, climbed to the top of a jungle gym, tied the rope to the top of the apparatus, started to swing down, fell and broke his arm." (458) The court stressed that the student had been taught about the use of playground equipment and knew his action was dangerous. The court ruled that the teacher was not negligent, that ordinary care had been exercised and that the teacher had no previous indication that the student would perform such a stunt.

Another case in which the teacher (defendant) succeeded is *Green v. Orleans Parish School Board* (1978). A 16-year-old student was permanently paralyzed as a result of an injury received in a wrestling bout in a required physical education class. The issue which turned the case was whether a 30-second drill to wrestle "hard" used on the fourth day of class (day of injury) created an unreasonable risk of harm. All of plaintiff's expert witnesses said "yes;" all of defendant's expert witnesses said "no." The court provided the following guidance for professionals working in human movement:

> A teacher has the duty to conduct his classes so as not to expose his students to an unreasonable risk of injury. (836), and

> When an activity is dangerous or has a potential for being dangerous, students should receive instruction before attempting the skill, they should become aware of basic rules and procedures in executing the skill and they should be aware of the risks involved. (836)

No guidelines, national or local, were available which showed how to teach wrestling. The court concluded that the drill in which the student was injured did not fall below a standard acceptable to the profession. Note: the court relied upon the testimony of experts (in this case the defendant's experts), as there were no guidelines to base its opinions.

In one case, the teacher was able to make specific statements with reference to the skill which caused the injury, and the injured student was able to identify how the skills should have been executed. This case resulted in a verdict for the teacher, which later was affirmed by the court of appeals. A 19-year-old high school senior, in *Berg v. Merrick* (1974), was rendered a paraplegic as a result of a neck fracture sustained during a faulty back pullover on a trampoline in a regular physical education class. The student jumped, failed to execute a seat drop, flipped over and landed on his head and neck.

The court ascertained, as a result of testimony by the teacher and a number of students, that each member of the class had been instructed to "stand at one end of the trampoline, jump up slightly and drop down to the trampoline on his seat. The trampoline would then propel his legs over his head and he would land on his stomach, hands and knees or feet." (224, footnote 2) It was further established that the teacher had an adequate, if not superior, background for teaching trampoline and the class members knew that there was to be no horseplay. An expert witness, a well-known university coach and gymnastics instructor, testified that the spotting was appropriate for the size of the class. It was also established that the teacher had used an adequate progression of instruction.

In reference to spotting, the *Segerman v. Jones* (1969) ruling noted that the teacher's presence could not have prevented the accident. In

Segerman, the court stated that the teacher, who left the classroom while young children were doing fitness exercises, was not liable for an injury sustained by one of the children during her absence. The court noted that her presence could not have prevented the accident (804-805).

The incidence in *Berg* ". . . indicates that Mickey Berg's injury was caused by his failure to follow the coach's . . . instruction." (225) Had Berg executed the stunt as directed, the fact that he might land on his head or shoulders was unforeseen. It was an "act which a reasonable, careful and prudent gym teacher could not have anticipated under the circumstances." (227)

Important to all teachers was the court's statement in *Berg* that "teachers who conform to every educational standard known to them should also know that they are protected by legal standards from the frailty of human judgment oft affected by emotion and compassion." (227) Another fact to be noted in this case and in many other cases was the size of the class. The class of 38 students was not mentioned as a large class, nor did the court make any reference to class size.

Standards for Negligence Influence Malpractice Decisions

Standards of negligence differ from state to state. As previously mentioned, many states use negligence as the means of determining liability on the part of the teacher. Some states require a much higher standard of wilful and wanton neglect; mere negligence is not enough. The appeal in *Kobylanski v. Chicago Board of Education* (1976) involved two cases which presented the common issue of whether teachers and school districts could be held liable for injuries to students resulting from allegedly negligent conduct, or whether the greater burden of wilful and wanton misconduct had to be proved before liability was imposed.

Barbara Kobylanski brought an action against her physical education instructor for a spinal injury which resulted from a fall from a knee hang on steel rings suspended from the ceiling, in a regular physical education class. The second case involved Linda Walton, who also sustained a spinal injury, but as a result of performing a front drop on a trampoline. Complaints against the teachers were that they failed to provide proper instruction and supervision. However, neither of the students were able to find wilful and wanton neglect. The court ruled that in the absence of proof of wilful and wanton misconduct, teachers and school districts could not be held liable.

Another Illinois case of gymnastics in the physical education classroom, in which the plaintiff failed to make the wilful and wanton misconduct standard, is *Montague v. School Board of Thornton Fractional Township* (1978). Michael Montague fell while attempting "to vault a horse," and fractured his arm. Prior to the accident, the student had successfully executed the stunt approximately 33 times; in fact, he had executed five or six vaults that day. Facts presented in the case included statements that the teacher:

> at the outset of the tumbling segment, gave the students oral instruction on the use of the horse; he personally instructed each student on his vaults; he reminded the students before each class to be careful when using the vaulting horse . . . and there had been no previous accidents involving the equipment. (831)

The teacher was found liable for wilful and wanton misconduct in *Landers v. School District No. 203, O'Fallon* (1978). Michelle Landers, an overweight 15-year-old, sustained serious injury while executing a backward roll. She was 5'6" tall and weighed 180 pounds. The teacher was found to have wilful and wanton misconduct as a result of ignoring Michelle's statement of fear and her body size, and providing only a brief demonstration of the backward somersault. This case should be read in depth by curriculum planners, and effort should be made to establish teacher rights in light of situations where students are not capable of executing basic skills.

Teacher Becomes Class or Team Member

Another situation which could result in malpractice is the instructor's decision to become a playing or participating member of the class or team. *O'Dell v. School District of Independence* (1975) is such a case. A high school student brought action against his high school wrestling coach for injuries received when the coach applied an illegal hold. Although the case was decided on a theory of immunity rather than the merits of the facts, it issues a warning to teachers to consider their size and skill before joining class participants or young athletic team members.

Most of the malpractice cases have occurred in organized physical education settings. As a result, physical educators should be aware of the tort (educational malpractice) and sensitive to the fact that the profession has been a model for successful plaintiff decisions. Although early decisions were against the teacher, recent decisions have provided positive precedent for teachers and guidance in preparing for litigation.

Whether the decisions rendered in schools and institutions of higher education will carry over to corporate and recreational fitness is unclear. What is certain is that most corporate fitness programs and spas are not enticing clients to extend themselves to maximum potential; they appear to discourage risk activities or the acquisition of elite performance. Schools, on the other hand, continue to strive for student achievement and elite performance. As a result of the difference in emphasis, the pattern of litigation may be different. Insufficient cases exist to draw conclusions.

Another case in which the teacher was part of the classroom was *Schnepf v. Andrews* (1952). This case involved an Arthur Murray Studio of Dancing instructor who allegedly gave the student a push in a turn in the jitterbug and then released her into the turn. Plaintiff (the student) lost her balance, fell into a wall, slipped to the floor and fractured bones in her wrist. Defendant said the plaintiff assumed the risk of injury when enrolling in dance classes. The trial court agreed with the defendant. However, the court of appeals reversed the decision, saying though the plaintiff assumed the foreseeable risk involved in dancing the jitterbug, she did not assume the risk of the push from the negligent instructor.

Participant in Pain

McKinley v. Slenderella (1960) alerts instructors to the practice of permitting clients or students to continue to participate in activity after complaining of injury. In this case, a 51-year-old woman complained of pain following a series of Slenderella treatments. (Slenderella was a set of reducing treatments in which the subject was stretched out on a table containing oscillating equipment. The entire body was subjected to various sequences of oscillating.) She alleged the equipment was faulty, she was not examined for medical problems prior to treatment, she was never told the treatment could cause injury and the treatments were continued after she complained of injury. The court ruled the equipment was in satisfactory condition and the plaintiff was provided a brochure and other information on the treatments; but, Slenderella was negligent in permitting the treatments to continue after the plaintiff complained of pain.

The results of this case are significant to all agencies in which "pain is considered gain." Should people complaining of pain or injury be prohibited from activity? Certainly, the idea of the instructor continuously telling the client that the pain could not possibly be related to the slenderella activity, when in fact it was, was a basis for liability.

FAILURE TO SUPERVISE

Failure to supervise often is credited for injuries in physical activity. Whether it be failure to warn participants of the dangers inherent in certain activities or failure to properly spot in sports such as gymnastics, it has provided the basis for considerable litigation. Supervisors feel they cannot leave the gymnasium or field to take care of personal needs. But remember, results of court cases support the premise that a supervisor or teacher is only accountable for those injuries which they could have prevented had they been present. A well-organized learning and recreational play environment should permit the teacher to move from one area of the room to another, and to even leave the room if necessary.

Another factor commonly mentioned in physical activity cases is failure to render adequate first aid and to immediately seek medical assistance. Procedures for such emergency care should be well planned and efficient.

Play Within Established Rules and Matched Teams

Whether the athlete should be forced to play within the confines of established rules, and whether teachers and operators of facilities should be held liable when participants ignore those rules was the basis of the suit in *Dillon v. Keatington Racquetball Club* (1986). A 38-year-old man was injured while acting as a member of a five-person "pick-up team" in a walleyball game. (Walleyball is the game of volleyball played on a racquetball court. The official rules state that teams shall consist of two, three or four people.) During play, he collided with a teammate and was injured. He alleged that his injuries were a result of too many people on the playing court.

The question to the court was "whether a recreational facility and its agents owe a duty to its members or customers to supervise informal games to ensure compliance with the games' rules." (213) In other words, was defendant under a legal duty to enforce the rules of the game? The court made note of the fact that had there been young children involved, there may have been a duty to specify numbers. The court concluded that "the facility has no obligation to supervise the patrons to ensure that they play the game according to the rules or otherwise in a safe manner." (214-215)

The courts, in their effort to look for established standards, often look to the rules of games. In intentional torts in professional athletics, the fact that the athlete ignores the rules has become a basis for finding liability. Whether rules should be used as a standard outside of professional athletics is a question which should be examined by the physical activity professional. In *Dillon*, the court refused to impose such liability on a recreational agency. Had the game and the environment been more formal, would the court have behaved in the same manner?

A recent case in which the agency was held liable for assigning teams of unlike players to a common match has great significance. In *Benitez v. City of New York* (1986), a 19-year-old high school student suffered a broken neck, fractured vertebrae and a slipped disc while making a block during game play on his high school's football team. Benitez alleged that the New York Board of Education was responsible for the injury because it was negligent in allowing mismatched teams to compete. In this case, a high school "B" division team was matched with an "A" division team. The jury found the Board of Education 70 percent liable for negligence of its employees in assigning "A" and "B" division teams to the same match, and the plaintiff 30 percent liable as a result of agreeing to participate. $875,000 was awarded to the plaintiff.

Use of Safety Equipment

The importance of using the safest equipment available in risk sports has been another concern of the court. Dental damage and injuries to the mouth were the injuries sustained in *Berman v. Philadelphia Board of Education* (1983). Brad Berman, an 11-year-old fifth-grade student, was injured in a floor hockey game when an opponent made a backhand shot and followed through, causing his stick to make contact with Brad's mouth. Considerable expense and pain were endured, as a number of Brad's teeth had to be capped and repaired.

In response to questions from the court, the teacher made satisfactory explanations of his safety procedures and his instructions to prohibit slapshots and raising the stick above the waist. When asked if aware of safety equipment used in such play, the teacher said he was. He also reported that safety equipment was not required in ordinary play. No such standard existed, nor was it a typical pattern in other schools engaged in floor hockey.

The trial court held, and the appellate court affirmed, that despite no requirements to provide safety equipment, the school board, in failing to provide such equipment, failed to assure the safety and welfare of the student during the game. Therefore, the school was negligent for the injuries to the student's mouth. Further, the court ruled that the student's youth and lack of experience precluded a finding of contributory negligence or assumption of risk. An interesting point was made when the court noted that no serious accidents had occurred in the floor hockey games prior to Brad's encounter; therefore, Brad had no experience which would indicate to him the severity of the risk.

A school district's responsibility to ensure that students have adequate protective equipment was the issue in *Gerrity v. Beatty* (1978). Mathew Gerrity suffered severe injuries when making a tackle in a football game. His complaint was filed against the manufacturer of the helmet, the attending physician, the hospital, the fire department safety squad who transported him to the hospital and the school district. The school district was granted a motion to be stricken from the case. Gerrity appealed that motion to the Supreme Court of Illinois. The Supreme Court held that where a school district carelessly and negligently:

(a) Permitted and allowed the plaintiff to wear an ill fitting and inadequate football helmet;

(b) Refused to furnish adequate and proper football equipment upon the plaintiff's request;

(c) Furnished and provided the plaintiff with an ill fitting and inadequate football helmet when it knew or in the exercise of ordinary care should have known said helmet was liable and likely to cause plaintiff injury. (1325)

The school district was not immune from suit and the student was not required, under Illinois statute, to prove wilful and wanton misconduct. The district was held responsible for issuing ill-fitting gear for the athletic contest.

Role of Teacher in Extracurricular Activities

What is the role of teachers and supervisors in extracurricular events? *Verhel v. Independent School District No. 709*, a 1984 Minnesota case, provides some interesting points on that subject. Twelve cheerleaders from a Duluth, Minnesota public high school were involved in a serious car accident at 5:00 a.m. on August 30, 1980, while bannering football players' homes before the opening game of the season. The cheerleader driver of the van testified that she was very tired and in a hurry, and ran a stop sign at the scene of the accident. The driver of the second car admitted to considerable drinking prior to the incident, but no specific statement was made as to his level of intoxication at the scene of the accident.

Suit was brought by head cheerleader and her father against the school district, the faculty advisor and the driver of the car. However, this discussion will focus on the faculty advisor. The advisor, a second-year teacher, had been assigned supervision of the cheerleaders the previous spring; however, she was not under contract to assist them in practice nor to meet with them during the summer.

The incident occurred prior to the opening of school, or the beginning of the advisor's teaching contract. The advisor did, however, attend some of the practice sessions. The case against the teacher hinged on whether she had knowledge of the bannering and whether bannering was a recognized school activity. Although school officials recognized the cheerleaders as an official group, they presented evidence to suggest that bannering was not one of the group's recognized activities.

It was concluded that even though the teacher was not yet under contract as team advisor nor did she participate in the bannering, she should have stopped the event if she was aware it was going to occur. The teacher claimed she was not present during the discussion and heard of the bannering only as an offhand remark.

The plaintiffs' evidence included a purchase order the teacher signed for the students to obtain materials for the bannering, and the fact that the students borrowed tape and scissors from the principal's office, thus alerting the principal or school district to their activity.

The court concluded that not only was the cheerleading advisor inexperienced, but she had not been properly supervised by the school district. As a result, the teacher was not found liable. The district court, under comparative negligence, allocated the responsibility accordingly:

School district	35 percent
Driver of second car	26 percent
Driver of cheerleader van	39 percent
Faculty advisor	0 percent

The Supreme Court of Minnesota affirmed the decision of the district court. It should be noted that this precedent would affect only Minnesota because it is a Minnesota State Supreme Court decision. This decision points out the responsibility the Minnesota Court feels a school district has for any event of which they are aware. Even though school officials refuse or do not participate in an activity or event, they will be held accountable for those actions of students of which they are aware.

A case in which the responsible parties were difficult to define, and one that many professionals in physical activity can identify to, was *Swanson v. Wabash College* (1987). Dan Taylor, a varsity baseball player, decided to organize a fall practice schedule for students interested in becoming varsity baseball players. He contacted the baseball coach for help, but was informed the coach was busy with football practice. The baseball coach told the varsity baseball player that as far as the athletic department was concerned, he was on his own (328). The coach did, however, give the varsity baseball player access to the baseball equipment, and the Dean of Men of the College provided money for the purchase of baseballs for practice.

Freshman Eric Swanson was hit in the eye while playing the position of shortstop. He filed a claim against Wabash College for the eye injury. The trial court found that: "(1) The College had no duty to supervise the baseball practices, (2) Dan Taylor was not an agent of Wabash College, and (3) Eric incurred the risk of his injury." (329)

The First District Court of Appeals of Indiana affirmed the trial court, stating that the college could not be held liable for a group of students getting together for recreational play, particularly when some of them were not varsity team members. No evidence was available to support the claim that the varsity player taking charge was an agent or employee of the school.

In *Lovitt v. Concord School District* (1975), two high school football players suffered heat prostration during football practice; one died, and one suffered permanent injury. The families brought action against the school and the teachers/coaches. At the time, governmental immunity prohibited the plaintiffs from recovering against the school; the trial court ruled accordingly. The court of appeals upheld the governmental immunity with reference to the school district but found the teachers/coaches liable for negligence. The court, in recognizing the role of personal negligence on the part of the teachers stated that, "the liability of the teacher is not based upon negligence imputed to them as public functionaries, but rather it arises from their individual conduct. They must be held accountable for their own actions." (483) When teachers are found to be negligent, they may not be protected under governmental immunity. The courts may choose to find them personally liable.

Accidents Involving Crossing of Streets

Injuries sustained by students crossing streets or entering parking lots are often encountered in the teaching of physical activity. Though the classroom or gymnasium may be fully supervised and all precautions taken, student movement between the school and other facilities should be carefully monitored. Cases in which movement between facilities became a problem include *Flournoy v. McComas* (1971), in which a junior high school student was killed crossing a street to a physical education class; *Taylor v. Oakland Scavenger Company* (1941), in which a 15-year-old girl sustained permanent foot and leg injuries when she ran into a garbage truck as she lead her classmates out the door of the school to a nearby playing field; and *Lunday v. Vogelmann* (1973), in which a student was run over by a lawn mower while chasing a ball during a physical education class.

Supervision of Students Excused From Participation

Students who report to class unable to participate because of failure to properly dress, medical excuse or parent permission to refrain from activity, present problems to the professional. Whether teachers should be responsible for individuals who have been prohibited from instruction is a question that has never been addressed by the courts and is seldom answered in school policy. *Siau v. Rapids Parish School Board* (1972) provides guidance and advice to the teacher given the responsibility of supervising such students.

William Siau, a 10th-grade student, attended a physical education class without the proper dress. He was assigned to sit in the bleachers.

That day, the class was running a 880-yard track event. Siau discovered that if he did not complete the run, he would be prohibited from trying out for softball. Siau decided to run on the outfield, alongside his classmates; he was immediately told by an instructor to stop. Ignoring the teacher's caution, Siau ran at full speed. Looking back at his classmates, he ran into a javelin (which was properly stored), impaling himself.

Evidence introduced in court was that the student was not wearing his glasses, thus restricting his vision; that the space in which he chose to run was not used for running; and that the student was well aware the space was not used for running. The court ruled that the student was negligent and that his contributory negligence was the proximate cause of the injury.

CASES IN GENERAL

Golf and gymnastics are activities that place students and teachers at a high level of risk. Golf injuries usually involve students of junior or senior high school or college age; few cases exist in elementary settings or with professional instruction groups.

Brahatcek v. Millard School District #17 (1979) is a case in which a 14-year-old died as a result of being struck by a golf club in a junior high school physical education class. A student teacher had replaced the full-time teacher the day the accident occurred. The question for the court was the adequacy of the supervision and the negligence of the deceased student. The court ruled that the supervision was inadequate, that the only instructions the student had received in golf were from the student who delivered the fatal blow and that Brahatcek did not know enough about the activity to be contributarily negligent. The class consisted of 34 boys, 23 girls, and two teachers. Note: no mention was made of the problems that might occur in permitting nearly 60 students to swing golf clubs.

Catania v. The University of Nebraska (1983), where a judgment for the student in the District Court was reversed in the Supreme Court of Nebraska, is a case that illustrates the need for the instructor to be aware of alternative strategies and the merits of the strategy selected for use. The issue in the case was the organization of the class for indoor golf practice. The plaintiff was injured when hit in the eye by a plastic golf ball driven by one of his fellow students. The teacher, who had considerable experience and academic credentials, convinced the court that the oval formation used met accepted physical education standards and was superior to the double line formation recommended by the expert witness.

Note that many of the malpractice cases discussed also alleged failure to supervise. In the learning environment — spa, physical education classroom or athletic practice field — the courts will fully examine instruction before looking at supervision. When the environment is a "free play" or playground situation, no instruction is expected to be imparted thus causing the court to focus on the elements of supervision. Also, the courts attempt to determine the number of participants in these "free play" areas under the supervision of a single instructor; one supervisor to 100 students is a typical ratio.

In *Collins v. The Bossier Parish School Board* (1986; writ denied Feb. 7, 1986), a kindergarten boy fell from the monkey bars and sustained a severe leg injury after another child wrapped his legs around Collins. Both children fell; apparently, the other child was not injured. Collin's father brought suit against the father of the child who did the leg wrapping for causing the fall, and against the school board for failing to supervise the playground during recess. The district court awarded judgment against the father of the boy causing the injury of $13,141.05, and dismissed the suit against the school board. Collins appealed the decision of the board.

The Court of Appeals of Louisiana affirmed the trial court's decision, saying the one to 80 student ratio was adequate and there was no indication that had another teacher been present the action would have stopped. The employees were not negligent in their supervision of the children during recess. The court pointed out that the children had been told only one person was to be on the equipment at any one time.

Students suing other students and adult participants suing other participants for injuries occurring in physical activity is not uncommon. In *Collins*, the boy who wrapped his legs around the plaintiff knew he was not to be on the monkey bars and had been informed that the type of activity he was engaging in was unsafe and could bring harm to himself and others. Other similar cases will be discussed under intentional torts in Chapter Six.

Failure to warn students about injuries is negligence that can be classified under supervision. It should be considered among the supervision responsibilities in a risk management program. Warnings and how to use warnings are discussed in Chapter Seven, Product Liability.

FAULTY EQUIPMENT

In addition to educational malpractice and failure to supervise, faulty equipment can place physical activity professionals at risk. Faulty equipment and faulty facilities set precedent for much of the early litigation in physical activity. Weakened climbing ropes, defective trampoline springs, poorly-maintained gymnastics equipment, splinters on bats and arrows, holes in fields and tennis courts and leaking roofs contributed to facility and equipment risks. Response to these dangers has caused supervisors and teachers to rid the profession of many of these problems; thus, the number of faulty equipment cases has decreased. Equipment and facilities will be discussed separately; note how facilities, on occasion, may be influenced by property law as well as negligence.

Bleachers create many problems in sport and physical education. It is not uncommon for spectators to fall off bleachers, and occasionally for bleachers to collapse during competitive events. Far more difficult a problem is the placement of bleachers on the perimeter of the classroom playing area. Curricular planners agree that all wall and peripheral playing space should be used for practice, making most portable bleachers an obstacle.

Children injured by protruding bleachers is not uncommon; *Tijerina v. Evans* (1986) is such a case. The student was injured when she ran into the protruding last row of the bleachers during a whiffle ball game in a physical education class. She brought action against the teacher for wilful and wanton misconduct. The teacher allegedly required students to participate in a game in close quarters which produced a danger of injury, failed to warn students of the danger of the game, failed to inspect the gym for dangers and failed to put the bleachers into proper position. Tijerina's action against the school district was for failure to use reasonable care in providing safe facilities. All actions were dismissed, as the student was unable to build a case for wilful and wanton neglect or misconduct under Illinois statutes.

In *Hornyak v. The Pomfret School* (1986), a 15-year-old was injured when she lost her balance on the bench during the Harvard Step Test. She brought action against the school. The bench used in the test was allegedly placed on uneven ground. The trial court dismissed the case. The first circuit of appeals reversed and held that the question of negligence should be decided by a jury.

In *Tiemann v. Independent School District #740* (1983), a student fell and injured her leg during a physical education class. While vaulting over a horse, she caught a finger in the hole left by the removal of a pommel from the horse. She sued the teacher, the school district and the manufacturer of the equipment. The district court granted a directed verdict and a judgment in favor of all the defendants. The Plaintiff appealed. The Supreme Court of Minnesota affirmed the trial court's decision only against the manufacturer; it reversed the decision against the school and the teacher and remanded for a new trial. In reversing the trial court's decision against the school and the teacher it pointed out:

> We do not intimate that use of the horse with holes exposed was necessarily negligent, for we hold only that where reasonable minds might differ with respect to whether the harm was one which the

teacher should reasonably have anticipated, the question of negligence is one of fact for the jury. (251)

The concept of prevailing custom should be noted here. A teacher or a school district has a good argument when their behavior is typical of the physical education industry. Also note that Tiemann mentions that in the event that the jury ruled that the custom represented conduct below a standard of reasonable care, the defendant would be liable.

In *Jackson v. Board of Education* (1982), a child who was injured when she fell from a swing on a school playground brought action against the Chicago Board of Education for negligence in "failing to supervise the playground properly; failing to maintain the swings adequately; and failing to provide and maintain adequate mats for the protection of children falling from swings." (121) The circuit court entered judgment for defendant, but plaintiff appealed. Appellate Court of Illinois, First District Third Division, affirmed. (Unfortunately, the court never discussed the details of the potential need for mats under swings.)

A 34-year-old man was injured when he jumped to catch a pass during a basketball game, in *Pedersen v. Joliet Park District* (1985). As he came down with the ball he fell to the floor, tearing ligaments in his knee. Pedersen filed a complaint against the Joliet, Illinois School District No. 86, who owned the building and the Joliet Park District, who had leased the building for the activity. Pederson charged the defendants with inadequate cleaning and maintenance of the floor and for failure to warn him of the dangerous condition. However, the plaintiff's deposition stated the floor did not have any visible defects, did not appear dirty or slippery and appeared in "good shape."

The court ruled the plaintiff's deposition or "account of the accident indicated that he did not slip on the floor." (24) The trial court and the court of appeals both ruled for the defendant.

In *Chase v. Shasta Lake Union School District* (1968), an adult playing in a recreational league softball game ran into a concrete incinerator adjacent to the field on the grounds of an elementary school. Chase suffered severe skull injuries. The trial court found the school district negligent in knowingly maintaining a dangerous condition, but stated that Chase had assumed the risk. Chase appealed. The court of appeals reversed.

DUTY OF CARE OF PROPERTY OWNERS

A person owning land, or considered in possession of land as a result of a lease or some other business arrangement, may be liable to persons entering the land. Generally, the possessor of land is not liable for natural conditions which might be dangerous. There are three levels of duty owed by those in possession of land to the various publics who might enter the land: invitee, licensee and trespasser.

Invitee

An invitee is a person who has either expressly or implicitly been invited onto the land for an economic benefit to the person in possession of the land. On occasion, particularly in state and federal recreation areas, the public at large has been invited onto the land. Even though no economic motive may influence the invitation to the public, the person or agency in possession of the land is responsible at an invitee level. Duties owed to the invitee include keeping the premises in a reasonably safe condition and when dangerous conditions exist, natural or artificial, providing warning of such conditions. The possessor of land is not only responsible for reasonable care and adequate warning to invitees about known dangers but also about those conditions of which the invitee should have been aware. For example, amusement park participants are invitees; the owner of the park is responsible for reasonable care and adequate warnings about known dangers and conditions of which the invitees should be aware.

Licensee

A licensee also is a person who is on the land with expressed or implied permission, for no economic benefit. A social guest is a licensee, as is an individual who goes onto someone's land with the owner's knowledge and is not asked to leave. If a farmer knows hunters are on the farmer's land and fails to ask them to leave or fails to post signs, the person entering the land might be considered a licensee. Duties to the licensee are the same as duties to the invitee, with one very important exception: the licensee is to be warned or protected only from harms of which the possessor of the land is aware.

Trespasser

The trespasser is a person who goes onto land without permission and without the knowledge of the possessor. The possessor of land owes no duty of care to the trespasser. Owners need not warn trespassers of danger, nor have a need to use reasonable care in anticipating trespassers. However, when owners become aware that a trespasser may be on their property, they cannot create a harm which the trespasser could not have anticipated. For example, someone has trespassed into an equipment hut; the possessor of the equipment hut would not be responsible if the trespasser sprained an ankle on the uneven floor. However, the possessor of the hut could be liable if he or she thought some-one was in the hut and decided to burn it down.

When the trespasser is a minor, the reason for trespassing takes on importance. If the condition of the land, or of an object on the land, presents an attraction and a danger to the minor there may be liability under the theory of attractive nuisance. In order for the theory to apply, the possesser of the land must foresee the potential attractiveness and the fact that a child could be seriously harmed. No defense is available in attractive nuisance, as the child is considered too young to appreciate the danger.

Whether one was an invitee or a licensee and the duty of care pro-vided each category was the issue in Light et al. v. Ohio University (1986). A child, playing in a locker room, pulled a number of lockers over on her body, sustaining serious injuries. The mother was in the locker room at the time the accident occurred. The complaint charged Ohio University with negligence in the placement, maintenance and operation of the lockers in the recreation facility.

The trial court found that the Lights, mother and daughter, were licensees and that no legal duty had been breached. The court of appeals reversed the judgment and remanded for a new trial, saying the Lights were invitees. The court of appeals gave business invitee status on the fact that there was a charge for the coin-operated lockers, even though Mrs. Light hadn't the chance to put a coin in the locker. In the new trial, the court supported the finding of the trial court; the Lights were licensees. Further, the court noted that "the duty owed by a licensor is to refrain from wantonly or wilfully causing harm to the licensee. There is no charge of wanton or wilful misconduct ... and no evidence in the record which would support such a finding." (168) Ohio University had breached no duty of care to the little girl who pulled the lockers over.

CASES INVOLVING FACILITIES IN GENERAL

In Curtis v. Ohio State University (1986) the issue was the safety of the glass in the door on which the plaintiff was injured. Curtis, a member of the football team, was practicing an exercise referred to as "a liner" in the French Field House on the Ohio State University campus. He ran beyond the designated area and struck a wire-reinforced glass door, pushing his foot and leg through the glass and sustaining injuries.

The court noted that, "A great deal of factual conflict exists in the record as to whether Curtis' contact with the door was unavoidable, or a diversion, consisting of a jumping kick turn off the glass door's push-bar type door handle." (366) This issue never was resolved. The court found that Ohio State University had met the standard required by law for safety glass in the area and had no reason to believe a student would be injured in that manner in that area of the building.

Negligence per se for violation of a department of Health rule concerning swimming pool safety was found in *First Overseas Investment Corp. v. Cotton* (1986). Cotton, a hotel guest, went swimming in the shallow end of the hotel pool and drowned. The water in the pool was so cloudy that persons in the pool, who noticed Mr. Cotton missing, spent 20 minutes looking for him by swimming lengths of the pool. The cloudy pool condition was caused by an inoperative filtration system that dumped large quantities of ash into the water. When Cotton was brought up, no rescue equipment was available.

The suit for wrongful death alleged that Cotton would not have drowned if the hotel had complied with the Florida Department of Health rules which included specifications for swimming pool filtration and chemical systems. The awarded negligence per se is automatic negligence. There need not be a finding of negligence or a search for the four factors of negligence. (Violation of a statute is considered automatic negligence or negligence per se.)

Sloppy maintenance was also the alleged injury in *Gatti v. World Wide Health Studio of Lake Charles, Inc.* (1975). Plaintiff, a 59-year-old businessman, in his testimony stated that "after sitting on the top step of the steam room for a few minutes he attempted to get up where upon his feet slipped out from under him causing him to fall down all three steps." (820) He sustained a back injury. He said he thought he slipped on lotion left by someone earlier in the day. His complaint alleged negligence on the part of the spa for failure to keep the steps clean, use non-skid tape on the steps, warn of slippery conditions, provide hand rails, and maintain and inspect the steam room.

Both trial court and court of appeals agreed that the plaintiff fell and sustained a back injury; however, they stated the plaintiff failed to prove the fall was caused by lotion on the steps and to establish actionable negligence. This case points out the court's behavior when an injury occurs and there is no concrete evidence as to how the injury occurred.

In *Markowitz v. Arizona Parks Board* (1985), a mother brought action against the State of Arizona for injuries her son sustained when he took a dive into shallow water in a lake in a state recreation area. David Markowitz, a 15-year-old boy who had taken both life-saving and scuba instruction, dove into the cove without checking the depth of the water or the condition of the bottom. It was the first time he had seen the cove. He did notice, prior to diving, about 15 people swimming and wading in the water. His companion took a flat dive and swam away unharmed. David hit his head on a ledge or a sandbar (details were not specific). In his testimony, David admitted that as a result of his previous swimming experience he knew he should check the bottom before going into unknown water.

David's argument was that the cove should have been marked. Had he observed a sign warning of dangerous diving conditions he would not have entered the water in a dive. The trial court and the court of appeals agreed that the state "owed no duty to David, and even if it did, the injuries were not proximately caused by any breach of that duty." (1985, 366) The fact that the boy was aware of a need to check the bottom before diving into the water means he had a warning. Therefore, the park had no requirement to notify him of the need for prevention.

The court discusses the duty of the state in this negligence case the same as the duty of an individual, by noting that:

> . . . we must contemplate the possession of 45 miles of shoreline and 13,000 plus acres of undeveloped land as though held in possession by an individual but at the same time open to the public for use as a park. There is no dispute that members of the public, including the injured plaintiff, were permitted freely to enter upon the lands and waters of Lake Havasu Park and to use its resources for recreation. As such, they are classified as 'invitees' for purposes of tort law. There is no dispute about this in the present case.
>
> In considering the duty of the State, it is necessary to give some perspective to the physical and geographical circumstances involved. Lake Havasu Park is not a small, confined area with supervised facilities for campers and picknickers, constantly within view of park rangers and supervisory personnel. The area is essentially undisturbed and unimproved rolling desert terrain down to the water's edge. (939 & 940)

The trial court and the court of appeals agreed on this decision. The Supreme Court of Arizona reversed and remanded their decision for further proceedings. The Court agreed that David was an "invitee." It noted that the invitee relationship imposed a duty on the state to take "reasonable precautions for David's safety." (1985, 367) The court concluded, after considerable discussion, that the concept of reasonable precautions was that the state or park should have posted the dangerous area to warn visitors that diving was prohibited. The court concluded that due to the state's inability to inspect the vast area of shore available for diving, all diving should be prohibited.

SUMMARY

Negligence is the legal theory most often encountered in sport and physical activity. The reason for this is related to the risk involved in physical activity — risk within the activities, and risks created by poorly prepared and poorly skilled people choosing to engage in complex sports. Injuries occur; those who engage in the provision and supervision of sport and physical activities are held to a standard of care which will decrease injuries. When injuries occur as a result of their negligence, they may be expected to participate in the expenses incurred by persons sustaining injuries.

Negligence may be a result of malpractice or faulty teaching, failure to supervise or failure to warn of potential risk and faulty equipment. In addition to the expected duties of care, professionals in sport and physical activity need to be aware of the duties of care expected of a property owner; invitee, licensee and trespasser require a specific duty of care.

References

Bellman v. San Francisco High School District, 11 Cal. 2d 576, 81 P. 2d 894 (1938).
Benitez v. City of New York, Bronx Supreme Court, Index No. 7407/85 (May 29, 1986).
Berg. v. Merrick, 20 Md. App. 666, 318 A. 2d 220. (1974).
Berman v. Philadelphia Board of Education, 456 A. 2d 545 (Pa. Super. 1983).
Brahatcek v. Millard School District #17, 202 Neb. 86, 273 N.W. 2d 680 (1979).
Catania v. The University of Nebraska. 213 Neb. 418, 329 N.W. 2d 354 (1983).
Chase v. Shasta Lake Union School District, 66 Cal. Rptr. 517 (1968).
Clark v. Furch, 567 S.W. 2d 457 (1978).
Collins v. The Bossier Parish School Board, 480 S. 2d 846 (1985) (Writ denied Feb. 7, 1986).
Curtis v. Ohio State University, 29 Ohio App. 3d 297 (1986). A motion to certify the record to the Supreme Court of Ohio was overruled on January 21, 1987 (case no. 86-1865).
Dibortolo v. Metropolitan School District of Washington Township, 440 N.E. 2d 506 (1982).
Dillon v. Keatington Racquetball Club, 151 Mich. App. 138, 390 N.W. 2d 212 (1986).
First Overseas Investment Corp. v. Cotton, 491 So. 2d 293 (Fla. Dist. Ct. of App. 1986).
Flournoy v. McComas, 488 P. 2d 1104 (1971).
Gatti v. World Wide Health Studios of Lake Charles, Inc., 323 So. 2d 819 (1975).
Gerrity v. Beatty, 71 Ill. 2d 47, 15 Ill. Dec. 639 (1978).
Green v. Orleans Parish School Board, 365 S. 2d 834 (1978).
Hornyak v. The Pomfret School, 783 F. 2d 284 (1st Cir. 1986).
Jackson v. Board of Education, 441 N. E. 2d 120 (1982).
Kobylanski v. Chicago Board of Education, 63 Ill. 2d 165, 347 N.E. 2d 705 (1976).
Landers v. School District No. 203, O'Fallon, 66 Ill. App. 3d 78 (1978).
Larson v. Independent School District No. 314, Braham, 289 N.W. 2d 112 (1979) (Rehearing denied, 1980).
Light et al. v. Ohio University, 28 Ohio St. 3d 66 (1986).
Lovitt v. Concord School District, 58 Mich. App. 593, 228 N.W. 2d 479 (1975).
Lueck v. City of Janesville, 57 Wis. 2d 254, 204 N.W. 2d 6 (1973).
Lunday v. Vogelmann, 213 N.W. 2d 904 (1973).
Markowitz v. Arizona Parks Board, 705 P. 2d 937, 146 Ariz. 260 (1984).
Markowitz v. Arizona Parks Board, 706 P. 2d 364, 146 Ariz. 352 (1985).
McKinley v. Slenderella, 63 N.J. Super. 571, 165 A. 2d. 207 (1960).
Montague v. School Board of Thornton Fractional Township North High School District 215, 57 Ill. App. 3d 828 (1978).
O'Dell v. School District of Independence, 521 S.W. 2d 403 (1975).
Pedersen v. Joliet Park District, 136 Ill. App. 3d 172, 90 Ill. Dec. 874 (1985).
Restatement of The Law of Torts, (Second), (1965).

Rutter v. Northeastern Beaver County School District, 496 Pa. 590, 437 A. 2d 1198 (1981).
Schnepf v. Andrews, 333 Mich. Rpts. 510 (1952).
Segerman v. Jones, 256 Md. 109, 259 A. 2d 794 (1969).
Siau v. Rapids Parish School Board, 264 S. 2d 372 (1972).
Smith v. Vernon Parish School Board, 442 So. 2d 1319 (La. App. 3rd Cir. 1983).
Swanson v. Wabash College, 504 N.E. 2d 327 (Ind. App. 1 Dist. 1987).
Taylor v. Oakland Scavenger Company, 17 C. 2d 594 (1941).
Tiemann v. Independant School District #740, 331 N.W. 2d 250 (Minn. 1983).
Tijerina v. Evans, 150 Ill. App. 3d 288, 103 Ill. Dec. 678, 501 N.E. 2d 995 (1986).
Verhel v. Independent School District, No. 709, 359 N.W. 2d 579 (Minn. 1984).

6

Intentional Torts

Intentional torts are injuries caused by a deliberate act, or a failure to act. Intentional torts possess distinct characteristics; as a result, different responses are advanced by the defending party to each tort. The following discussion will identify each intentional tort and include a list of the elements of the tort. Examples of the tort and suggestions for avoiding occurrence of the tort also will be provided.

Intentional torts most often encountered in sports, athletics and physical activity are torts to persons and property. Managers in private enterprise also will encounter intentional torts in economic relations. By intentional, tort is meant that the person executing the act intends to do the act. A person intentionally hitting another in the heat of competition expects the act to be carried out; however, the person does not intend that an injury will be sustained as a result of the act. For example, a linebacker intended to sack the quarterback, but didn't mean to injure that player's neck. Intent is a factor to be considered. Was there intent only to do the act, or was there intent to do the act as well as intent to harm the plaintiff?

In reckless misconduct, there is an intent to commit the act, but no intent to harm the plaintiff. Substantial damage is not required; in fact, the person need not be injured. However, an act executed with an intent to harm another is not only an intentional tort, but could become a criminal offense. If a substantial injury or death should occur, the actor could be accountable for a criminal act.

INTENTIONAL TORTS TO PERSONS

Intentional torts to persons include battery, assault, false imprisonment and reckless misconduct. They may occur between persons engaging in an activity, or between a coach, teacher or supervisor and a player or client. Physical discipline of students also will be discussed as an aspect of intentional torts.

Battery

Battery is an intentional harmful or offensive contact with another person, without that person's consent. The physical contact must be intentional; however, there does not need to be intent to injure, and injury or damage does not need to occur. Note: in defining battery, all extensions of the body such as golf clubs, hockey sticks, rackets or paddles, are considered part of the person.

Continuous, intentional tagging and pushing in a basketball game; engaging in locker room pranks; hitting another in the heat of competition or pushing a player out of the way could, given the right circumstances, become battery. Teams fighting with opponents at the conclusion of game play is a battery often observed on television. Throwing team members into a swimming pool in celebration of success is a battery.

Numerous batteries, seldom recognized as such, exist in the traditional rituals of recreational and competitive sport and in other collegiate activities, particularly those involving fraternities. Many of these collegiate activities take place in public or university sport arenas. When they take place in facilities under the supervision of physical activity specialists, they become our responsibility.

One does not commit a battery if the other party consented to the act. The element of consent, however, is a difficult one to assess. For example, does competing in and winning a swim meet give consent to fellow team members to toss one into the water in celebration?

For years, the courts found it difficult to assess sports injuries as intentional torts. They usually held that an individual engaging in sport, particularly body contact sport, had agreed to any hazard that might occur. Attitudes started to change as the courts faced severe injuries, particularly when rules had been created to deter injuries and offenses that would be considered assault and battery or criminal under ordinary circumstances. The tort, reckless disregard for others (discussed in later chapters, has become a popular category for sport litigation in which the action resembles battery but the court is hesitant to label the action a battery.

One case clearly identified as battery was *Griggas v. Clauson* (1955). Griggas was an action by a mother on behalf of her minor son for injuries he sustained in a recreational basketball league game. The court ascertained that the injury occurred when:

defendant was standing directly in back of plaintiff . . . that plaintiff was about to receive a pass of the ball from a team mate when defendant pushed him and then struck him in the face with his fist and, as plaintiff fell, struck him again, knocking him unconscious. (364)

As a result of the blow he received, the plaintiff lay on the ground unconscious for 15 minutes, spent 20 days in the hospital and sustained many injuries, some permanent. A jury award of $2,000 against the young man who injured Griggas was affirmed on appeal.

Another case, which occurred in an even more informal environment, was *Kabella v. Bouschelle* (1983). Vance Kabella sustained a hip dislocation in a "friendly game of tackle football." The boys previously had agreed that when a "ball-carrier announced that he was down," the opponent would let go of his body. Gregg Boushelle apparently failed to let go of Kabella after Kabella announced numerous times that he was down.

Although the request to the court was on the theory of negligence, the court analyzed the case as an intentional tort and later returned to negligence in arriving at the decision. The court found that Bouschelle had no intention of hurting Kabella. Conclusions were that "the players had agreed to stop play activity when the ball carrier yelled 'I'm down.' Kabella's complaint does not allege that this practice or rule was for the protection or safety of a participant or that violation of the rule constituted an intent to harm." (294) The claim was dismissed; the dismissal was affirmed on appeal.

In *Bourque v. Duplechin* (1976), one softball player injured another player during a double play in a recreational league game. As Duplechin ran full speed into second baseman Jerome Bourque, Duplechin brought his arm up under Bourque's chin, fracturing Bourque's jaw and breaking seven teeth. The umpire removed Duplechin from the game as a result of the contact. Bourque brought suit against Duplechin and Allstate, the defendant's liability insurer.

The lower court found for Bourque. Duplechin appealed to the Court of Appeals of Louisiana. The Court of Appeals rejected the *Duplechin* decision, saying Bourque had assumed the risk of the injury. The Court said Bourque had assumed the normal risk of injury from a ball, bat, or spike; however, he did not assume the risk of an opponent acting in an unsportsmanlike fashion. It also ruled that there was no evidence of contributory negligence on the part of Bourque.

Note that Allstate Insurance Company claimed on appeal that its insurance plan covered only negligence, not an intentional tort. Allstate said that the policy it had on the defendant covered only negligence (Chapter Four); if the court concluded that the defendant's actions were an intentional tort, the policy would not cover his actions. Allstate would not pay the damage award. Allstate's position in this matter should serve as an alert to professionals to carefully examine their insurance policy coverage.

These cases are the results of litigation over intentional torts in sports, and differ from the cases on intentional torts in general. An intentional tort requires only an intent to execute an act; results of court decisions in sport seem to require that there be both an intent to act and an intent to injure. Given the nature of sport, an event in which participants, agree to certain risks, the courts have been reluctant to find an intentional tort unless evidence of intent to injure existed.

In addition to battery occurring within the competitive arena, there are batteries occurring as a result of athletes injuring spectators. Sometimes it is negligence on the part of the stadium owner, and other times the team or a team member may be held for an intentional tort as a result of hitting a spectator.

In *Manning v. Grimsley* (1981), a spectator at a professional baseball game was injured by a ball thrown by the pitcher. He brought an action of battery against the pitcher and his employer, the professional team. Defendant succeeded in district court. Plaintiff appealed. Important to note is that the pitcher was being heckled by the audience at the time of the accident. The question was whether the pitcher, looking directly into the audience, intentionally fired the pitch into the crowd, or accidentally fired the pitch into the crowd? It was vacated and remanded for a new trial on the battery count.

One of the most publicized cases of spectator violence was *Bearman v. University of Notre Dame* (1983). Christenna Bearman suffered a leg fracture when she was knocked down by a drunken spectator as she returned to her car following a football game at the South Bend campus. The Circuit Court, St. Joseph County granted the university a motion for judgment on the evidence. Bearman appealed. She argued that:

> she was a business invitee of the University of Notre Dame; therefore, Notre Dame owed to her a duty to protect her from injury caused by the acts of other persons on the premises. On the other hand, Notre Dame argues that absent notice or knowledge of any particular danger to a patron, the University can not be held liable for the acts of third persons. (1197)

The Court of Appeals of Indiana reversed the judgment of the trial court and remanded for further proceedings based on the statement that:

The University is aware that alcoholic beverages are consumed on the premises before and during football games. The University is also aware that "tailgate" parties are held in the parking areas around the stadium. Thus, even though there was no showing that the University had reason to know of the particular danger posed by the drunk who injured Mrs. Bearman, it had reason to know that some people will become intoxicated and pose a general threat to the safety of other patrons. Therefore, Notre Dame is under a duty to take reasonable precautions to protect those who attend its football games from injury caused by the acts of third persons. (1198)

Assault

Assault is the apprehension of imminent contact, rather than the contact itself. Again, the person has not consented or agreed to the act. For example, when a person is threatened by an action enough to believe another is preparing to hit him/her and in retreat steps backwards, falls and hits his/her head on bleachers, no battery or physical contact has caused the fall; but, an assault has occurred. The person threatened need not be in fear of the other's actions; only apprehension is required. The threat must be physical; words alone will not constitute an assault.

In *Hogenson v. Williams* (1976), an action in assault was brought on behalf of Rory Hogenson, a seventh-grade football player, against his coach. The coach was "displeased with Rory's performance of blocking assignments, and as a result started yelling at Rory, then struck the boy's helmet with force sufficient to cause him to stumble and fall to the ground, and then grabbed his face mask." (457) Rory weighed 115 pounds; the coach weighed 195 pounds. Rory sustained a severe cervical sprain and bruising of the brachial plexus. The jury found that the coach did not commit an assault and that the actions were "done for instruction and encouragement without any intent to injure." (457) The privilege of force as a purpose of instruction and encouragement is based on a Texas statute and would not be applicable in many states.

When an intentional tort is between a teacher and a student, privileged force often comes into play. Privileged force permits a teacher, acting in loco parentis, to use a physical act to enforce compliance, to control, to train or to educate a child or to punish a student for engaging in a prohibited activity. This privilege usually is regulated by state statutes, causing a measurable difference from state to state.

False Imprisonment

False imprisonment is the unjustified, unlawful, intentional confinement, restraint or detention of a person within specific boundaries against that person's will. Wrongful intent need not exist, nor is there a need for substantial damages. For example, store managers restraining shoppers suspected of shoplifting could be charged with false imprisonment. No court decisions exist in the physical activity profession; however, coaches and teachers who routinely restrain students in locker rooms or gymnasiums as punishment could be liable for false imprisonment.

Reckless Misconduct

Reckless misconduct is conduct creating "an unreasonable risk of physical harm to another." (Restatement of The Law of Torts [Second] §500 (1965) Closely allied with reckless misconduct is quasi-intent, or wilful, wanton and reckless misconduct. This category serves to bridge the gap between outright intent and negligence, as:

> Wilful, wanton and reckless means that the actor has intentionally done an act of an unreasonable character in disregard of a known or obvious risk that was so great as to make it highly probable that harm will follow (Restatement of The Law of Torts. [Second] §500, 1965)

In the past, reckless misconduct was a tort of professional sports; today, we can see the tort occurring in collegiate and scholastic competition.

Historically, most sports related injuries were considered to be part of the risk an individual assumed in participating in such an activity. Injuries were expected in body contact sports such as football. In recent years players have sustained severe injuries which were in direct violation of the rules of game play and which would be considered intentional torts in society in general. Just how far beyond the rules of the game can a player, even a professional player, be expected to assume a risk of injury? The courts appear to sense a need to declare that a player assumes all risks of injury up to the limit of the rules; but, when the injury is a clear violation of the rules, it could become a tort.

In *Tomjanovich v. California Sports Inc.* (1979), a fight involving a number of team members occurred following an intense play in a National Basketball Association game between the Los Angeles Lakers and the Houston Rockets. Kevin Kunnert of the Lakers and Kermit Washington of the Rockets were involved in the play. Members of both teams, including Tomjanovich, swarmed onto the floor to take part in the fight. Washington pushed Tomjanovich in the mouth, knocking him unconscious. The push caused fractures of the nose, jaw and skull; lacerations of the face; a concussion and leakage of spinal fluid. Tomjanovich sued the Lakers on the theory that as Washington's employer they were responsible for "curbing his dangerous tendencies." A jury award of $3.3

million was appealed by the Lakers, and later settled out of court for an undisclosed sum of money.

Another highly visible case which helped to establish the concept of reckless disregard, is *Hackbart v. Cincinnati Bengals, Inc.* (1979). On September 16, 1973, Dale Hackbart, a veteran free safety for the Denver Broncos, was involved in a play that resulted in a pass interception by the Broncos. Acting as an offensive player, Hackbart attempted to block Charles Clark, an offensive back for Cincinnati, by throwing his body in front of him. Clark struck Hackbart, who was still on his knees, with a blow to the back of his head. No penalty was called and Hackbart continued to play. Later, Hackbart had pain, and when he sought medical attention he discovered a neck fracture.

The trial court judge resolved the liability issue in favor of the Cincinnati team and Clark reasoning that:

> professional football is a species of warfare and that so much physical force is tolerated and the magnitude of the force exerted is so great that it renders injuries not actionable in court; that even intentional batteries are beyond the scope of the judicial process... Despite the fact that the defendant Charles Clark admitted that the blow which had been struck was not accidental, that it was intentionally administered, the trial court ruled as a matter of law that the game of professional football is basically a business which is violent in nature, and that the available sanctions are imposition of penalties and expulsion from the game. (518-519)

This case weighs the notion of violence, consent and assumption of risk. The court of appeals reversed and remanded for a new trial holding, among other reasons, that the tort law was applicable to an athletic event and that recklessness, not assault and battery, was a standard for measuring liability in this situation.

Reckless misconduct was applied in scholastic sport in *Nabozny v. Barnhill* (1975), in recreational sport in *Borek v. Schmelcher* (1985), in collegiate sport in *Hanson v. Kynast* (1987) and in the physical education classroom in *Oswald v. Township High School District* (1980).

In *Nabozny,* the goal keeper of the Hansa soccer team was kicked in the head by a midfielder on the Winnetka team while the goal keeper was on his left knee in the penalty zone. Experts agreed that the contact in question should not have occurred. The court stated:

> that when athletes are engaged in an athletic competition; all teams involved are trained and coached by knowledgeable personnel; a

recognized set of rules governs the conduct of the competition; and a safety rule is contained therein which is primarily designed to protect players from serious injury, a player is then charged with a legal duty to every other player on the field to refrain from conduct proscribed by a safety rule. A reckless disregard for the safety of other players cannot be excused. To engage in such conduct is to create an intolerable and unreasonable risk of serious injury to other participants. We have carefully drawn the rule announced herein in order to control a new field of personal injury litigation. Under the facts presented in the case at bar, we find such a duty clearly arose. Plaintiff was entitled to legal protection at the hands of the defendant . . .

It is our opinion that a player is liable for injury in a tort action if his conduct is such that it is either deliberate, wilful or with a reckless disregard for the safety of the other player so as to cause injury to that player, the same being a question of fact to be decided by a jury.(260-261)

The case was reversed and remanded to the circuit court for a new trial.

In *Borek v. Schmelcher*, 18-year-old Schmelcher threw a stick over his head into the crowd following a roller hockey game. The stick flew into the crowd and struck Borek. Borek sustained loss of one tooth and fractures of four others. He succeeded on an action of careless disregard.

In *Hanson v. Kynast* (1987), Hanson received paralyzing injuries while playing lacrosse for Ohio State University. Hanson believed his teammate Allen was being threatened by opponent Ashland University's Kynast, so he went up to Kynast and clinched him in a bear hug to stop Kynast from hurting Allen. When Kynast pushed him off, Hanson fell and hit his head. The court ruled that Kynast's act could not be an intentional tort, as he had no intention of hurting Hanson. Kynast was trying to release his own body from Hanson's bear hug. The court said that Kynast's actions during this activity breached no duty recognized at law. Kynast was not found liable.

Intentional tort analysis moved into the classroom in *Oswald v. Township High School District* (1980). Plaintiff Oswald was kicked in the leg by another student in a physical education class. Oswald sued the boy who kicked him and the school. The circuit court dismissed the case against the boy. He appealed. His complaint was that he was:

injured when kicked while playing basketball in a required high school gym class. In count III, it is alleged that at the time of the occurrence, the National Federation of State High School Association rules governing the protection and safety of participants in basketball games were in effect; that defendant knew or should have known of these rules; that defendant owed a duty to play the game in accordance with those rules and to exercise care to avoid causing injury to other participants; that defendant violated, failed to comply with, or failed to conduct himself in a manner consistent with the rules and that, as a proximate result thereof, plaintiff was injured. (158)

The court chose to examine the decisions obtained in professional athletics under the holdings of *Nabozny* and *Hackbart*. The court ruled that the plaintiff failed to state a cause of action for which recovery would be granted.

INTENTIONAL TORTS TO PROPERTY

Physical activity professionals should be aware that trespass to land is an intentional tort to property. An intentional entry, walking onto land or the projection of an object (shooting an arrow or hitting a golf ball) onto land in possession of another, is trespass to land. The action must have been executed without permission, either implied or expressed, from the owner of the property. The intent need only be to enter; there need not be an intent to harm.

Suggesting students pass through a property owner's yard enroute to an outdoor field, use the grounds of a private agency as a practice field or continue an activity in which an object from game play is known to enter private property may constitute trespass to land. When a baseball is hit and breaks competitive records of the school and also breaks a neighbor's window, negligence will be the tort. When the baseball diamond is set up so most good hits enter the neighbor's yard, it is an intentional tort. Substantial damage is not required in the intentional tort. The ball does not have to go through a window or hit someone to constitute an intentional tort.

FRAUD, DECEIT AND MISREPRESENTATION

Fraud and deceit are torts seldom found in physical activity, but often appear in athletic recruiting at all levels. Fraud and deceit also may appear in the purchase of equipment, or in the construction of a building. The elements of fraud and deceit are:

1. a false representation of a material fact,
2. knowledge that the fact is false,
3. intention to induce the other party to rely on the representation,

4. the other party's reliance on the representation, and
5. substantial damage as a proximate result of the other parties reliance. (Restatement of the Law of Torts, [Second], §525)

Schools explaining league laws and health spas explaining improve-
ments a customer can expect from taking their courses are examples of
situations that might be vunerable to litigation. Note that false representation of a material fact is not: (1) a promise, unless the person making the
promise has absolutely no intention of keeping the promise; or (2) an
opinion, unless the person giving the opinion has the confidence of the
listener. Coaches', teachers', doctors', and lawyers' opinions, on issues
they are expected to be knowledgeable about, may be considered fact.

A misrepresentation of a law will not be actionable unless it is made
by a person in a position of confidence, or by one expected to have
knowledge of the law. Will a college coach, administrator or recruiter be
actionable for misrepresenting the National Collegiate Athletic Association (NCAA) code? Could the code be considered a law? Could an athletic recruiter be liable for misrepresenting the out of state university
requirements to a potential student athlete?

Material, as used in fraud and deceit, means the facts played an important role in convincing the person to do the act. Reliance need not be
the only reason for making a decision, but it must play a strategic role. If
the persons harmed are found to have conducted their own investigation
of the matter, the court will find it difficult to claim the harmed persons
relied upon someone else's material statement.

The difference between fraud and misrepresentation is that fraud
involves the intent to deceive. The deception was planned. Note that
there may not be any attempt to injure, as is true of all intentional torts.
Misrepresentation is:

1. falsely denying knowledge of the facts,
2. actively concealing the facts,
3. disclosing only parts of the facts, or
4. providing a false picture.

Persons claiming misrepresentation need to assess the difference between non-disclosure and misrepresentation. If the question was never
asked, the person making the representation may not have been obligated to disclose the facts. Non-disclosure or failure to disclose is usually
not actionable unless there is a relationship between the plaintiff and the
defendant which required that there be disclosure, or the plaintiff relied
on the defendant's special skill and knowledge in making the decision.

Damages

Unlike the other torts, there must be substantial damages before one can make a claim under fraud, deceit or misrepresentation. Damages usually include everything that was lost as a result of the injury. It may be lost work time, lost customers, lost time in school or lost money. Some courts award costs only for out-of-pocket expenses or expenses which can be verified by receipts; others may permit more abstract losses to be covered. Only when wilful and wanton misconduct is involved are punitive damages awarded.

DEFENSES TO INTENTIONAL TORTS

Defenses to intentional torts are excuses or reasons to justify the actions of the actor. They include consent, self-defense, defense of others or property, necessity and discipline. Assumption of risk is not a defense to an intentional tort; however, the tort, reckless misconduct, referred to as both an intentional tort and as negligence, does permit the defense of assumption of risk. The *Hackbart* decision, for example, covers the court's decision, as it examined the assumption of risk doctrine in light of intentional sport torts.

Consent

Consent may be verbal or implied as a result of silence. If a reasonable person should have objected or attempted to stop an action of another, consent will be attributed to the owner of property or person upon whom the tort was committed. According to section 50 of the Restatement Second of Torts, "consent applies even where there is an intentional invasion of personal interests." Comment b to section 50 specifies, "that participation in a game involves a manifestation of consent to those bodily contacts which are permitted by the rules of the game." (86) One question often raised, though not supported by recent decision, is whether the mere participation in the event constituted consent. It should be noted that a person must know the risks involved in an activity and the extent of the damage that could occur before giving an informed consent.

In horse-play situations, the extent of the person's consent is often a factor in determining liability. Consent is ineffective if the person lacked capacity to give consent, if the consent was coerced, if the person was mistaken about the nature of the act or if the conduct was of such a nature that no reasonable person would give consent. A child must be of an age adequate to give consent to a particular situation. Capacity exists when a minor has the ability of the average person to understand and weigh the risks involved.

Self-Defense and Defense of Others

Self-defense and defense of others rest upon the necessity of permitting persons, under attack, to take reasonable steps to prevent harm to themselves or to others, when there is no time to resort to a legitimate legal effort. Reasonable force may be used to prevent threatened harm or offensive body contact. Individuals must know that they or others, are in extreme danger. Revenge is not a defense.

Necessity

Should a sailing group be hit by threatening weather and consider tying their craft to a private dock and making camp on a private shore, they may do so because it is necessary to their safety. In this case, necessity is seeking shelter in a life-threatening situation. If damage is done by group members they are responsible for the extent of their damage; however, they are not liable for having entered the property without permission.

Discipline

Striking another is permitted in certain jurisdictions as the privilege of discipline. Historically, a school teacher had the authority to control any activity that affected the decorum and morale of the school. Acts of corporal punishment by public school teachers have been challenged, and numerous states have changed their codes with reference to spanking and disciplining school age children. Knowledge of local statutes and the district code is essential to physical educators. Knowledge of agency codes and the state statutes are equally important to all persons employed in physical activity.

Two cases involving student discipline in the context of intentional tort are *Frank v. Orleans Parish School Board* (1967) and *Ingraham v. Wright* (1974). Frank sustained a broken arm in a confrontation with his physical education teacher. The confrontation followed Frank's third refusal to sit down after being disruptive during the teaching of a basketball skill. The court never discerned whether the teacher was threatened by Frank and acted in self-defense, but allowed that the difference in size of Frank and the teacher would make it difficult to believe the teacher ever thought he was in jeopardy. The court of appeals ruled that:

the evidence preponderates and the trial court obviously concluded that therefrom that Henderson's physical effort went further than mere restraint and that he actually lifted the boy from the ground, shook him in anger and then dropped him to the floor. . . . these actions were clearly in excess of that physical force necessary to either discipline or to protect himself, and subjects the defendant to liability for the injuries. (453)

. . . general rule permitting physical contact between teacher and student in any instance without qualification would obviously encourage the one who occupies a position of superiority to take advantage of those who are in a less favorable position since they are subject to their authority. (454)

A relationship exists between the right a student might have to a hearing, a due process right and an award of a physical punishment. *Ingraham v. Wright* (1974), another physical punishment case involving a teacher and a student, is studied in depth in this text under the Fourth Amendment of the Constitution.

SUMMARY

Intentional torts are injuries caused by a deliberate act, or a failure to act. Intentional torts to persons include battery, assault, reckless misconduct and false imprisonment. Other intentional torts include intentional torts to property and fraud and deceit. These torts occur most often in professional sports, although they are beginning to appear in collegiate and scholastic sport. Defenses to intentional torts include consent, self-defense and defense of others, necessity and discipline.

For years society in general and the courts held that the person engaged in physical activity assumed all risks inherent in the sport. In some cases they even assumed that participants assumed the risk of intentional torts which might occur in the heat of battle. In *Nabozny*, the courts began to question the merit of forcing the athlete to assume the risk of injury resulting from intentional torts and from reckless disregard for safety. *Rutter*, an important decision in the area of assumption of risk in sport, pointed out the need for a court to be able to base the assumption of risk on knowledge and voluntariness of the risk.

Assumption of risk has been extensively modified or abolished in twenty states: Alaska, California, Delaware, Hawaii, Idaho, Iowa, Kansas, Kentucky, Michigan, Minnesota, New Hampshire, New Jersey, New Mexico, North Carolina, Oregon, Pennsylvania, Texas, Washington, Wisconsin and Wyoming. In states in which assumption of risk remains, courts have resorted to rule books as a means of clarifying or identifying the risks. It is assumed the participants are knowledgeable about the rules and the rightful privilege awarded aggressive players on occasion as a result of those rules. A player violating the rules, and in the act injuring another, will be in a potentially liable situation. Persons called upon to enforce the rules and failing to do so also will be subject to close scrutiny.

References

Bearman v. University of Notre Dame, 453 N.E. 2d 1196 (1983).
Black, Henry Campbell (1979). *Black's Law Dictionary*. (5th Ed). St. Paul, MN: West Publishing Company.
Borek v. Schmelcher, N.Y. Oneida County Supreme Court, Index No. 85-866, (Dec. 3, 1985).
Bourque v. Duplechin, 331 So. 2d 40 (La. Ct. App.) (1976).
Frank v. Orleans Parish School Board, 195 So. 2d 451 (1967).
Goldberger, Alan S., (1984). *Sports Officiating, A Legal Guide*. New York: Leisure Press.
Griggas v. Clauson, 128 N.E.2d 363, 6 Ill. App. 2d 412 (1955).
Hackbart v. Cincinnati Bengals, Inc., 601 F. 2d 516, cert den (US) 62 L. Ed. 2d 188, 100 S. Ct. 275 (1979).
Hanson v. Kynast., Court of Appeals of Ohio, 5th Appellate District No. CA-870 (April 9, 1987).
Hayes, Jacquelyn K. (1980). Professional Sports and Tort Liability: A Victory for The Intentionally Injured Player. *Detroit College of Law Review*, 686.
Hogenson v. Williams, 542 S.W. 2d 456. (1976).
Ingraham v. Wright, 498 F. 2d 248. (1974).
Kabella v. Bouschelle, 672 P. 2d 290, 100 N.M. 461. (1983).
Keeton, W. Page, Dan B. Dobbs, Robert E. Keeton, and David G. Owen. (1984). *Prosser and Keeton On Torts*, 5th Ed. St. Paul, MN: West Publishing Co.
Manning v. Grimsley, 643 F 2d 20 (1981).
Nabozny v. Barnhill, 31 Ill. App. 3d 212 (1975).
Oswald v. Township High School District, 84 Ill. App. 3d. 723, 40 Ill. Dec. 456, 406 N.E. 2d 157 (1980).
Restatement Of the Law Of Torts (Second) (1965). Pamphlet One and Pamphlet Three. St. Paul, MN: American Law Institute Publishers.
Rutter v. Northeastern Beaver County School District, 437 A.2d 1198 (1981).
Tomjanovich v. California Sports Inc., No. H-78-243 (S.D. Texas 1979).

7

Product Liability

Athletes and sports participants place a great deal of faith in the equipment they choose to use. As technology has enhanced competitive athletes' chances for success, products have become significant in the sports world. At the same time, the average physical activity participant expects a sophisticated product for the expense incurred in such purchases. Product liability imposes liability on the manufacturer, wholesaler, retailer and supplier for defective products placed on the market that cause injury. This liability theory is based on the concept that the manufacturer, or seller, is in a better position than the consumer to become aware of and eliminate the defect and to absorb whatever loss occurs.

Teachers, coaches, administrators, owners of fitness and spa establishments, corporate fitness managers and any persons responsible for purchasing equipment need to be aware of product liability. They must be able to protect their agencies against the purchase and installation of faulty products, be astute in claiming the agencies' rights when products fail and be effective in providing clients and students with the manufacturers' warnings.

Product liability may be found under negligence, breach of warranty or strict liability in tort. Negligence occurs when the manufacturer or retailer, who has a duty of care, violates the reasonable standard of care in placing a deficient product on the market. Breach of warranty exists when the object fails to function according to its written specifications, advertising brochures or any other material statement about the product. In breach of warranty, there is no need for the injured person to prove negligence or recklessness.

Strict liability in tort makes a seller liable for any and all defective or hazardous products which unduly threaten a consumer's personal safety.

State and federal laws govern product liability; therefore, states may differ on the details of product liability. The concepts presented in this chapter are general and will be applicable in nearly all situations.

NEGLIGENCE IN PRODUCT LIABILITY

Wittenburg (1986) notes that "one focus of the negligence-based recreation and sport product claim has been on the legal responsibility to inspect or test where a failure to do so may allow a dangerous and latently defective product to cause harm that might otherwise have been prevented." (1-13, §1.02) The manufacturer must have a system for inspecting and testing products, and that system must be in continuous use. This system must effectively identify the defective product.

Once a product has been identified as defective or as highly dangerous, the manufacturer must decide whether to (1) halt production and alter the product, reducing its danger, or (2) continue to produce and market the product, alerting customers to its unsafe potential. The manufacturer's decision making process, often referred to as the evaluation component of the risk management system, will be examined by the courts under negligence theory. The manufacturer has a substantial burden of responsibility to discover dangerous defects and to evaluate the options.

In defining negligence, a court will tend to use a balancing test. This test will equate the likelihood of substantial harm from the product defect with the value to the public of the product in its present condition and with the cost of removing the defect. The court will consider: Is the product of importance to the public? Is the cost of the product a factor in the public being able to use the product? Will removal of the defect increase the cost of the product so the public will no longer be able to use it? Can the public be adequately warned of the product's potential danger? The balancing consists of examining the likelihood of harm and the severity of harm of the product in relation to the cost of protecting the public against the product's potential harm.

In most states a manufacturer cannot delegate the duty to inspect or test the product to another agency. Though they may employ someone else to carry out the task, they retain responsibility and liability. The duty to inspect does not require the product to be perfect, only that it function in a reasonable manner. However, a manufacturer, having received reports of product malfunction, has a duty to inspect with greater diligence.

The product seller usually relies on the manufacturer's expertise. Therefore, a product seller is not required to inspect or test a product as long as the seller is dealing with a reputable manufacturer. When dealers become aware of complaints about a particular product, they should take steps to inspect and test the product or seek assurance from the manufacturer that such steps have been taken and the product has been rendered safe. Dealers are not responsible for testing or inspection unless they have reason to believe a problem exists. When sellers assemble, install or repair a product, they take a more active role in the product and increase their liability for a defect in the product.

When manufacturers and sellers become aware of a dangerous product, they have an obligation to warn the user about the specific dangers involved. A simple product such as a butcher knife can be dangerous, but not defective. Defective products should be removed; dangerous products should carry warnings. Products may be dangerous only when used or misused in certain ways. Manufacturers must simulate how products will be used and whether the product could be dangerous in its present or potential use. If manufacturers and sellers can foresee any of these uses or misuses, or a court decides they should have foreseen them they must warn with reference to the dangers. The object of a warning is to alert the user to a danger of which the user is not aware.

Manufacturers and dealers are under no duty to warn of obvious injuries. For example, in *Dixon v. Outboard Marine Corp.* (1971), the manufacturer of a golf cart was not held to a duty to warn the owner not to stand up in the cart while it was in motion.

In *Hensley v. Muskin Corp.* (1975), the court said the manufacturer, seller and owner of a four feet deep, above-ground swimming pool had no duty to warn the 28-year-old who took a dive into the pool from the roof of a seven feet high garage. There is no duty on the part of the manufacturer or seller to warn the user of a product who possesses professional knowledge that the product was dangerous. For example, persons trained to be teachers and supervisors of physical activity would be expected to know the dangers involved in the use of typical athletic equipment. Managers of health spas would be expected to have professional knowledge or know the dangers accompanying the use of various exercise equipment. Also, a duty to warn does not exist when the product is misused, unless the manufacturer had reason to know the product would be misused in that manner.

Manufacturers, sellers and owners — including teachers, athletic directors, coaches and fitness and sport consultants — using a product, may be held to a duty to warn. Teachers, coaches and recreation personnel need to be aware of warnings and need to establish a process for informing clients and students about the warnings. An adequate warning is:

1. conspicuous, so it attracts the users eye;
2. specific, so it's understood by the user and

3. forceful, so it convinces the user of the range and magnitude of
   the potential harm.

Other examples of adequate warning cases are *Rawlings Sporting
Goods Co. Inc. v. Daniels* (1981), *Gentile v. MacGregor Mfg. Co.* (1985)
and *Durkee v. Cooper of Canada Ltd.* (1980). In *Rawlings*, the plaintiff was
injured in football practice when the helmet he was wearing collapsed as
he hit another player. Daniels brought an action against the manufacturer of the helmet on product liability and negligence. Plaintiff alleged
the helmet was defective, exposed him to an unreasonable risk and the
manufacturer failed to warn him of the defect. The district court entered
a judgment against the manufacturer for $1,500,000; the manufacturer
appealed. The Court of Appeals of Texas at Waco affirmed the decision.
   One point the Court made was that "the primary purpose of a football helmet is to protect against 'head' or 'brain' injuries of the wearer of
the helmet." (439) Some interesting facts presented by the court were:

> In the instant case, defendant fully understood the dangers which
> were incidental to the use of its helmets. Testimony of defendant's
> own witnesses revealed defendant knew: 1) A practical helmet could
> not be designed that would prevent all head injuries; 2) there are
> limitations on the protection capabilities of any helmet; 3) it has
> been known for a long time that helmets will not protect against all
> brain injuries; 4) defendant's helmets would not protect against all
> subdural hematomas; 5) laymen believe the purpose of the helmet is
> to protect the head; 6) almost all fatal football injuries are related to
> head and neck injuries; 7) 200,000 to 4 million football players are
> injured each year; 8) you can receive a brain injury while in a helmet
> that performs all the functions that it was designed to perform; 9) the
> helmet has severe limitations on protecting the brain; it will not pro-
> tect against subdural hematomas; 10) total football deaths are be-
> tween 30 and 40 a year from subdural hematoma; 11) parents of high
> school players don't have this detailed knowledge of the dangers of
> subdural hematoma. (440-441)

The court ruled that since the helmet was purchased for protective purposes, and Rawlings knew that it would not protect the player's head and
neck under certain conditions, Rawlings had a duty to warn purchasers.
   In *Gentile*, the court held the reconditioner of a football helmet to
the same standard of warning as it did the manufacturer of the helmet.
The court noted that under strict liability, those who service a product are
responsible not only for the service they provide but for any pre-existing
defects.

The plaintiff in *Durkee* was injured when a hockey puck hit the chin strap, part of the helmet he was wearing. Durkee had engaged in an "over 30" recreational league, and was an experienced hockey player. Durkee alleged the manufacturer failed to warn him of the risk involved in wearing a hockey helmet. The court of appeals ruled that the danger of the helmet was obvious, therefore there was no duty to warn an experienced player about the use of the helmet. On the issue of the design of the particular helmet Durkee was wearing, the court remanded the issue be returned to the lower court for trial on product defect.

A case in which the court found no duty to warn the user of the danger of the use of a product was *Garrett v. Nissen Corp.* (1980). Garrett, an experienced gymnast and a high school senior, was seriously injured while performing a stunt on a trampoline. The court determined, as a result of his testimony, that Garrett was well aware of the danger inherent in the activity. The court stated that given the fact the product was not found to be defective, the manufacturer was not liable.

Note that under negligence in product liability, users must use ordinary care to protect themselves from injury or be barred from recovery on contributory negligence or assumption of risk theory. These defenses can be used only in negligence in product liability; they are not applicable in warranty or strict liability in tort.

BREACH OF WARRANTY

Sections 2-313, 2-314 and 2-315 of the Uniform Commercial Code (UCC) cover express or verbal warranty, implied warranty of merchantability and implied warranty of fitness for a particular purpose. Liability in warranty exists without regard to fault. If the product does not meet the specifications of the warranty, liability of the manufacturer or seller is automatic. Also, there is no need of investigation of the intention of the manufacturer.

Express Warranty

UCC 2-313 explains the express warranties that a manufacturer, wholesaler, retailer or supplier may make:

(1) Express warranties by the seller are created as follows:
    (a) Any affirmation of fact or promise made by the seller to the buyer which relates to the goods and becomes part of the basis of the bargain creates an express warranty that the goods shall conform to the affirmation or promise.
    (b) Any description of the goods which is made part of the basis of

the bargain creates an express warranty that the goods shall conform to the description.

(c) Any sample or model which is made part of the basis of the bargain creates an express warranty that the goods shall conform to the description.

(2) It is not necessary to the creation of an express warranty that the seller use formal words such as "warrant" or "guarantee" or that he have a specific intention to make a warranty, but an affirmation merely of the value of the goods or a statement purporting to be merely the seller's opinion or commendation of the goods does not create a warranty. (UCC §2-313)

In proving a breach of an express warranty, the plaintiff must establish that:

1. the warranty was made, and the seller made the statement;
2. the seller's statement was part of the bargain (the purchaser relied upon the seller's statement in making the decision to purchase, and the seller's statement was in the form of a brochure, blue print, written specification, sample model or the seller's own words);
3. the product did not conform to the warranty and
4. a causal connection between the breach of the warranty and the plaintiff's injury exists. (Injury here can be both economic and physical).

Implied Warranty: Merchantability and Fitness

Merchantability means the product is suitable for the purpose for which it was created. The level of suitability need not be perfect; however, it should be reasonable. UCC §2-314, under implied warranty, merchantability, notes "a warranty that the goods shall be merchantable is implied in a contract for their sale if the seller is a merchant with respect to goods of that kind." Further, the Code notes that the goods should "pass without objection in the trade, . . . be fit for the ordinary purpose for which they were intended . . . be adequately contained, packaged and labeled as the agreement requires" and conform to the promises of fact made on the container or label.

Fitness of the product means that product has been made for a particular purpose and should serve that purpose. UCC 2-315 describes fitness in the following:

Where the seller at the time of contracting has reason to know any particular purpose for which the goods are required and that the buyer is relying on the seller's skill or judgment to select or furnish suitable goods, there is unless excluded or modified under the next section an implied warranty that the goods shall be fit for such purpose.

Case Analysis of Breach of Warranty

Plaintiff was able to recover as a matter of law for breach of express and implied warranties, misrepresentation and defective product design in *Hauter v. Zogarts* (1975). The facts are that:

defendants manufacture and sell the "Golfing Gizmo" (hereinafter Gizmo), a training device designed to aid unskilled golfers improve their games. Defendants' catalogue states that the Gizmo is a "completely equipped backyard driving range." In 1966, Louise Hauter purchased a Gizmo from the catalogue and gave it to Fred Hauter, her 13 1/2-year-old son, as a Christmas present.

The Gizmo is a simple device consisting of two metal pegs, two cords - one elastic, one cotton - and a regulation golf ball. After the pegs are driven into the ground approximately 25 inches apart, the elastic cord is looped over them. The cotton cord, measuring 21 feet in length, ties to the middle of the elastic cord. The ball is attached to the end of the cotton cord. When the cords are extended, the Gizmo resembles the shape of a large letter "T," with the ball resting at the base.

The user stands by the ball in order to hit his practice shots. The instructions stated that when hit correctly, the ball will fly out and spring back near the point of impact; if the ball returns to the left, it indicates a right-hander's "slice"; a shot returning to the right indicates a right-hander's "hook." If the ball is "topped," it does not return and must be retrieved by the player. The label on the shipping carton and the cover of the instruction booklet urge players to "drive the ball with full power" and further state "COMPLETELY SAFE BALL WILL NOT HIT PLAYER." (379)

On July 14, 1967, Fred Hauter was seriously injured while using defendants' product. Evidence showed that the device required the ball be hit solidly, a skill not often found among novice golfers, the target market of the device.

This case should impress upon physical activity professionals the importance of carefully studying the written statements made by the manufacturers, and should caution those entrusted with making such statements to be certain the statements are fact.

Disclaimers

One of the major defenses in breach of warranty is the disclaimer. Manufacturers and sellers may use disclaimers, statements declaring they are not responsible or liable for the product if the product is used for a purpose or in a manner beyond the limits of those uses recommended by the manufacturer. Despite the opportunities to disclaim the use of the product, the product must be both merchantable and fit.

Some disclaimers literally state that the product, as is, cannot be used. Although litigation dealing with these disclaimers has not occurred, one wonders if such a disclaimer would hold up in a court of law. Another unfortunate aspect of these absurd disclaimers is their appearance on inexpensive sporting goods. The public, after purchasing the product, ignores the disclaimer and in so doing, learns to ignore all other disclaimers.

STRICT LIABILITY IN TORT

United States courts apply the *Restatement of The Law of Tort (Second)* 402A definition of strict liability which states that:

> One who sells any product in a defective condition unreasonably dangerous to the user or consumer or to his property is subject to liability for physical harm thereby cause to the ultimate user or consumer or to his property if
> a) the seller is engaged in the business of selling such a product, and
> b) it is expected to and does reach the user or consumer without substantial change in the condition in which it was sold.

Therefore, liability of the seller under strict liability exists, though the seller has exercised the maximum care possible in the preparation and sale of the product.

Strict liability requires proof of a product's defect and evidence that it was unreasonably dangerous. There are three types of product defects:

1. manufacturing defect,
2. design, and
3. lack of proper instruction or warnings.

Manufacturing Defects

A manufacturing defect is when the product does not perform or was not built as the manufacturer originally planned; a defective design means that the product was built according to the manufacturer's specifications, but a problem within the design will cause an unreasonable risk of harm. In the latter situation, examination of the manufacturer's schematics would reveal a flaw in the design and analysis of the manufacturing protocol would show the product was created according to the faulty design. A manufacturing defect is an unreasonably unsafe product created in the construction process.

Design

A design defect exists when the original plans or specifications were faulty and will cause an unreasonable risk or harm. Those persons who created the design and specifications will become ultimately responsible. The manufacturer's, seller's or distributor's failure to note the design flaw will be based upon whether they had expertise or reason to know, through complaints, personal use or other sources, that a design flaw might exist. Manufacturers, sellers and distributors involved in repair or general service of the product also assume a greater or higher level of responsibility and liability. Product disclaimers are often ineffective in strict liability in tort because the courts are interested in controlling the stream of unsafe products on the market. The object is to remove the unsafe product from the market.

Instructions and Warnings

Manufacturers, retailers and supervisors of activity also have a duty to instruct participants on the safe use of the equipment and to warn against dangers. The extent of the warning must be sufficient to enable the average person to understand the probability, frequency, and magnitude of the occurrence of the risk. Swimming, rafting and small craft instructors and supervisors, for example, must be sure participants recognize the differences in life jackets and know the appropriate model for each activity.

When a manufacturer supplies a warning to a teacher, principal, coach, corporate fitness executive or others working in physical activity, it gives responsibility to that person to properly inform or pass the warning on to those who will use the equipment. Warnings are to be placed on the face of the equipment or on the wall above the equipment; they are not to be thrown out in an empty carton.

Usually, the courts will determine the adequacy of the warning on a case by case analysis, allowing its adequacy to be determined by the judge or the judge and jury. A warning must be: ACCURATE, CLEAR, and STRONG. It must capture the attention of those who will use the article and inform them of the potential dangers. Experience, expertise and knowledge of the foreseeable product users may have an impact on the warning. However, even in situations when the user is highly educated, a warning is in order.

An example of the importance of warning is found in *Anderson v. Heron Eng. Co. Inc.* (1979). Donald Anderson, a ski instructor, was injured while riding a chair lift at the Keystone ski area. The chair in front of him slipped back along the cable, struck his chair and knocked him 30 feet to the ground. His action was brought on theories of breach of warranty and strict liability in tort. The strict liability in tort related to the requirements posted in the repair manual for the chair lift. In essence, the manual failed to state the magnitude of the problem that could occur if directions contained in the manual were not properly followed.

The district court entered judgement for the manufacturer; the instructor appealed. The court of appeals affirmed the district court. The Supreme Court of Colorado engaged in considerable discussion of strict liability and ruled the case be remanded to the district court for a new trial.

Failure of an adequate product warning was a major factor in the decision of *Pell v. Victor J. Andrew High School and A.M.F. Inc.* (1984). Lauren Pell, a 16-year-old beginning gymnast, was injured as a result of a faulty somersault performed on a mini trampoline. The facts of the case state that:

> On the day of the injury, plaintiff had first performed two somersaults off the mini-tramp. Both of the school's coaches, Charlene Nutter, the varsity gymnastics coach, and Cathi Miles, were present in the gymnasium. Miles, who worked primarily with the freshmen and sophomore students, witnessed plaintiff's third somersault from a distance of approximately 10 feet. Plaintiff testified that she took a few running steps up to the mini-tramp and jumped onto the bed. When she went into the air, at the point when her feet were straight up and down above her, plaintiff said she felt a sharp pain in her knee and was unable to properly complete her somersault. She collapsed onto a nearby mat severing her spine . . .
>
> The mini-tramp was sold to the School District 230 with a heat-laminated caution label affixed to the bed which stated: "Caution. Misuse and abuse of this trampoline is dangerous and can cause serious injuries. Read instructions before using this trampoline. Inspect before using and replace any worn, defective, or missing parts. Any activity involving motion or height creates the possibility of accidental injuries. This unit is intended for use only by properly trained and qualified participants under supervised conditions. Use without proper supervision can be dangerous and should not be undertaken or permitted . . .

When the mini-tramp was assembled by a faculty member at the high school, the bed was placed so that the caution label was on the bottom, facing the floor, as opposed to the top where it would be visible to a performer. There were printed warnings also on the frame of the mini-tramp, however they were covered by frame pads on each of the four sides. (861)

The school district settled out of this case early, so the responsibility of the teacher for informing the student was not litigated. The case does, however, make clear the point of the importance of passing on instructions to users. With all of the sophisticated equipment used in today's health spas and other areas, warnings will take on an even greater importance. Teachers, coaches and physical activity specialists will be held to a high standard in passing on warnings.

Wade, in a 1973 *Mississippi Law Journal*, listed seven factors to be considered in determining the duty owed by the manufacturer to the user of the product.

(1) The usefulness and desirability of the product — its utility to the user and to the public as a whole.
(2) The safety aspects of the product — likelihood that it will cause injury and the probable seriousness of the injury.
(3) The availability of a substitute product which would meet the same need and not be as unsafe.
(4) The manufacturer's ability to eliminate the unsafe character of the product without impairing its usefulness or making it too expensive to maintain its utility.
(5) The user's ability to avoid danger by the exercise of care in the use of the product.
(6) The user's anticipated awareness of the dangers inherent in the product and their avoidability, because of general public knowledge of the obvious condition of the product, or of the existence of suitable warnings or instructions.
(7) The feasibility, on the part of the manufacturer, of spreading the loss by setting the price of the product or carrying liability insurance.(837-38)

Defenses

Assumption of risk is recognized to some extent in all three product liability situations; manufacturing defect, design and lack of proper instructions or warnings. Under assumption of risk the defendant must prove the plaintiff knew of the risk of danger or had facts from which they could comprehend that a danger might exist. Defendant must have:

1. known of the danger;
2. appreciated the significance and magnitude of the risk associated with the use or consumption of the product; and
3. voluntarily undertaken the risk.

Knowledge and appreciation of the danger means the defendant must actually have known of the danger, rather than the fact that they should have known. This also means that the injured person was properly informed of the danger. When the injured persons are elite athletes, experience and observation of others sustaining injury should serve to inform them of potential hazards.

The fact that the performer is expected to have undertaken the risk voluntarily needs to be examined in the context of certain attitudes existing in physical activity settings. Students cannot be commanded to execute a skill; they must voluntarily execute the skill. An athlete cannot be commanded to run a certain distance in a certain time; they must voluntarily accept the challenge. Requiring a certain feat for a grade or as part of the class requirements could be construed as requiring an activity, thus eliminating student voluntary participation.

Another question to consider is whether the skills required or the instruction itself is voluntary in a required physical education program. Unless students are explicitly forced to execute a risk skill without regard for their current level of competence, or placement in the skill progression most professionals believe the activity is voluntary, even in required programs or when being considered as a grade. This issue should be very carefully studied as part of tests and measurements in all human movement environments including exercise testing.

Under the Uniform Product Liability Act (1979), comparative fault has made product liability judgments more palatable to the manufacturers. Section 112 of the Act sets forth conduct which affects comparative fault. They are:

1. Failure to discover a defective condition — claimant is under no duty to inspect, but is expected to discover a defect that would be apparent to an ordinary person without inspection; 2. Use of a product with a known defective condition — generally, claimants may not create their own product liability claims by using a product with a known defective condition, but there may be circumstances justifying such conduct (for example, when a person discovers a welt in a tire, it may be reasonable to proceed cautiously to a nearby service station rather than to stop and immediately call for assistance); 3. Misuse of a product — damages are reduced to the extent that the misuse caused the harm; 4. Alteration or modification of a product

— generally, damages are reduced to the extent that product alteration or modification, by someone other than the product seller, contributed to or caused the harm.

Damages

Damages in product liability are usually compensatory and punitive. Compensatory damages cover the expenses incurred in sustaining the injury and the accompanying rehabilitation. Compensatory payments of large sums leveled as a result of the documented financial injuries can cause a business to lose its financial stability. Some of this has occurred in the football helmet industry.

Punitive damages are those money awards assessed against the perpetrator of the harm which will cause the injured persons to change their lifestyles. Punitive damage awards sums are usually arrived at with a very thorough understanding of the financial situation of the defending agency. An award of a large sum, such as $1.5 million, might relay to society that the company has so many assets that a substantial sum is demanded so the company will hurt sufficiently to discontinue its ill behavior. Punitive damages in and of themselves seldom bring the company into bankruptcy. Physical activity professionals should note the difference between the two damages.

SUMMARY

Product liability imposes liability on the manufacturers, wholesalers, retailers and suppliers for defective products placed on the market that cause injury. This liability is premised on the assumption that manufacturers, wholesalers, retailers and suppliers are in the best position to become aware of and eliminate defects, and to absorb whatever loss occurs. Product liability may be found in negligence, breach of warranty or strict liability in tort.

Negligence in product liability relates to the inspection and testing of equipment. It also relates to actions taken by the industry when the equipment is known to have created injury or behaved in such a way that injury could be a result of its use. The industry is charged with creating and passing on a warning system to be used when the equipment is dangerous or when certain use makes the equipment dangerous. Professionals in physical activity must heed such warnings and, when appropriate, pass them on to participants.

Breach of warranty means that the products are warranted for merchantability and fitness for the use specified by the manufacturer. Merchantability means the product is suitable for the purpose for which it was created. Fitness means that the purpose for which the product was created is clearly stated and that the product meets that purpose. If the product does not meet the specifications of the warranty, liability of the manufacturer or seller is automatic.

Strict liability in tort means that the seller has exercised maximum care in the preparation and sale of the product. Product defects tend to be in manufacturing, design and lack of proper instruction or warning.

Damages in product liability are compensatory and punitive.

References

Anderson v. Heron Eng. Co. Inc., 604 P. 2d 674 (1979).
Dixon v. Outboard Marine Corp., 481 P. 2d 151 (Okl. 1971).
Durkee v. Cooper of Canada Ltd., 99 Mich. App. 693, 298 N.W. 2d 620 (1980).
Garrett v. Nissen Corp., 84 N.M. 16, 498 P. 2d 1359 (1980).
Gentile v. MacGregor Mfg. Co., 493 A. 2d 647 (N.J. Super L. 1985).
Hauter v. Zogarts. 14 Cal 3d 104, 534 P. 2d 377, 120 Cal. Rptr. 681 (1975).
Hensley v. Muskin Corp. 65 Mich. App. 662, 238 N.W. 2d 362 (1975).
Pell v. Victor J. Andrew High School and A.M.F., Inc., 123 Ill. App. 3d 423, 462 N.E. 2d 858 (1984).
Rawlings Sporting Goods Co. Inc. v. Daniels, 619 S.W. 2d 435 (Tex. Civ. App. 1981).
Restatement of The Law of Torts, 1965. Pamphlet 2 §§281-503. St. Paul, MN: American Law Institute Publishers.
Uniform Commercial Code 2-313, 2-314, 2-315.
Uniform Product Liability Act, 44 Fed. Reg. 62, 714 (1979).
Wade, John W. (1973). On the Nature of Strict Tort Liability for Products, 44 *Miss. L.J.*, 825, 837-38.
Wittenberg, Jeffrey D. 1986 (update 1987). *Product Liability: Recreation and Sport Equipment.* New York City, NY: Law Journal Seminars Press.

8

Strict Liability In Physical Activity

Strict liability in tort means that a person can be liable by virtue of an act, action, event or incident. Intention to harm is no longer important. (Remember, intention played a significant role in negligence; negligence meant that one did not intend for the injury or the event to occur. Intention also played an equally important role in intentional torts; intention had to be proved as one of the elements in order to establish that the tort existed.) Proximate cause or a direct relationship between the injury and act is important in strict liability. The injury must be a direct result of the incident.

Strict liability also is limited to foreseeable events and to foreseeable persons or victims. It does not extend to unforeseeable events such as the events of nature or to situations in which the unforeseeable acts of someone caused the harm. Strict liability torts mentioned most often in sport and physical activity litigation are defamation, liability of employers to employees, vicarious liability and worker's compensation.

DEFAMATION

Defamation is the "holding up of a person to ridicule, scorn or contempt in a respectable and considerable part of the community. . . . A communication is defamatory if it tends to do harm to the reputation of another as to lower him in the estimation of the community or to deter third persons from associating or dealing with him." (*Black's Law Dictionary*) Defamation may be of a living person, a corporation or a business or an association. Publication of the derogatory information must be made to a third person. If the communication is oral it is slander; if the communication is in print it is libel.

Defamation does not exist unless the statements are communicated to a third person. Telling someone facts of an incident does not constitute the third person publication. The third person must have heard a defamatory remark. Derogatory information may be accusing someone of a serious crime, such as murder. Once the defamatory meaning is apparent, it is assumed the person's reputation will be damaged.

To establish liability for defamation, the following elements must be present:

1. a false and defamatory statement concerning another must be made;
2. the statement must be published to a third person (publication can be in writing, spoken to the person or overheard by the third party);
3. the person publishing the statement must intend to publish the statement (there is no need of intention to hurt someone); and
4. damage must occur.

A plaintiff must show evidence that her or his reputation was damaged, and that respect has been lost by some people in the community.

Status of Person as a Factor in Defamation

Whether the person is widely known or known only by a few is a factor in what can be said about a person in a public forum, or what can be revealed about the same individual to a third party. People are classified into two categories: public figures and public officials, and private individuals. This differentiation is extremely important in analyzing a fact pattern for the elements of defamation. Public figures are people known to the community. Athletes, sports figures and administrators are public figures. Private persons are those not widely known in the community. The decision of whether a person will be considered a public or a private figure will be determined by a judge, using federal law.

The public figure-private individual comparison also is related to First Amendment Constitutional questions of the individual's right to maintain her or his reputation and to the interest of the public in preserving free speech. A need exists for the public to be informed about its leaders; at the same time, an individual's personal life should be secured. As a result of the decision in *New York Times Co. v. Sullivan* (1964), the courts permitted a statement that was true to be made against a public official and public figure. The source of this restriction was the First Amendment to the Constitution.

Private individuals continue to have a cause of action under defamation, even though the statement may be true. A 1974 case, *Gertz v. Robert Welch, Inc.*, extended the idea of a public figure from one who was known by all, to one who voluntarily injected oneself or was drawn into a particular controversy. Being drawn into the controversy, one became a public figure for a limited period of time or a range of issues. (345)

Narol, a noted author, lawyer and past officer of the National Association of Sports Officials, writing in the January 1987 *Trial* magazine described a public figure-private individual continuum for sports officials. He placed professional officials at one end of the spectrum and called them public figures; placed Amateur Athletic Union (AAU), semi-professionals and collegiate officials in the middle; and categorized high school and little league officials at the opposite end of the continuum. The latter group was called private persons. (69)

Defenses and Damages in Defamation

The only defenses to defamation are truth and privilege. The defendant must establish that what was said was the truth. Defendant may be excused under privilege if his or her conduct was an act in furtherance of some socially useful interest. Privilege is a difficult element to establish. Like truth, it must be established by the defendant.

Damages in defamation may be compensatory and punitive. They may be a result of the damage to one's business or reputation (compensatory), or they may involve punitive damage, awarded to discourage similar actions on the part of the plaintiff or others.

Cases in Defamation

One sports-related defamation case that received great publicity was *Curtis Publishing Co. v. Butts* (1967). Curtis Publishing, publishers of the *Saturday Evening Post*, printed an article that alleged Butts, athletic director at the University of Georgia, was involved in fixing a football game between Georgia and the University of Alabama. Butts, a former football coach at Georgia, was a well-known and respected person and at the time of the defamation, was a candidate for a professional team position. The case revealed that:

> George Burnett, an Atlanta insurance salesman, had accidentally overheard, because of electronic error, a telephone conversation between Butts and the head coach of the University of Alabama, Paul Bryant, which took place approximately one week prior to the game.

Burnett was said to have listened while "Butts outlined Georgia's offensive plays . . . and told . . . how Georgia planned to defend . . . Butts mentioned both players and plays by name." The readers were told that Burnett had made notes of the conversation, and specific examples of the divulged secrets were set out.

The article went on to discuss the game and the players' reaction to the game, concluding that "[t]he Georgia players, their moves analyzed and forecast like those of rats in a maze, took a frightful physical beating," and said that the players, and other sideline observers, were aware that Alabama was privy to Georgia's secrets. It set out the series of events commencing with Burnett's later presentation of his notes to the Georgia head coach, Johnny Griffith, and culminating in Butts' resignation from the University's athletic affairs, for health and business reasons. (136, 137)

Georgia was sorely defeated by Alabama.

Butts brought a libel action in federal court for $5 million in compensatory and $5 million in punitive damages. All parties involved conceded that Butts was a public figure. Curtis Publishing's only defense was substantial truth. The evidence showed that Butts and the Alabama coach had discussed football, but failed to prove that what had been discussed would have been of value to the Alabama coach. Butts' contention was that the magazine's investigative reporting was reckless and wanton misconduct. The jury returned a verdict of $60,000 in general damages and $3 million in punitive damages. The latter was later reduced to $460,000.

Of particular importance in the *Curtis* case is the fact that what might appear to be "kidding around" could be taken seriously and completely misconstrued by another. One responsible for reporting information must be diligent in checking the accuracy and reliability of all sources used.

EMPLOYER-EMPLOYEE AND VICARIOUS LIABILITY

Employers have certain responsibilities for the persons they employ. Among those is the provision of a safe work environment or a system of warning about dangers that cannot be eliminated. Although few physical activity-related cases have been filed under the theory of strict liability, it is a very real possibility for suit.

Under the doctrine of respondent superior, the principal, as master or corporate entity, is responsible or vicariously liable for the torts of employees committed within the scope of their employment. Vicarious liability means one is responsible for the torts of another.

Administrators are liable for the torts of their employees, even though the administrator may not be aware of the circumstances under which the tort occurred. Also, the administrator may be held personally liable for having employed an incompetent person.

To hold the administrator liable, there must be evidence that the administrator had control of the employee and that the incident under question was done within the scope of the person's employment. For example, a campus recreation coordinator or an intramural director is usually under the direction of a vice-president for student affairs. Should the coordinator be held liable as a result of an injury in an intramural competition, the vice-president usually will be vicariously liable. If the injury is alleged to be related to the inadequacy of the referee, the intramural director may be both vicariously liable and personally liable for employing an official that could not control game play.

The test for the existence of the master-servant relationship is the master's right to control the servant. Scope of employment includes the specific tasks set by the master and the additional responsibilities incidental to these tasks. Masters are not responsible for employees' torts beyond the scope of their employment, nor are they responsible for employees' intentional torts unless they have either ratified or told the employee to commit the intentional tort. Sport management personnel employed in spas or professional athletic events in which liquor is sold should be sensitive to the role of bouncers. Bouncers will, on occasion, use force in removing people from the premises. As a result of their actions, they may commit an intentional tort. Employers also will be held liable for the same intentional tort if they told the employee to commit the tort, or if they ratified the tort that was committed.

A servant in a master-servant relationship, or an agent in a principal-agent association is a person who works directly with the employer. The employee answers to the employer, or to someone in the employer's chain of command. The employer possesses the legal right to control the employee and to actively direct the work that is to be accomplished. As employers they dictate the specific job duties and how the work will be performed.

The employer is also responsible for the actions of the employee. For an agency relationship to exist, the parties agree to the relationship, the employee knows she or he is acting on behalf of the employer and the employer assumes a fiduciary duty to pay the employee. The employer maintains records, pays unemployment insurance and worker's compensation and provides benefits.

Independent Contractor

An independent contractor is an employment relationship in which the employer has a contract right only to the result to be achieved. The employer has no right of control over the employee or how the employee is to accomplish the work. In an independent contract situation, the employer pays for the project in a lump sum payment; the employer does not pay wages or fringe benefits or furnish supplies or equipment. Independent contractors carry their own insurance; cover compensations, wages and employee benefits; and withhold income tax. They are responsible for their actions; the employer is usually not responsible for independent contractors action on the job.

Test to Determine Difference Between Principal-Agent and Independent Contractor

In an effort to establish a master-servant or an independent contractor status, the courts will ask a number of questions. A finding of master-servant or independent contractor will be based upon the response to the majority of the questions. It is not necessary to fulfill all of the requirements to be designated as one or the other; a majority of affirmative answers to one category will serve to identify the status. The questions are provided to guide the professional in identifying existing relationships and creating new relationships.

1. *What is the extent of control?*
   - Is control mentioned in the contract?
   - Was control discussed and agreed upon in the preliminary meetings?
   - If control was addressed, how much and by whom?
   - Who evaluates the employees?
   - Who hires the employees?
   - Who fires the employees?
   - In an unforeseen situation, who is expected to become the leader?

   The courts have found that the employer has a right to inspect and to observe the tasks being performed, as long as the inspection is infrequent and does not result in a request to change the methodology. If the employer participates in the hiring and firing of individuals, sets up the daily work schedule or controls the method used in carrying out the tasks, the independent contractor status will be lost. When the employer has control, a principal-agent situation is created.

2. *Is the employee engaged in a distinct occupation or business?*
   - Does the employee's job require special certification or is it recognized as an unique area of specialization?
   - What certificates or qualifications are required?
   - Would such qualifications prohibit the employer from being

able to evaluate the employee?

When the employer would not be able to evaluate the employee because of the unique type or level of skill or specialization, a case can be made for a distinct occupation.

3. *What is the custom in the industry?*
   - What is the generally accepted custom in the industry?
   - How do others view a particular employee-employer relationship?

   Industry precedent should be considered when attempting to differentiate between relationships. What is the relationship used by most clubs for a tennis pro, or by most school systems for a part-time coach?

4. *What skills are required?*
   - What is the level of skill required?
   - Does an employee orientation exist? If yes, what does it include?
   - Are progressions and syllabi required?

   As noted, the requirement of a high level of skill often places the employee in a position where the employer is prohibited from supervision because he or she does not have adequate knowledge of the task. Spas and corporate fitness centers wishing to claim independent contractor status should obtain highly trained and fully certified employees. The higher the level of competence for a particular job, the better the case for autonomy for the employee.

   A business claiming independent contractor relationships should avoid all but the minimal orientation and training for employees. The provision of a syllabus or the use of training tapes and records will suggest a principal-agent or master-servant relationship. A requirement that a specific progression be followed nearly guarantees such status. The actions of the parties will determine the relationship.

5. *Who provides the tools and supplies for work?*
   - What equipment is necessary?
   - Who owns the equipment?
   - Who maintains the equipment?

   Much of the law in this area has come from the construction industry, where ownership of tools has been an important factor in determining status. The owner of equipment in the sports industry takes on considerable responsibility and liability for injuries that may occur as a result of the use of the equipment. However, it is unclear that such ownership would be a major factor in differentiating a master-servant from an independent contractor status.

6. *What is the length of employment?*
   - Is the period of time short or extended?
   - Is it interval or continuous?

   If the employment period is short, it raises less suspicion. A long employment period suggests a master-servant relationship. When the employee's business is such that the employer only requires the service at certain intervals or for specific purposes, arguments can be advanced that the form of employment is not continuous, and thus of an independent contract status.
7. *What is the method of payment?*
   - Is payment by job or lump sum?
   - Is payment by hour, week or month?

   Payment by job suggests independent contractor; payment by the hour, week or month suggests master-servant status.
8. *What is the employer's regular business?*
   - Do the tasks performed by the employee relate to the core of the employer's business?
   - Are the tasks specialized or unique services?

   Teaching of dance in a dance studio is an example of a task relating to the core of the business, thus suggesting regular employee status. An example of a specialized service that could be viewed as an independent contract would be the teaching of dance in a racquet club.
9. *What did the parties think they were creating?*
   - Did each of the parties understand what they were negotiating?
   - Was the representation accurate?

   Even though an employer sets out to create an independent contractor situation, the employer may have assumed control sufficient to prohibit the status. Both parties should fully discuss the previous eight elements. They should also identify the party who will be responsible for providing worker's compensation, withholding required taxes, adhering to civil rights rules (age, race and sex discrimination), labor laws and employee safety. Also, employers should be aware that even though their employees have met the requirements of independent contractor status, the employer may be held liable for an employee under other legal theories. An employer may be personally liable for:
   a. negligence in selecting a contractor with a history of carelessness,
   b. allowing a hazardous situation to exist.
   c. failing to perform a duty which the employer cannot delegate by law, or
   d. allowing the party to do inherently dangerous work.

The reason for differentiating among the various employment relationships is based upon a need to identify an individual who will be responsible for the legal, financial and social obligations of the relationship. Employers and employees should identify the relationship that will best meet their needs, create a contract using the questions provided and acquaint all parties with information sufficient to enable each to make an informed decision.

WORKER'S COMPENSATION STATUTES

Worker's compensation is a statutory provision of benefits and medical care for employees and their dependants for injuries arising of and in the course of their employment. Each state has its own worker's compensation act and system. A compulsory insurance program is also provided by the statutes. It is not necessary to prove negligence on the part of the employer under worker's compensation. The worker is injured, and following proof of injury the worker is compensated.

A number of athletes have made claims against worker's compensation as a result of injuries sustained in intercollegiate athletics. In most cases, the athlete has sustained such severe injuries that the cost of rehabilitation is prohibitive and worker's compensation could serve to cushion the financial blow. In addition to athletes attempting to obtain worker's compensation, numerous other persons associated with sports on a part-time basis are often unclear as to whether they are covered by the institution's worker's compensation. Examples of these unclear situations are presented in *Rensing v. Indiana State University Board* (1982, 1983) and in *Coleman v. Western Michigan University* (1983).

Rensing and Coleman were football players seriously injured who attempted to claim worker's compensation. Although the players were not successful in their claims, they raised numerous issues of significance to the scholar athlete world.

Rensing signed a player/athlete financial aid agreement with Indiana State University. The agreement was to be renewable each year for a total of four years, if Rensing continued to actively participate in football. He was to receive tuition, room, board, laboratory fees, book allowance, tutoring and a limited number of football tickets. The agreement also specified that in the event of an injury that in the opinion of the school's health authority made it advisable to discontinue play, he would not be required to play football but to render other service to the institution.

Rensing's injury was sustained when he tackled a teammate during a punting drill in a spring football practice scrimmage. He suffered a fractured dislocation of the cervical spine at the 4th through 5th vertebrae which rendered him 95 percent to 100 percent disabled. Much of the $120,449 medical and rehabilitation expenses were paid by the university's insurer.

Rensing then filed a worker's compensation benefit claim stating that he was an employee of the university at the time of the accident. He used his student/athlete agreement as his employment contract. The Industrial Board denied his worker's compensation claim for benefits for injuries sustained in spring football practice, stating that he did not have an employee-employer relationship with Indiana State University within the meaning of the Indiana Worker's Compensation Act.

Rensing appealed the Industrial Board decision to the Court of Appeals of Indiana. The court found that his letter of agreement was in fact a contract and had established an employer-employee relationship. The court stated that the:

> Trustees did contract with Rensing to play football, regardless of whether one views the various documents submitted to Rensing and signed by him as constituting an express contract, or merely as evidence of the parties' understanding in support of an implied contractual relationship. In this regard, we note the settled law that [a]ny benefit, commonly the subject of pecuniary compensation, which one, not intending it as a gift, confers on another, who accepts it, is adequate foundation for a legally implied or created promise to render back its value. (1982, 85)

The court also focused on the contract wording which described the athlete's obligation to provide assistance to the university in the event that he could no longer play football. Further, the university had

> also retained their right to terminate their agreement for Rensing's services under certain prescribed conditions, a factor tending to distinguish his grant from an outright gift and which has previously been noted by this court as a significant indicia of an employer-employee or master-servant relationship. (1982, 85)

The Court of Appeals of Indiana held that the varsity football agreement was an employee-employer relationship, thus entitling Rensing to worker's compensation. The case was reversed and remanded to the board to determine Rensing's benefits. Indiana State University Board petitioned for a transfer of the case from the Court of Appeals of Indiana to the Supreme Court of Indiana. In the petition to transfer, the trustee successfully argued that an athlete who accepted a grant-in-aid was not under a contract of employment. The argument was based on the National Collegiate Athletic Association Constitution and By-Laws which stated that collegiate athletics is an educational program and the athlete cannot accept pay for playing athletics. The court also noted that Rensing had not identified his grant-in-aid income on his income tax return. Sports educators should be aware that contemporary tax law has changed the reporting of student income and could affect the value of the above statement made by the court.

Although the results in *Coleman* were the same, the court took a different approach in analyzing the employer-employee relationship. The court noted that an employer-employee relationship had to exist before a person could file for worker's compensation. One significant aspect of the employment relationship is the right of the employer to control the employee.

Plaintiff's and defendant's testimonies confirmed that even if Coleman had not played satisfactory football, he could not have been fired nor could his athletic scholarship have been removed. Therefore, the university did not have control over whether he was paid to play football. With reference to whether the scholarship constituted wages, the court found that it did constitute wages. And, in response to the test of whether the task performed by the football player was an integral part of the university's business, the court ruled the university's business was academic, not athletic. (226)

CASES UNDER MASTER-SERVANT AND WORKER'S COMPENSATION

Referees, who were injured in the course of their work as referees, have presented some interesting cases to worker's compensation. In *Ford v. Bonner County School* (1980), the referee, trapped in a football play, sustained a knee injury that caused disability for 13 weeks. The Industrial Commission awarded the referee worker's compensation for medical bills and income benefits. The school district appealed. Using a right to control theory, the court held that the school district had control over the referee, therefore he could qualify for their worker's compensation.

A wrongful death award from worker's compensation was hotly contested in the Court of Appeals of Southeast Oklahoma in *Warthen v. Southeast Oklahoma State University* (1982). Warthen, teacher, head of the drama department and certified basketball referee, died of a heart attack while refereeing an interfraternity basketball game. The administrator of his estate brought a wrongful death claim on behalf of the 38-year-old man's two dependent daughters. The claim was awarded. "The

University and its insurer petitioned for review, claiming that the trial judge erred in finding that death arose out of and in the course of (his) employment." (1126) The court ruled for the professor/referee stating that he was in the course of his employment when refereeing the game, as faculty members were encouraged to become involved in university extracurricular activities.

In *Ehehalt v. Livingston Board of Education* (1977), Calvin Ehehalt, another referee who injured his teeth while officiating a basketball game in the Livingston School system, was denied worker's compensation. He appealed. The appellate division upheld the decision of the lower court stating that he was an "independent contractor," and therefore, not entitled to compensation.

SUMMARY

Strict liability in tort means automatic liability. Strict liability torts most often occurring in sport and physical activity are defamation, employer-employee relationships, vicarious liability and worker's compensation.

Defamation is the holding up of a person to ridicule, scorn or contempt in the presence of a third person. If the communication is oral, it is slander; if it is in print, it is libel. Whether the person is widely known or known only by a few people is a major factor in what can be revealed about the person. When a person is classified as a public figure or a public official, most any fact that is true may be revealed. Private individuals who have been defamed have a cause of action even though the statement is true.

Employers have a responsibility to provide a safe work environment and to warn employees of dangers which cannot be eliminated. Employers are responsible for the torts of their employees under vicarious liability and personally responsible for hiring incompetent people.

An independent contractor is a worker in an employment relationship in which the employer has a contract right only to the results to be achieved. The employer has no control over the employee, or how the work is to be accomplished.

Worker's compensation is a statutory provision of benefits and medical care for employees and their dependants for injuries that occur in the course of employment. Each state has its own system.

References

Black, Henry Campbell (1979). *Black's Law Dictionary*. (5th Ed). St. Paul, MN: West Publishing Company.

Coleman v. Western Michigan University, 336 N.W. 2d 224 (1983).

Curtis Publishing Co. v. Butts, 388 U.S. 130, 87 S. Ct. 1975, 18 L. Ed. 2d 1094 (1967).

Ehehalt v. Livingston Board of Education, 371 A. 2d 752, 147 N.J. Super 511 (1977).

Ford v. Bonner County School, 612 P. 2d 557 (1980).

Gertz v. Robert Welch, Inc., 418 U.S. 323, 94 S. Ct. 2997, 41 L. Ed. 2d 789 (1974).

Narol, Mel. Protecting the rights of sports officials. *Trial* 64. (January, 1987)

New York Times Co. v. Sullivan., 376 U.S. 254, 84 S. Ct. 710, 11 L. Ed. 2d 686 (1964).

Redeker, James R. and James O. Castagnera. Labor Relations, The Legal Nightmare of Employee Leasing. *Personnel Journal*, February, 1985, 58-62.

Rensing v. Indiana State University Board, 437 N.E. 2d 78 (1982).

Rensing v. Indiana State University Board, 444 N.E. 2d 1170 (1983).

Stephenson v. College Misericordia, 376 F. Supp. 1324 (1974).

Tuma v. Kosterman, 682 P. 2d 1275 (1984).

Warthen v. Southeast Oklahoma State University, 641 P. 2d 1125 (1982).

9

First and Fourth Amendments To The Constitution

The United States Constitution is the supreme law of the land. Judges in every state are bound by the Constitution and by the constitutions of their respective states. The First, Fourth and Fourteenth amendments to the Constitution are the aspects of Constitutional law most often affecting participants and managers of sport and physical activity. This chapter will address First and Fourth Amendment law. Chapter Ten will address Fourteenth Amendment law.

It is important to note that the Constitution can be amended. An amendment to the United States Constitution may be proposed by a two-thirds vote of those present in each house of Congress, or by a committee of the legislatures of two-thirds of the states. Amendments may be ratified by the legislature of three-fourths of the states or by conventions in three-fourths of the states. (Chapter Two provides the details of amending the federal or a state constitution.) There are times when an amendment may be acceptable within a particular state but will not be acceptable to the entire country. The Equal Rights Amendment's success in numerous states and failure at the federal level is such an example.

The Constitution guarantees, or enforces, individual rights only with reference to the federal government and to state actions as incorporated in the Fourteenth Amendment. When a complaint involves a guarantee of a personal right, a court must determine whether the action challenged is a federal or state action. A person challenging a privately owned and operated agency forces the court to determine whether the agency is subject to state protection and regulation. If the court determines the agency is subject to state protection and regulation, that agency is subject to various Constitutional elements such as procedural due process. Tribe (1978) describes the situation in the following:

> The Court has gone about this task frequently enough over the years to develop a body of case law to which it can look in resolving new controversies, and to develop catch phrases such as "public function" and "nexus" in terms of which it can characterize various situations. But despite the precedents, and despite the vocabulary, the Supreme Court has not succeeded in developing a body of state action "doctrine", a set of rules for determining whether governmental or private actors are to be deemed responsible for an asserted constitutional violation. (1148-1149)

FIRST AMENDMENT

The First Amendment states that "Congress shall make no law respecting an establishment of religion, or prohibiting the free exercise thereof; or abridging the freedom of speech or of the press; or the right of the people peaceably to assemble, and to petition the government for a redress of grievances." Historically, the First Amendment applied only to actions of the federal government. However, in recent years the Courts, through the process of incorporation, have made the First Amendment applicable to state actions.

First Amendment actions of concern to those involved in the teaching and supervision of physical activity focus on freedoms of speech, press and privacy. As these rights are also considered privileges, persons suing a public elementary or secondary school or an institution of higher education will tie their cause of action to the Fourteenth Amendment. The Fourteenth Amendment forbids any state to make or enforce any law which denies either a privilege or an immunity to a citizen of the United States.

When challenging First Amendment rights, an individual requests that a court of law examine the facts with respect to the particular situation and balance the personal rights in relation to the authority of the state, federal government or a private agency to effect a particular rule, law or regulation. Personal or individual rights are balanced against the rights of the state.

Freedom of speech and freedom of the press are considered to be absolute freedoms. Freedom of speech is freedom to speak, to remain silent, to discuss with others, to advocate and communicate ideas. Freedom of the press includes freedom to write, draw and create models. Ideas may be published and circulated. One is free to convey ideas in the theater and movies and on television.

Freedoms of speech and press do not protect language that is libelous or slanderous, lewd or obscene. The possibility of creating a breach of peace, or advocating the commission of a crime is not protected. The free expression of speech, press and religion can occur within the confines of a rather liberally established set of boundaries. Court decisions serve to illuminate these boundaries.

Students, athletes, teachers, government employees and employees of private industry possess all First Amendment rights available to citizens. Despite these general First Amendment rights, professionals in education also are expected to retain an atmosphere in which all persons can learn at their maximum potential. Sometimes, the First Amendment is perceived to be in conflict with the mandate to maintain the learning environment in which all can achieve at maximum potential.

Freedom of Speech

Speech may be verbal or expressive (protests, demonstrations). Speech cannot be suppressed in the educational environment unless the activity will materially and substantially interfere with the operation of the learning environment. In order to determine whether speech merits protection, the courts examine:
   A. the subject of the speech,
   B. to whom it was directed,
   C. forum in which it occurred, and
   D. manner of delivery.

Speech as Symbolic Protest: Symbolic protest has received considerable attention in general school cases and in athletic events. Symbolism, in the following cases, has been exercised in violation of predetermined rules. This symbolism takes on two very distinct characteristics: the first is the use of a symbolic gesture in order to influence or alert the public to ideas; the second is the selection of a method of personal grooming unacceptable to predetermined standards. Grooming rules tend to be enforced more often in extracurricular activities than in the formal school setting.

Tinker v. Des Moines School District (1969) is the case most often cited in symbolic protest. Results of the court decision can be traced to the display of certain symbolism among winning athletes at various competitive events, including the Olympics. In *Tinker*, three Des Moines, Iowa, junior and senior high school students wore black armbands one December, 1965 day in public protest of the United States government's participation in the Vietnam war. School authorities, knowledgeable about the proposed armband protest, had established school policy on armbands only a few days prior to the event.

The three students were asked to remove their black armbands. The students refused. School authorities then suspended the students from school and told them not to return until the armbands were removed. The students sought injuncture relief from the courts but were unsuccessful in their quest.

The United States District Court "upheld the constitutionality of the school authorities action on the grounds that it was reasonable in order to prevent disturbance of school discipline." (505) The United States Court of Appeals for the Eighth Circuit, in reversing and remanding the lower courts' decisions, made a number of points.

1. the meaning of armbands in the circumstances of this case was entirely divorced from actually or potentially disruptive conduct by those participating in it. It was closely akin to "pure speech" which we have repeatedly held, is entitled to comprehensive protection under the First Amendment. (505-506)
2. It can hardly be argued that either students or teachers shed their constitutional rights to freedom of speech or expression at the school house gate. (506)
3. the prohibition of expression of one particular opinion, at least without evidence that it is necessary to avoid material and substantial interference with school work or discipline, is not constitutionally permissible. (511)

The court went on to state that the Constitution did not permit state officials to deny a form of expression which "neither interrupted school activities nor sought to intrude in the school affairs or the lives of others." (514) The court saw the activity as one to stimulate discussion outside of the classroom rather than to disrupt the learning environment.

In *Williams v. Eaton* (1970), the subject of black armbands moved into collegiate football. Fourteen members of the University of Wyoming football team announced they would begin wearing and would continue to wear black armbands in protest of the University's scheduled game with Brigham Young, a Mormon institution of higher education in Utah. The athletes met with the head football coach, explained their opposition to claimed religious beliefs of the Mormon church with reference to blacks and announced their protest. Head football coach Eaton dismissed the athletes from the team, citing a long-standing coaching rule which prohibited team members from engaging in protests.

Following the dismissal, the university president conducted a hearing over the dispute and interviewed all parties involved. The president then submitted the dispute to the university's board of trustees. Various hearings established that the athletes had been well aware of the coaching rule prohibiting protests prior to their actions, that all athletes retained full value of their scholarships after dismissal and that some of the athletes, if reinstated, had decided not to return to play unless the head coach was fired. The board of trustees formally dismissed the 14 athletes for violating the coaching rule.

The athletes then filed a civil rights action in the United States District Court of Wyoming against the State of Wyoming, the football coach, the athletic director, each member of the board of trustees and the university president. The plaintiffs complained that their dismissal from the team,

> constituted a deprivation of the plaintiffs' right to peaceably demonstrate under the Constitution of the United States and that the plaintiffs were suspended and dismissed from the University of Wyoming football team without cause and for the sole reason that they wore armbands in peaceable and symbolic demonstration, thus exercising their rights protected by the First, Ninth and Fourteenth Amendments. (1348)

The Court stated that had the university, an agency of the State,

> acceded to the demands of the 14 plaintiffs . . . , such action would have been violative of the First Amendment of the United States Constitution prohibiting the establishment of religion, mandating upon the states the principle of separation of Church and State and the requirement of complete neutrality and that it would have been further violative of Article 7, Section 12 of the Wyoming Constitution's directory that no sectarian tenets or doctrine shall be taught or favored in any public school or institution. (1352)

In ruling for the university, the court said that the facts of the case rendered the plaintiffs' complaint insubstantial and without merit under decisions rendered by the United States Supreme Court. The plaintiffs appealed.

The United States Court of Appeals, Tenth Circuit upheld a number of the trial court's orders, but remanded the First Amendment issues for further proceedings (*Williams v. Eaton*, 1971). On remand, the Tenth Circuit held that the athletes' First Amendment rights to freedom of speech could not be considered more important than the right of Brigham Young University to practice its religion (*Williams v. Eaton*, 1972).

In *Boyd v. Board of Directors of the McGehee School District* (1985), black football players, believing the selection of a homecoming queen was rigged by their coach, walked out of a pep rally and refused to play in the game scheduled for that evening. They were suspended from school. Plaintiffs contended they were suspended as a result of race and as punishment for their exercise of the right to freedom of expression.

The court found evidence that the black football players had reasonable grounds to believe the coach had manipulated the results of the vote for homecoming queen. He had denied the black candidate, the woman with the highest number of votes, the opportunity to become queen. Punitive damages were awarded against the coach.

Results of these cases demonstrate that protests are permissible when they do not disrupt the educational or the collegiate environment and when the expression of the protests are not in violation of the rights of other members of society. The cases also illustrate the fact that school policy or disciplinary rules could be challenged in a court of law, and if found to violate the rights of a specific population, could be overruled.

Expression and speech can be regulated when the expression may cause an obstruction of justice. If there is clear and present danger of serious harm of which the public has a right to be made aware, it may be permitted. When the speech or expression could easily cause a breach of peace or a riot it may be suppressed.

Personal Grooming: Elements of grooming were a chief source of First Amendment litigation among young people in the 1960s and 1970s. The extreme hair and dress styles of the late 1980s could lead agencies to return to grooming rules.

In an early United States Court of Appeals, Tenth Circuit decision, *Freeman v. Flake* (1971), the Court examined three cases — one each from Utah, New Mexico and Colorado — in which the issue was the suspension of students for violation of school regulations on the length of hair of male students. The Court stated that all of the cases were similar; "students desired to express their individualities and the school board offered justification for the regulation." (260) Students' lawyers relied on a number of Constitutional provisions; the First Amendment was one.

All of the cases quoted *Tinker*, and argued that hair was a form of symbolic speech. The U.S. Court of Appeals, Tenth Circuit stated that "the wearing of long hair is not akin to pure speech. At the most it is symbolic speech indicative of expressions of individuality." (260) In ruling, the Court went on to say that "complaints which are based on nothing more than school regulations of the length of a male student's hair do not 'directly and sharply' implicate basic constitutional values . . ." Therefore, each of the complaints "should have been dismissed for failure to state a claim on which relief can be granted." (262)

Many of the cases of the 1970s revolved around dress and grooming codes designed explicity for athletic teams and extracurricular activities.

As these cases often isolated a specific school population, they were litigated under the equal protection and the due process elements of the Fourteenth Amendment. These will be discussed in Chapter Ten.

Grooming regulations, under the First Amendment, may be established for disciplinary or other reasons but must have a basis or reason for existence. For example, in *Long v. Zopp* (1973), the Court refused to support a high school football coach who denied a player an earned "letter" and an invitation to the spring athletic banquet as a result of the athlete's failure to maintain the football grooming standard following completion of the playing season. The court noted that even though, "there might be some hygienic or other reasons to support a 'hair code', as promulgated by the football coach during football season, such reason would plainly not justify the enforcement of the code after the football season had ended." (181)

Grooming cases under the First Amendment require that the rights of the individual student to determine his/her own personal appearance be balanced against the rights of the state to require conformity to a standard regulation. *Bishop v. Colaw* (1971), established a standard for First Amendment analysis in grooming situations. Stephen Bishop, a 15-year-old, was suspended from school solely because of his hair style. He brought an action for readmission and a declaratory injunction, overturning the regulation governing hair length and style for male students. The district courts denied the plaintiff relief.

The United States Court of Appeals, Eighth Circuit reversed the district court's decision, noting the following facts: the Seventh and First Circuits had concluded that students possess a Constitutional right to wear their hair as they choose, while the Fifth, Sixth and Ninth Circuits had sustained school dress codes or denied students the opportunity to wear their hair as they pleased. In those cases in which the codes had been sustained, the reasonableness and necessity of the regulation had been the factor. The Fifth Circuit, for example, suggested that the "reason for sustaining the regulation is the demonstration that they are necessary to alleviate interference with the educational process." (1073)

Bishop argued that his rights included the First Amendment and the equal protection clause of the Fourteenth Amendment, and his parents' rights were in the Ninth Amendment. The Court was unable to recognize hair style as a symbolic expression or as a First Amendment right. The Court passed on the equal protection, or Fourteenth Amendment attack, and found that the regulation did not invade the parents' Ninth Amendment rights. The court held that Stephen had a Constitutional right to "govern his personal appearance," (1075) thus finding that the school failed to demonstrate the necessity of the regulation of male hair style and length. The student succeeded in his quest for personal grooming.

In *Dostert v. Berthold Public School District* (1975), Mark Dostert was prohibited from engaging in extracurricular school activities because of his refusal to trim his hair above the ears. As a result of the denial he filed a complaint against the school district, members of the school board and the superintendent.

The school presented the following reasons for requiring the grooming policy:

1. Since students have no constitutional right to participate in extracurricular activities, as opposed to academic programs, a school can impose a hair policy as a condition of participation;
2. The band director and the FFA adviser asserted that judges in band and FFA contests might take long hair into consideration in marking down the school in general appearance;
3. The basketball coach asserted that long hair can interfere with one's play on the basketball court;
4. The football coach (and the basketball coach to some degree) asserted that a hair policy was necessary in building successful athletic teams, in that it contributed to the discipline, dedication and unity of team members. (879)

In response to the four items, the court noted:

1. This "right-privilege" argument misses the point. The Plaintiff's constitutional challenge of the hair policy cannot be answered by an argument that participation in extracurriculars is a privilege and not a right. Regardless of whether participation in extracurriculars is a "privilege" or a "right", it is still a fact that, in excluding Mark from fully participating in extracurriculars because of his long hair, the Defendants are infringing upon his constitutional right to govern his own appearance. (880)
2 and 3. Although hair could be a factor in the success or failure of the school in a competitive environment the leaders could not cite an instance in which that had been a factor in competition nor could they justify the failure to use less restrictive methods. The coach even agreed that a hair band would have adequately met the basketball situation. (881)
4. With reference to reason number four:
   A. The most substantial justification for the hair policy advanced by the Defendants is that, insofar as athletics is concerned, it is necessary in building successful teams. A hair policy is said to contribute to the discipline, dedication and unity of an athletic team." (882)

B. That requiring uniformity of hair length is rationally related to obtaining an extra degree of success for their athletic programs. They must show that requiring uniformity of hair length is necessary to obtain an extra degree of success, and that their interest in obtaining this extra degree of success is such a compelling part of the public educational mission as to outweigh Mark's constitutionally protected interest in determining his own hair length. (882)

C. Even if an athletic team's success could be increased by requiring all its members to have uniform hair lengths, we do not think that winning is such an important interest that it outweighs all others. Winning should not be the be-all and end-all. And it certainly should not be of more importance in the educational process than the teaching of toleration of individual differences. (882)

The court ruled for the student, stating that the justifications for the grooming policy failed to demonstrate the necessity of the hair policy.

In *Lowman v. Davies* (1983), Larry Lowman, a park naturalist, was fired from the park service when he refused to trim his hair within the regulations of the agency. Lowman alleged that the regulation violated his Constitutional right to govern his personal appearance, and ultimately deprived him of a right to a due process hearing prior to being removed from his job.

The park service stated that the grooming standard was essential to enable the public to recognize the employees, to maintain order and to promote "esprit de corps." The court ruled that the uniforms should enable employee recognition by the public, that Larry's right to personal appearance was more important than "esprit de corps" and that the due process aspects of the case were to be remanded for further proceedings.

Freedom of Speech for Government Employed Teachers, Coaches and Others: Speech is often the issue of litigation, especially among government employees. The following discussion will chronicle events in the evolution of free speech. Emphasis will be placed on the role of the teacher; however, the results of these decisions have an impact on all federal and state employees, including recreation workers, sport managers and others.

Keyishian v. Board of Regents of the University of the State of New York (1967) has been referred to as the turning point in the rights of teachers to speak out. In this case, Keyishian challenged the Feinberg Law, a combination of two early forms of legislation. One part of this legislation established a system for implementing a 1917 statute providing for removal of teachers at the high school or college level for "the utterance of any treasonable or seditious word or words or the doing of any treasonable or seditious act or acts." The other form of legislation incorporated into the Feinberg Law was a 1939 ban on teaching the overthrow of the government. A 1953 amendment extended the Feinberg Law to higher education.

In 1962, when faculty members of the privately-owned University of Buffalo were taken into the State University of New York system, they were required, as part of the statutory and administrative regulations of the state, to sign a statement to the effect that they were not nor had ever been a communist. Keyishian and others refused to sign the statement and were notified that their failure to conform to the requirement would result in their dismissal. They brought an action for declaratory and injuncture relief, alleging that the state requirement violated the Constitution. The United States Supreme Court found the requirement to be unconstitutional, citing the statutory and administrative regulations as vague and threatening to the teacher's First Amendment rights.

Pickering v. Board of Education (1968) created a change in the United States Supreme Court's recognition of the rights of teachers under the First Amendment. Pickering, a tenured public school teacher and a resident of the school district in which he was employed, authored a letter to the local newspaper critical of the board of education's allocation of school funds, with reference to athletic and non-athletic programs. Pickering was terminated as an employee of the system.

The Court identified the problem as the need to "arrive at a balance between the interests of the teacher, as a citizen in commenting upon matters of public concern and the interest of the state, as an employer, in promoting the efficiency of the public services it performs through its employees." (568) The Court noted that the first step in the analysis was to determine that the teacher was in fact engaged in a Constitutionally-protected activity. Note: as a resident, the teacher was also a citizen of the local community.

The Court held that the letter was protected by the First Amendment, and ordered Pickering reinstated. The Court also used the *New York Times Co. v. Sullivan* (1964) defamation standard in determining that Pickering's statements concerned issues which were the subject of public attention, and not issues that could have interfered with the performance of his teaching duties. Pickering was thus entitled to the same protection as any member of the general public. The Court also held that had Pickering's statements been made with actual malice, or a reckless disregard for their truth, they would not have been protected. Under the holding of *Pickering*, a teacher will prevail when the teacher can demonstrate that the speech at issue is protected under the First Amendment and that the speech was one of the factors that led to the negative action against the teacher.

The Court, in *Pickering*, gave three situations in which the legitimate interest of the state might limit a teacher's right to speak freely on a topic, and two situations favoring a teacher's right to freely criticize his or her employer. Legitimate interests of the state include the following situations. A. "Need to maintain discipline and harmony among superiors and co-workers."(570) For example, did the teacher's actions interfere with the operation of the educational process? The decision also supports the idea that the closer the proximity of the working relationship, the lesser the protection. B. "Proper performance of daily duties in the classroom." (572, 573) Substandard teaching or the use of the classroom to air academic grievances, or failure to meet contractual duties is not accorded First Amendment protection. Disruptive speech is tolerated outside the classroom when a teacher is effective within the classroom and avoids using the learning environment as a forum for disruptive speech. C. "Freedom from interference in the regular operation of the school." (572) An unpopular view is not adequate, the activity must substantially interfere with the operation involved.

Legitimate interests of the teacher include: A. "Free and unhindered debate on matters of public importance," (568, 574) and B. "Recognition of the teachers' expertise in school matters making it essential that they be able to speak out freely on matters without fear of reprisal." (572)

It was not until 1975 that a standard was articulated for use in situations where speech was protected by the First Amendment. In *Mt. Healthy City School District Board of Education v. Doyle* (1975), a non-tenured public school teacher (Doyle) gave a local radio station the contents of an administrative memo about teachers' dress and appearance. Soon after the radio station announced the contents of the memo, Doyle was advised he would not be rehired.

The District Court, the Sixth Circuit and the Supreme Court (*Doyle v. Mt. Healthy City School District Board of Education*, 1982) held that Doyle's call was protected by the First Amendment. The teacher proved that the activity was Constitutionally protected and that it was a substantial and motivating factor in the school's decision not to hire, renew or transfer him. Doyle met the burden of proof for the First Amendment rights; but, the board of education presented adequate justification that Doyle would have been terminated absent his protective rights. Although teachers' Constitutional rights are to be protected, teachers will not retain their positions merely as a result of their constitutional rights; they must also be meeting the entire obligations of the jobs. In this case, Doyle had failed to maintain the obligations of his job and was dismissed for that reason, not for publishing the administrative memo.

Whether public employees, particularly teachers, have the same protection in private speech as they possess in public speech was examined in *Givhan v. Western Line Consolidated School District* (1979). (Review Chapter Eight for an analysis of private speech versus public speech.) Givhan, a junior high school English teacher, was alleged to have made petty and unreasonable demands to her principal in an "insultry, hostile, rude and arrogant" manner (412). She criticized the school for being racially discriminatory. She was dismissed after the incident.

The District Court held that the dismissal violated her First Amendment right of free speech and ordered her reinstated. The Court of Appeals reversed, saying that "because petitioner had privately expressed her complaints and opinions to the principal, her expression was not protected under the First Amendment." (413) The U.S. Fifth Circuit Court of Appeals said that "they were unable to agree that private expression of one's views is beyond constitutional protection and therefore reverse the Court of Appeals' judgment and remand the case so that it may consider the contentions of the parties freed from this erroneous view of the First Amendment." (413)

The Court went on to say the:

First Amendment forbids abridgement of the "freedom of speech." Neither the Amendment itself nor our decisions indicate that this freedom is lost to the public employee who arranges to communicate privately with his employer rather than to spread his views before the public. We decline to adopt such a view of the First Amendment. (415-416)

Previous to *Givhan*, private speech did not appear to be as well protected as did public speech. In *Givhan*, the Court held that private communication was to be afforded the same degree of First Amendment rights. The Court also said that while it was willing to tolerate a substantial interference in the working relationship between employer and employees before the speech would be considered unprotected, it was also necessary to consider manner, time or place of the private speech.

A case having merit, as it may have a significant impact on future First Amendment litigation, is *Connick v. Myers* (1983). Myers, an employee of the New Orleans Assistant District Attorney, was offered a transfer, which she did not approve. Myers also had several complaints about continuing office problems. In discussing her situation with a superior she was told that her perception of office problems was not widely held by other employees. She therefore devised and executed a questionnaire to research the issue. She was dismissed for refusing the transfer and for insubordination in conducting the research. Myers brought suit in federal court under the First Amendment Freedom of Speech. The federal court ruled in her favor, reinstated her and awarded compensatory damages. The Fifth Circuit affirmed.

The United States Supreme Court reversed, finding lower court error on the use of the *Pickering* balancing test of equating the interest of the teacher in commenting on public matters with the efficiency of the public service. When discussing Myer's survey, reference was made to the fact that the items were of a personal nature, not public issues. The Court then inferred that the First Amendment would protect only those elements of speech which were of a public concern.

Another First Amendment case of significance is *Knapp v. Whitaker* (1983). Terry Knapp, a public school physical educator and coach who had become acquainted with various school board members through his collective bargaining involvement, filed a grievance over unequal mileage reimbursement and lack of car liability insurance provided for coaches. The grievance was denied. Knapp went to the school board. School officials reprimanded him for failure to follow proper channels and warned him that such action would result in his being found insubordinate. Knapp brought an action on the basis of his First Amendment right to free speech against the school district, the superintendent, principal and assistant principal. He was awarded $500,000 in compensatory damages, which were affirmed on appeal.

In *Marcum v. Dahl* (1981), student athletes at the University of Oklahoma made derogatory comments about their head coach to the press following the completion of their last basketball game of the season. Soon after their comments were printed, the plaintiffs were notified that their athletic scholarships would not be renewed. Marcum, Whitlock and Christian brought action against the athletic director for women and the general athletic director under the First and Fourteenth Amendments. They contended that their statements to the press, including references to the head coach's personal lifestyle and the fact they would not return to the team if she was allowed to continue to coach, were constitutionally protected by the First Amendment. They also asserted that the failure to renew their athletic scholarships was in violation of their First Amendment rights.

The United States District Court, relying on the results of *Doyle* and *Pickering*, found, "that the plaintiff's comments to the press were not on matters of public concern and therefore were not constitutionally protected by the First Amendment." (734) In affirming the lower court's decision, the United States Court of Appeals, Tenth Circuit noted that the controversy between the athletes and the coach, which had occurred all season, was an internal problem and not an issue of general public concern. Therefore, the student athletes could not invoke the First Amendment.

Freedom of The Press

A recent court decision involving a high school newspaper serves to inform professionals of their First Amendment freedom of the press rights and the need to permit others to exercise their lawful First Amendment rights. In *Kuhlmeier v. Hazelwood School District*, (1984), three Hazelwood East High School students and other members of the student newspaper staff prepared a series of articles on teenage pregnancy. A faculty advisor to the paper approved the publication of the three articles on teen pregnancy, which included personal accounts of pregnancies, marriages and divorces, as well as descriptions of certain federal regulations. A newly assigned advisor, read the articles and stopped the publication.

The student newspaper staff members brought action against the members of the school board, superintendent, principal and faculty advisor. Each defendant was sued in his or her capacity as administrator, and each was sued personally or individually. The students alleged denial of their First Amendment rights.

Plaintiffs "allege that the articles did not violate any pre-existing, objective standards for censoring articles of *Spectrum* [the newspaper]; that none of the articles contain any libelous, obscene or private material; and that none of the articles would have caused material and substantial disruption to the work and discipline of the school." (1289-1290) The Court found the allegations were sufficient to impose liability on the school officials. They also found a possibility that some of the articles violated the Buckley Amendment. (The Buckley Amendment prohibits schools from disclosing confidential information about its students.) The Court also noted that the students had failed to exhaust school administrative remedies.

Later, in 1984, when the students returned to the District Court they were told that their graduation had rendered their case moot; they no longer had a claim. Staff members of the school newspaper took the same claim to the District Court (*Kuhlmeier v. Hazelwood School District*, 1985). In the deliberation, attention was focused on the fact that the paper was a portion of a regular school course, a journalism class. Therefore the newspaper involved the compulsory learning environment of the high school and as a result of this placement could not be afforded the freedom granted other extracurricular activities. *Spectrum* was not a public forum for free expression by students. The court affirmed the earlier court decisions that as a result of the curricular implications and the fact that certain of the articles could create an invasion of privacy of students, the school district administrators were right in removing articles from the student newspaper. This case remains in the courts.

Invasion of Privacy

Invasion of privacy was defined and described in reference to libel and slander in Chapter Eight as one of the defamation torts. Invasion of privacy can be caused by public statements. It also can include one's right of freedom of choice regarding marital and child-bearing decisions. It is applicable to the protection of one's body from offensive intrusion. The right of privacy is used to prohibit state actions that interfere with matters of private choice. Blood and urine testing could be the subject of an invasion of privacy challenge.

Drug testing cases can often be reviewed under the First Amendment invasion of privacy, as well as the Fourth Amendment search and seizure. All performers in physical activity possess a right of privacy. This right accompanies the elite as well as the average athlete to the playing field, training spa and locker room. A state can limit a person's right of privacy only when there is a compelling state interest.

The state interests that exist with reference to drug testing are to maintain the natural competitive qualities of the participants and to assure athletes of good health. When drugs enhance an athlete's skill, the sport is no longer a test of the athlete's native capacity. If at the same time it is known that drugs may cause harm to the athlete, the state, in the name of the school or athletic governing agency, may see fit to control the use of the drugs.

LeVant v. N.C.A.A. (1987), the first drug testing case in athletics, involved a female diver at Stanford who challenged the NCAA drug testing program by refusing to sign a statement agreeing to the test. The trial judge issued a preliminary injunction for Ms. LeVant. The case is on appeal at the time of this book's printing. In issuing the injunction, the trial court said:

> The fact that an athlete volunteers to compete in NCAA competition does not vitiate the reasonable expectation of privacy. The NCAA cannot require Ms. LeVant under these particular circumstances to give up a very valuable right — the right of privacy. The NCAA regulations are pervasive and manifold, but the fact that an athlete may have to give up the right to play poker for money because gambling is not permitted by the NCAA, does not equate with giving up the right to urinate in private. The urinalysis test may reveal lifestyle, or other irrelevant but deeply personal matters, such as the use of birth control medication. (Slip Opinion)

Additional drug testing cases will be reviewed under Fourth and Fourteenth Amendments discussions.

FOURTH AMENDMENT

The Fourth Amendment to the Constitution states: "The right of the people to be secure in their persons, houses, papers, and effects, against unreasonable searches and seizures, shall not be violated, and no Warrants shall issue, but upon probable cause, supported by Oath or affirmation, and particularly describing the place to be searched, and the person to be seized." Searches of students purses, lockers and hotel rooms have been the subject of various Fourth Amendment cases. As lockers are necessary in the physical activity system, and because professionals may be responsible for the lockers, a knowledge of the results of litigation on search and seizure will be helpful. Search and seizure is an equally important topic to the area of drug testing.

The discipline of a student, an athlete, a team participant or an employee for an infraction of a rule may be enforced when there is sufficient evidence to support the fact that the rule has been violated. The purpose of reviewing the following cases is to identify the limits of authority allocated to certain persons and agencies. Police and certain security officers have one set of rules for conducting searches, but teachers, principals, coaches and managers of health spas have an entirely different set of rules for conducting searches. In fact, there may be reasons why someone will be prohibited from conducting a search.

The system for analyzing facts with reference to the Fourth Amendment is the same as the one used in analysis of the First Amendment: a system of balancing. The student's, athlete's or participant's interest in privacy is balanced against the agency's right to maintain order and an environment in which others can safely participate. In order to establish or maintain order, it may be necessary to suspend or discipline a participant; however, valid evidence must be obtained before a complaint can be filed. The following discussion and cases will assist the supervisor or manager in deciding the merits of conducting such a search, creating written policy for searches, briefing workers on the proper system and actually conducting the search.

System for Searching

New Jersey v. T.L.O. (1985) was a case which has influenced many contemporary decisions. A teacher discovered five young women smoking cigarettes in a school washroom, violating school policy. The teacher escorted the girls to the principal's office. There, the assistant vice principal questioned them. When asked about smoking, one girl admitted to smoking. T.L.O., a 14-year-old, denied that she had been smoking and claimed she never smoked. T.L.O. was then invited into the assistant vice principal's office where he demanded to see her purse. Upon opening the purse, he not only found cigarettes but noticed a certain type of paper, often associated with rolling marijuana cigarettes. He then thoroughly searched the purse and located marijuana, a pipe, a substantial sum of money, lists of debts and two letters which implicated T.L.O. in the selling of drugs.

The assistant vice principal notified T.L.O.'s mother and the police, and gave the evidence gathered from the purse to the police. T.L.O., accompanied by her mother, went to police headquarters and confessed to drug use and sale.

As a result of T.L.O.'s confession to the police, the state brought delinquency charges against her. They also held that the Fourth Amendment applied to searches conducted by school officials and that the search in question was reasonable (State ex rel. T.L.O., 1980). The Appellate Division of the New Jersey Superior Court affirmed the trial court's findings that the search was within the Fourth Amendment, but vacated the adjudication of delinquency, and remanded for a determination of whether T.L.O. had voluntarily waived her Fifth Amendment rights before confessing (State ex. rel. T.L.O., 1982). The Supreme Court of the United States reversed the lower court's decision on the Fourth Amendment search and ordered suppression of the evidence found in the search (New Jersey V.T.L.O., 1985).

In this case the United States Supreme Court established that searches could be conducted by persons other than law enforcement officers; the "Fourth Amendment is applicable to the activities of civil as well as criminal authorities." (740) The Court also attempted to establish a standard which could be used to govern school searches. The question of balance in this situation was identified as an analysis of the individual's expectation of privacy and personal security versus the government's need for an effective method of dealing with breaches of order (741). In this case, order means to maintain an environment in which learning can occur.

The Court noted that the school setting required restrictions on searches different from those needed by other public authorities.

The warrant requirement, in particular, is unsuited to the school environment; requiring a teacher to obtain a warrant before searching a child suspected of an infraction of school rules would unduly interfere with the maintenance of the swift and informal disciplinary procedures needed in the schools. (743)

smoking. T.L.O., a 14-year-old, denied that she had been smoking and claimed she never smoked. T.L.O. was then invited into the assistant vice principal's office where he demanded to see her purse. Upon opening the purse, he not only found cigarettes but noticed a certain type of paper, often associated with rolling marijuana cigarettes. He then thoroughly searched the purse and located marijuana, a pipe, a substantial sum of money, lists of debts and two letters which implicated T.L.O. in the selling of drugs.

The assistant vice principal notified T.L.O.'s mother and the police, and gave the evidence gathered from the purse to the police. T.L.O., accompanied by her mother, went to police headquarters and confessed to drug use and sale.

As a result of T.L.O.'s confession to the police, the state brought delinquency charges against her. They also held that the Fourth Amendment applied to searches conducted by school officials and that the search in question was reasonable (*State ex rel. T.L.O.*, 1980). The Appellate Division of the New Jersey Superior Court affirmed the trial court's findings that the search was within the Fourth Amendment, but vacated the adjudication of delinquency, and remanded for a determination of whether T.L.O. had voluntarily waived her Fifth Amendment rights before confessing (*State ex. rel. T.L.O.*, 1982). The Supreme Court of the United States reversed the lower court's decision on the Fourth Amendment search and ordered suppression of the evidence found in the search (New Jersey V.T.L.O., 1985).

In this case the United States Supreme Court established that searches could be conducted by persons other than law enforcement officers; the "Fourth Amendment is applicable to the activities of civil as well as criminal authorities." (740) The Court also attempted to establish a standard which could be used to govern school searches. The question of balance in this situation was identified as an analysis of the individual's expectation of privacy and personal security versus the government's need for an effective method of dealing with breaches of order (741). In this case, order means to maintain an environment in which learning can occur.

The Court noted that the school setting required restrictions on searches different from those needed by other public authorities.

> The warrant requirement, in particular, is unsuited to the school environment; requiring a teacher to obtain a warrant before searching a child suspected of an infraction of school rules would unduly interfere with the maintenance of the swift and informal disciplinary procedures needed in the schools. (743)

The Court went on to state that

the legality of a search of a student should depend simply on the reasonableness, under all the circumstances, of the search. Determining the reasonableness of any search involves a twofold inquiry; first, one must consider "whether the . . . action was justified at its inception." Second, one must determine whether the search as actually conducted "was reasonably related in scope to the circumstances which justified the interference in the first place." (743-744)

Student Complaints

In *Zamora v. Pomeroy* (1981), a student filed a complaint saying the warrantless search of his school locker which identified marijuana was a violation of his Fourth Amendment rights. The school district had invited the police to bring in search dogs to sniff out the lockers. Vidal Zamora's locker was among those identified by the dogs as suspicious. The school stated it could enter the lockers because notice had been provided the students at the beginning of the year that the lockers were subject to inspection at any time. The court ruled that the search was legal, as the school needed some authority to handle the drug problem and that the student's education was not harmed. Zamora was not suspended from school, but transferred to a second school.

The lesson from this case is the importance of notifying holders of lockers that the lockers are subject to inspection at any time. Misunderstanding as to the privacy of a locker is a problem which can be avoided if both written and verbal instructions place the student on alert. Many agencies ask the locker holder to sign a release and a notice of agreement to the possibility of a search.

Persons conducting a school, playground or recreation search need to consider the age, sex and previous work or employment record of the individual being searched. They must also assess the importance of the problem that has created the need for the search and the value of time in conducting the search. It is recommended to obtain a search warrant or to turn the problem over to an authoritative body.

In *Webb v. McCullough* (1987), a Sixth District United States Court of Appeals' case, advisors of all extracurricular activities can study the Fourth and Fourteenth Amendments to the Constitution, and revisit the concept of "in loco parentis," a concept seldom employed in contemporary school litigation. The case developed after Wendy Webb and her three roommates were sent home from a high school spring break band trip to Hawaii, following alleged violations of the trip rules.

Webb was one of 140 students of Hixson High School selected to attend a band competition in Hawaii, in March of 1985. One day, as Webb and her roommates were preparing to go shopping, the male principal and a male chaperone entered the girls' hotel room without warning by using a key obtained from the desk. As one of the girls was clad only in bra and pants, the men left immediately, sending the principal's wife into the room to tell the girls to dress. After the girls dressed, the principal re-entered the room and, according to the testimony of Webb, informed them that the front desk had told him to search the girls' room for alcoholic beverages. Search of the room, bathroom, Webb's luggage and the rooms of a number of other students revealed no alcoholic beverages.

A second alleged violation involved Webb and her roommates visiting with two unknown boys in the hotel hall. (Whether the boys ever entered the hotel room was never established by the court.) The principal had heard there had been a party in the room adjacent to Webb's hotel room. Upon entering the adjacent room, he observed a boy leaping from the balcony. A check of the room's refrigerator revealed a six-pack of beer and a quart of wine.

Following this incident, the principal informed the four roommates to pack their bags, as they were being sent home on the first available flight. He also had called their parents, alerting them to the situation. Webb, distraught by the events, locked herself in the bathroom. One of the roommates informed the principal of the situation. The case reported that the principal,

> . . . was quite angry when he realized Webb was in the bathroom. He tried to jimmy the bathroom door lock, but Webb would not let him in. He then slammed the door three or four times with his shoulder. The door finally gave way, knocking Webb against the wall. McCullough then thrust the door open again, and it struck Webb again, throwing her to the floor. He then grabbed Webb from the floor, threw her against the wall, and slapped her. She then broke away and ran to her roommates. (Slip Opinion)

Early the next morning, the four girls were dropped at the airport with standby tickets. They obtained seats back to the states 24 hours later. After a detour to Chicago, they finally arrived in Chattanooga, 36 hours later. When school resumed, following spring break, Webb and her roommates were suspended from school for "violation of curfew, having a male in their room, having liquor in the next room, and trespassing into adjacent rooms of the hotel." (Slip Opinion) Meetings were held with the school board. Webb sought a federal injunction. Two weeks later, an agreement was reached permitting Webb to return to school; however, she was never permitted to return to the band.

Webb and her parents filed suit against the principal, the superintendent, the school system and the board of education alleging violation of her Fourth and Fourteenth Amendment rights. The district court granted the defendants (school, principal, superintendent) a summary judgment on all federal claims based on searches and suspensions. She appealed to the United States Court of Appeals for the Sixth District. When Webb reached the age of majority, the parents' claim was withdrawn and Webb proceeded on her own.

The Court of Appeals first examined the search of the room in the context of the two-part test in *New Jersey v. T.L.O.*: (1) were there reasonable grounds to suspect the search would turn up evidence that the student violating school law?, and (2) if such grounds existed, was the selected method of search the least intrusive, given the age and sex of the student and the nature of the alleged violation? The Court chose to provide the principal with a "limited scope of in loco parentis authority over Webb." (Slip Opinion) The court stated that a trip of this nature was not the regular school environment and that the travel and overnight accommodations permitted an in loco parentis legal theory to operate; thus, the situation provided immunity to negligence claims of the school authorities and allowed the claims to be treated the same as such claims would be treated for a natural parent. The principal was acting as both a representative of the state and in loco parentis in his task of searching Webb's room. The district court stated:

> It must be remembered that this case arose in the context of a "spring break" trip and that the school officials present were charged with the care and safety of the plaintiffs while they were more than 5,000 miles from home. . . . The crucial factual difference between the in-school search in *T.L.O.* and the search during a field trip in this case permits, indeed requires, the application of the in loco parentis doctrine. . . . Second, a greater range of activities occur during extracurricular activities than during school. . . . Third, there are many more ways for a student to be injured or to transgress school rules or laws during a non-curricular field trip than during relatively orderly school hours. To expose administrators and school districts to increased tort liability while denying them the authority necessary to lessen the likelihood of student injury would be inequitable and would probably decrease the range of extracurricular activities schools would offer. . . . Finally, this was a search of Webb's residence, albeit a temporary residence. Such a search simply could not occur in the course of an ordinary school day, the context to which T.L.O. applies. (Slip Opinion)

The United States Sixth Circuit Court of Appeals affirmed the earlier court's decisions on all but one issue: the blows that were struck in the bathroom the day of the violation. The Appeals Court reversed the decision, with reference to the alleged blows, and remanded for further proceedings.

The *D.R.C. v. State of Alaska* (1982) case involved a wallet that was taken from a student's pants pocket while the student was participating in a physical education class. On the day of the incident the teacher entrusted the locker room to a trusted student. The student was to lock the door upon leaving. Soon after the teacher left, D.R.C. entered the locker room. The entrusted student asked D.R.C. to lock the door upon leaving; the student left. However, the student, nervous about his responsibility, watched the locker room door and never saw D.R.C. leave.

At the end of the class a student reported his wallet, containing some $50, missing. The student entrusted with the responsibility of locking the locker room door identified D.R.C. in the hall and got into a fight with him. As a result of the fight, the boys were taken to the principal's office. After the questioning, the facts were assembled. The physical educator questioned D.R.C. about the wallet. D.R.C. was then searched, asked to remove his outer clothing and shoes, patted down, and frisked. One of his shoes contained money in the same bills as the identified missing money. D.R.C. was adjudicated a juvenile delinquent.

On appeal, D.R.C. alleged the evidence used in the delinquency hearing was seized in violation of his rights. The Court of Appeals of Alaska affirmed the earlier court decision that the search was legal. Lessons from the case are:

1. The school district's policy manual permitted school officials to search students for cause.
2. The assistant principal and the teacher knew D.R.C. was in the area prior to permitting the search. The questioning of D.R.C. occurred after his presence in the area had been established.
3. The school officials carefully discussed the search before conducting it.
4. As soon as the evidence was obtained, the police were notified. The school policy was to work closely with the police when stolen goods or illegal drugs were found.

Drug Screening

Drug screening has become popular in professional, collegiate and scholastic athletics. In fact, effort is being made to screen all school children for drugs during routine physical examinations.

Those in professional sports organizations are usually considered private employees, as are most employment organizations. They are not bound by the Fourth Amendment. Despite the fact that they were not government entities, the ruling in *Shoemaker v. Handel* (1985) upheld compulsory urinalysis under the administrative search standard for closely-regulated industries. This ruling suggested that, on occasion, private industry will be subject to drug testing the same as federal and state government.

Analysis of drug testing programs in industry shows that when the test was a part of the pre-employment examination of all employees, the courts tended to uphold the test; but, when the test was given to persons employed for many years, it was not upheld. In order for the test to be upheld among veteran employees, there has to be reason to believe that the employee is on drugs.

In *Patchogue-Medford Congress of Teachers v. Board of Education* (1987), the collective bargaining agreement between the school and the teachers required all probationary teachers to submit to a full physical examination in their first and in their final year of probation, prior to tenure. In 1985, all probationary teachers were asked to submit to urinalysis. The sole purpose of the test was to determine drug usage. The teachers' union brought an action to stop the test, saying it was unauthorized and constituted an unreasonable search and seizure in violation of the teachers' Constitutional rights. The union sought declaratory and injunctive relief and obtained an interim stay. School district arguments were that the "examination was authorized by the collective bargaining agreement, did not constitute a search or seizure and, in any event, was a reasonable requirement to impose on a tenured candidate." (458)

The trial court granted the petition, saying it constituted a search and seizure, and under the Constitution could be made only under reasonable suspicion. The court balanced the employees' right of privacy with the board of education's interest in employees who were fit to perform their jobs.

The court of appeals affirmed the trial court decision, saying that requiring public employees or job applicants to submit to a medical examination to demonstrate job fitness was acceptable and traditional. The addition of the single urinalysis for no basic reason was, however, not acceptable.

Society may choose to pressure for drug testing of athletes of all ages in the future. The following provides suggestions for the professional who will be forced to design and implement a drug testing program:

1. The first question the professional must ask: Is drug abuse in athletics a major social issue? Is it a physical issue? Is it a psychological issue? Next, is drug abuse in athletics among the age, sex and sport selection group with whom I work a major issue? For example, what is the probability that junior high school football players

are abusing drugs? That the same age tennis players are engaged in drug abuse?

2. Does the seriousness of the situation warrant an intrusive search such as collecting urine samples? (See Meloch, 1987, for further discussion of this issue).

3. When the setting — school, private team or municipal play environment — has been established, to foster moral and social development as well as physical skill accomplishment, consideration must be given to the entire message conveyed to persons undergoing a drug test. Alderman (1986) writing in the *Columbia Law Review* notes that:

> On one hand, when assessing the need to search, school officials are faced with the immediate and tangible dangers caused by student drug use. On the other hand, school officials must also consider, in a general sense, the coercive atmosphere generated by a program which enables them to extract students' bodily fluid upon command. (864)

4. When the decision is made to establish a drug testing program, all such programs must be investigated for cost efficiency and feasibility:
   a. The quality and accuracy of tests used in determining drug use must be of the highest standards possible. When accuracy is not maximum, several specimens should receive a battery of tests before a decision is given.
   b. Human error in testing and in the chain of custody of the drug must not be overlooked.
   c. Results of the tests must be understood by those receiving the results. For example, testing for marijuana has been known to pick up the fact that the subject merely breathed, but did not smoke marijuana. (Leal, 1984)

5. When the program has been established:
   a. Administrators of the program must know what is to be searched, how a search is to be conducted and the method for releasing results.
   b. Those who could be searched must be informed in writing that a search may be conducted, how it will be conducted, the treatment of the results and the impact of the results.

6. The above policies must be public information, readily available to those subject to the test and evidence obtained in which the subject notes that they have received such information.

7. The entire system should be created with legal advice. The coun-

sel for the agency should oversee the final plan, protocol for implementation and all paper work accompaning the plan.

SUMMARY

It should be noted that all Constitutional issues require a rule, regulation, statute or policy of the state or federal government be involved. First and Fourth Amendment analysis involve a balancing of the rights of the state with the rights of an individual. First Amendment actions involve freedoms of speech, press and privacy. Freedom of speech and freedom of press are considered to be absolute freedoms; however, the stipulation that a teacher must retain an atmosphere in which learning can occur may restrict a teacher's freedoms. In protecting speech, the court examines the subject of the speech, to whom it is directed, the forum in which it occurs and the manner of delivery. Freedom of the press is freedom to write, draw and create models. It is freedom to convey ideas in the theater, movies and on television. The right of privacy is the right to protect one's body from offensive intrusion.

The Fourth Amendment is the right of persons to be secure in their homes and personal effects. Systems for search and drug testing are under the Fourth Amendment. Within the cases presented are specific guidelines to assist the courts in balancing the rights and to enable professionals to understand the requirements involved.

References

Alderman, Ellen M. 1986. Dragnet drug testing in public schools and the fourth amendment. *Columbia Law Review, 86*, 852-875.
Bishop v. Colaw, 450 F. 2d 1069 (1971).
Boyd v. Board of Directors of the McGehee School District, 612 F. Supp. 86 (1985).
Connick v. Myers, 103 S. Ct. 1684 (1983).
D.R.C. v. State of Alaska, 646 P. 2d, 252 (1982).
Dostert v. Berthold Public School District, 391 F. Supp. 876 (1975).
Doyle v. Mt. Healthy City School District Board of Education, 670 F. 2d 59 (1982).
Freeman v. Flake, 448 F. 2d 258 (1971).
Gillow, Paul L. 1986. Compulsory urinalysis of public school students: an unconstitutional search and seizure. *Columbia Human Rights Law Review, 18*, 111-135.
Givhan v. Western Line Consolidated School District, 439 U.S. 410 (1979).
Gunther, Gerald. 1985. *Constitutional Law, Cases and Marerials,* 11th Ed. Mineola, NY: The Foundation Press, Inc.
Keyishian v. Board of Regents of the University of the State of New York, 385 U.S. 589, 87 S. Ct. 675 (1967).
Knapp v. Whitaker, 577 F. Supp. 1265 (1983).
Kuhlmeier v. Hazelwood School District, 578 F. Supp. 1286 (1984).
Kuhlmeier v. Hazelwood School District, 596 F. Supp. 1422 (1984).
Kuhlmeier v. Hazelwood School District, 607 F. Suppl. 1450 (1985).
Leal, Charles E. 1984. Admissability of Biochemical Urinalysis Testing Results for the Purpose of Detecting Marijuana Use. *Wake Forest Law Review, 20*, 391-412.
LeVant v. N.C.A.A. No. 619209, Superior Court of California, Santa Clara County (1987).
Long v. Zopp, 476 F. 2d 180 (1973).
Lowman v. Davies, 704 F. 2d 1044 (1983).
Marcum v. Dahl, 658 F. 2d 731 (1981).

Mayberry v. Dees, 663 F. 2d 502 (1981).

Meloch, Sally Lynn. 1987. An analysis of public college athletic drug testing programs through the un-constitutional condition doctrine and the fourth amendment. *Southern California Law Review, 60*, 815-850.

Mt. Healthy City School District Board of Education v. Doyle, 529 F. 2d 524 (1975).

New Jersey v. T.L.O., 105 S. Ct. 733 (1985).

New York Times Co. v. Sullivan, 376 U.S. 254 (1964).

Patchogue-Medford Congress of Teachers v. Board of Education, 70 N.Y. 2d 57, 517 N.Y. Supp. 2d 456 (1987).

Pickering v. Board of Education, 391 U.S. 563, 36 11. 2d 568 (1968).

Press v. Board of Regents of the University System of Georgia, 489 F. Supp. 150 (1980).

Shoemaker v. Handel, 608 F. Supp. 1151 (1985).

State ex rel. T.L.O., 178 N.J. Super. 329, 428 A. 2d 1327 (1980).

State ex. rel. T.L.O., 185 N.J. Super 279, 448 A. 2d 493 (1982).

Tinker v. Des Moines School District, 393 U.S. 503 (1969).

Tribe, Laurence H. 1978. *American constitutional law.* Mineola, NY: The Foundation Press, Inc.

Webb v. McCullough, United States Court of Appeals for the Sixth Circuit, Slip Opinion, (September 17, 1987).

Williams v. Eaton, 310 F. Supp. 1342 (1970).

Williams v. Eaton, 443 F. 2d 422 (1971).

Williams v. Eaton, 468 F. 2d 1079 (10th Circuit) (1972).

Zamora v. Pomery, 639 F. 2d 662 (1981).

10

Fourteenth Amendment to the Constitution

The Fourteenth Amendment to the Constitution provides the most important limitations on states and state action. Elements of the Fourteenth Amendment most important to the physical activity professional are the following:

> No state shall make or enforce any law which shall abridge the privileges or immunities of citizens of the United States; nor shall any state deprive any person of life, liberty, or property, without due process of law; nor deny to any person within its jurisdiction the equal protection of the law.

The Fourteenth Amendment protects acts, as well as failure to act. Equal protection and due process clauses apply to all persons, including aliens and corporations. However, the privileges and immunities stated in the Fourteenth Amendment apply only to citizens, not corporations, in the United States. Three areas of the Fourteenth Amendment will be addressed in this chapter: equal protection, substantive due process and procedural due process. Many cases involving equal protection and procedural due process are found in the area of physical activity. Sex discrimination will be treated separately, to highlight society's use of sport as a vehicle for social changes. Title IX of The Education Amendment of 1972, a federal statute in the area of sex discrimination, will be included, as it relates specifically to the equal protection clause. Although Title IX encompasses all school issues, its major impact was in the area of competitive athletics.

EQUAL PROTECTION

The Fourteenth Amendment, Equal Protection Clause states: "No state shall make or enforce any law which shall ... deny to any person within its jurisdiction the equal protection of the laws." (U.S. Constitution, Amend XIV, §1) An Equal Protection challenge must show that a group of people is being treated differently than the total population, without adequate justification. Legal analysis involves balancing the interests of the state with the interests of the individual. Precedent has created a complex set of guidelines that attaches different degrees of importance to the rights of certain classes of individuals.

A regulation which arbitrarily or unreasonably selects the group subjected to the regulation violates the Equal Protection Clause. The courts, in general, have ruled that whether or not a regulation is unreasonable depends upon the:

> rationale and conditions for which the regulation was originally created, and subsequent conditions that affect the regulation's reasonableness in practice.

If the regulation was unreasonable when adopted, it probably will be found to be unreasonable in practice.

On occasion, a regulation may provide optional benefits to the public. When members of the public have the opportunity to enjoy the benefit, but choose not to, they have not been denied equal protection under the law. Results of case law under the Fourteenth Amendment to the Constitution have been used by Constitutional scholars (see Tribe, 991-1136 and Gunther, 621-666) to create a system for analyzing the Equal Protection Clause.

This system contains three categories: traditional rational basis, middle tier or intermediate review and strict scrutiny. Each classification employs a process for weighing the need of the government in relation to the right of the individual or group:

1. *Traditional Rational Basis*
   The test requires the classification be reasonably related to a permissible government purpose. For example, what legitimate objective is served by the government's actions? Case decisions demonstrate that this approach usually results in finding a per-

missible purpose, thus making it difficult for a party to sustain a Constitutional challenge. This classification encompasses all cases not specifically identified in the other categories, including but not limited to poverty, medical, residency and license.

2. *Middle Tier or Intermediate Review*

This classification was originally identified in gender review in *Craig v. Boren* (1976). The Supreme Court said the equal protection clause required, "that classification by gender must serve important governmental objectives and must be substantially related to achievements of those objectives." (197) The requirement is that important governmental objectives bear a substantial relationship to the classification. Tribe (1978) uses a five-step technique to further explain the analysis.

A. Assessing the importance of the objective served by the challenged classification . . . insisting that the technique observed by a challenged classification or limitation on liberty be important. (1082)

Tribe takes from *Ulandis v. Kline* (1973) in stating that

it has become obvious . . . that, as the Court's assessment of the weight and value of the individual interest escalates, the less likely it is that mere administrative convenience and avoidance of hearings or investigations will be sufficient to justify what otherwise would appear to be irrational discrimination. (1083)

B. Demanding close fit . . . requiring, that the rules employed by government be, "substantially related to the achievement of . . . [the] objectives" involved to defend those rules. (1083)

C. Requiring current articulation . . . refusing to supply a challenged rule with a rationale drawn from judicial imagination or even from the rule's history, where the rationale is not advanced in the litigation in the rule's defense. (1083, 1084)

D. Limiting the use of afterthought is the fourth technique . . . If there are convincing reasons to believe that the objective is being supplied purely by hindsight - as one of several "after-the-fact" rationalizations it should not be used. (1085-1086)

E. Require that the legal scheme under challenge be altered so as to permit rebuttal in individual cases even if the scheme is not struck down altogether. (1088)

3. *Strict Scrutiny*

Under strict scrutiny, laws are subjected to detailed analysis and are held invalid unless shown to be necessary to a governmental purpose. There must be a compelling state interest in the law and no less restrictive means of satisfying the need. Laws, on their face, that blatantly discriminate against racial minorities, are usually invalidated. Laws that are facially neutral, but when applied in a discriminatory manner, are also unconstitutional. However, discrimination becomes much more difficult to prove in those instances. Strict scrutiny includes race and national origin.

Proponents of the Equal Rights Amendment have stated that sex would have been treated under the strict scrutiny analysis had the amendment passed. Note the results of case law under various state equal rights amendments to verify the validity of the above statement.

SUBSTANTIVE DUE PROCESS

Fourteenth Amendment Substantive Due Process limits the state regulatory powers, requiring such regulation to be for a proper legislative purpose, to bear a reasonable relationship to the purpose and not to be arbitrary or capricious. Modern day Substantive Due Process came as a result of *Roe v. Wade* (1973), a challenge to an anti-abortion statute in which the court ruled that the "right of privacy is the Fourteenth Amendment's concept of personal liberty . . . is broad enough to encompass a woman's decision whether or not to terminate her pregnancy." (153)

Although Substantive Due Process has not been applied by the courts to issues of importance to teachers or managers of physical activity, professionals should be aware of the difference between Substantive and Procedural Due Process.

PROCEDURAL DUE PROCESS

Fourteenth Amendment Procedural Due Process is a system that provides an opportunity for individuals to be heard. It differs from Substantive Due Process, a system for reviewing judgments of legislative branches. Procedural Due Process does not question the state's goals. It is a means for citizens to be assured of fair treatment. The extent and requirements of the process due to a particular individual have been the focus of considerable litigation. Legal advice must be sought to determine the extent of the process required in a particular situation.

```
FOURTEENTH AMENDMENT EQUAL PROTECTION ANALYSIS

                    Rational Basis
        Classification reasonably related to a
           permissible government purpose.


                     Middle Tier
                  Intermediate Review
           Classification is substantially related
          to an important government purpose.


                    Suspect Class
                   Strict Scrutiny
           Classification is necessary to a
          compelling government purpose.
```

Figure 10-1. *Fourteenth Amendment Equal Protection Analysis*

Professionals should be aware of the steps generally acceptable in Procedural Due Process and should be guided by legal counsel in forming policy for a particular situation. Individuals have:

1. a right to be informed of all charges and complaints brought against them,
2. a right to a hearing,
3. a right to secure counsel,
4. adequate time to prepare to respond to the complaint,
5. opportunity to present their side of the issue,
6. opportunity to call witnesses and to cross-examine opposing witnesses and parties and
7. opportunity for a fair trial.

TITLE IX OF THE EDUCATION AMENDMENTS OF 1972

In addition to the Fourteenth Amendment Equal Protection Clause, Title IX of the Education Amendment of 1972 provides statutory authority for similar protection. Title IX provides another avenue of redress in discrimination. Title IX states that: "No person in the United States shall, on the basis of sex, be excluded from participation in, be denied the benefit of, or be subject to discrimination under any education program or activity receiving Federal financial assistance." (Education Amendments of 1972) Appreciation of Title IX is acquired with an understanding of the difference between constitutional and statutory law (review Chapter Two).

Power to enforce Title IX is vested in the Department of Education, which has the authority to withdraw federal funding from institutions that violate the statute. In 1979, the Supreme Court (*Cannon v. University of Chicago*, 1979) recognized that an individual could also maintain a private cause of action under Title IX. In 1982, the courts (*North Haven v. Bell*), held that Title IX also applied to employment.

When violations of the United States or state constitutions are presented to a court of law, a long, complicated and sometimes costly process is involved. Court dockets are crowded, causing some cases to remain in the system beyond five years. The identity of the parties is well-known; therefore, rarely is a case kept a private matter.

Statutes, though, often provide an enforcement procedure within the regulation. Usually, an administrative body of the Federal or state government assumes such responsibility. A person may file a complaint without an attorney. In certain civil rights statutes, the complaint may be anonymous. When parties do identify themselves to the agency, the publicity is minimal. Agency personnel investigate the complaint as soon as possible — at agency expense. And, the resolution is by negotiation. The enforcement of a statute is inexpensive, fast and impersonal.

A constitutional claim, Fourteenth Amendment for example, cannot be taken to an Office of Civil Rights. However, a statute such as Title IX, can be taken to a court of law. Many statutes require an individual to seek redress under the statute prior to filing a complaint in court. If the parties are not satisfied under the ruling of the administrative body, they may go to court.

FOURTEENTH AMENDMENT EQUAL PROTECTION CASES IN ATHLETICS

Since the 1970s, women in the United States have looked to the courts for assistance in being treated as equals in athletics. Among the legal theories most often cited are the Fourteenth Amendment of the United States Constitution, Title IX of the Education Amendment of 1972, and state constitutions or state equal rights amendments. Note that sex discrimination also has been a factor in complaints filed under contract and antitrust law; however, the majority of complaints have been filed under one or more of the previously mentioned theories.

Challenges most often presented have been from females requesting membership on male teams, males seeking membership on female teams and females requesting equal expense and support for separate teams. The complaints have been taken directly to the state athletic association, or have been filed against a school or university and its board of education or trustees.

Females Requesting Membership On Male Teams

Among the early cases litigated under the Fourteenth Amendment Equal Protection Clause was *Hollander v. Connecticut Interscholastic Athletic Conference, Inc.* (1971). Susan Hollander challenged the Athletic Conference rule that denied her an opportunity to run on the men's cross-country team. At the time, no team existed for women. Although Hollander lost the case, Connecticut was required to integrate its non-contact sports as a result of a consent decree in January, 1973.

Debbie Reed (*Reed v. Nebraska Athletic Association*, 1972) brought a suit, similar to Hollander's challenge, against the Nebraska Athletic Association. Reed wanted to play on the men's golf team (again, there was no team for women). Reed's request for an injunction to allow women to participate on the men's team was granted. (Remember, an injunction is a judicial process requiring the person(s) to whom it is directed to do or stop doing a particular thing.)

The case cited more than any other is *Brenden v. Independent School District* (1973). Peggy Brenden, a student at St. Cloud Technical High School, and Antoinette St. Pierre, a student at Eisenhower High School in Hopkins, brought suit against the Minnesota High School League for barring females from participating with males in interscholastic sports. Brenden sought entry to the tennis team; St. Pierre wished to participate in cross-country skiing and running. Neither school provided teams for females in these sports.

The United States District Court for the District of Minnesota, under Judge Miles W. Lord, held that the "application of rule as to plaintiff was unreasonable." Minnesota High School League appealed. The Court of Appeals confirmed the U.S. District Court's decision in the holding as follows:

that where high schools attended by plaintiffs, two female students, provided teams for males in noncontact sports of tennis and cross-country skiing and running but did not provide such teams for females and where plaintiffs were qualified to compete with boys in such sports, application of rule prohibiting females from participating in the boys' interscholastic athletic program as to plaintiffs was arbitrary and unreasonable and in violation of equal protection clause of Fourteenth Amendment. (1292)

The court went on to note that:

There is no longer any doubt that sex-based classifications are subject to scrutiny by the courts under the Equal Protection Clause and will be struck down when they provide dissimilar treatment for men and women who are similarly situated with respect to the object of the classification. (1296)

Female golfer Johnell Haas (*Haas v. South Bend Community School Corp.*, 1972) filed for a permanent injunction to prevent enforcement of an Indiana State League rule which prohibited women from playing on men's teams. Haas was denied the injunction in the Indiana Trial Court. The Supreme Court of Indiana reversed, stating that the regulation, though facially fair, was discriminating in effect because there was no women's program and therefore, no opportunity for interscholastic competition.

A female tennis player brought action against the Michigan State Board of Education (*Morris v. Michigan State Board of Education*, 1973) on a similar rule. The lower court issued an injunction, and the state court affirmed. The Michigan legislature also adopted a provision allowing mixed competition in noncontact sports, regardless if separate teams existed for each sex.

In *Gilpin v. Kansas State High School Activities Association* (1974), Tammie Gilpin brought a similar complaint when denied the opportunity to participate in cross-country league competition after practicing all season. Gilpin first obtained a temporary restraining order enjoining the league from interfering with her competition. Later, the court ruled she could compete, stating the Association rule was overbroad in its reach as applied to female athletes.

Similar complaints were filed in Tennessee (see *Carnes v. Tennessee Secondary School Athletic Association*, 1976) and Nebraska (see *Bednar v. Nebraska School Activities Association*, 1976). There appeared to be a pattern among the courts allowing women to compete for positions on male teams when comparable teams for women did not exist, and denying such opportunities when comparable teams did exist.

Rittacco v. Norwin School District (1973), a class action suit, was brought to invalidate a Pennsylvania Interscholastic Athletic Association rule that prohibited mixed competition. In denying the request, the court said that separate but equal doctrine was justified and should be allowed to stand. Separate but equal doctrine in this context was the provision of a similar program for men and women. (It should be noted that separate but equal doctrine has not been permitted to stand in racial decisions.)

Rittacco, a class action suit, was denied by the courts. Class action suits in sports discrimination have not been successful because the courts are hesitant to accept the notion that all women are ready to compete on men's teams. However, the courts are willing to examine women's requests on a case-by-case basis. An example of this thinking on class action suits is found in *Darrin v. Gould* (1975), an action against the Washington Interscholastic Activities Association. The plaintiffs — a 212-pound, 5'9" 14-year-old and a 170-pound, 5'6" 16-year-old — demanded participation in contact sports. Both plaintiffs had completed all prerequisites for entry to the football team.

The issue was the constitutionality of the state regulation which denied females access to male teams and whether there was a reasonable basis to support the regulation. Expert witnesses testified that women in general were not physically capable of playing as equals on a football team. The court, ruling against the plaintiffs, suggested that had they filed individual suits, rather than the class action suit, they may have been successful. Individuals might have been capable of playing football, but girls in general were not capable of such a feat.

In *Hoover v. Meiklejohn* (1977), Donna Hoover brought a class action suit on behalf of all females her age and younger in the state of Colorado affected by a Colorado High School Activities Association rule. The rule limited participation in certain activities referred to as contact sports, including soccer, to males only. The court adopted a three-step analysis of the constitutional issue created by Harvie Wilkinson III, a professor of law. The three steps were: (1) importance of the opportunity denied; (2) strength of the state interest served and (3) character of the group whose opportunities were denied.

Under the first step, the importance of the opportunity, the court noted that "whether such games should be made available at public expense is not an issue . . . whether it is algebra or athletics, that which is provided must be open to all." (169) The second step, the interest of the state, was to create an environment in which injuries were minimal. "The failure to establish any physical criteria to protect small or weak males from the injurious effects of competition with larger or stronger males," was considered by the court, "to destroy the credibility of the reasoning urged in support of the sex classification." (169) In response to the third step, character of the group denied, the court stated that women must be allowed full participation in all educational programs.

The court ruled that the Association rule was unconstitutional on its face and ordered that the defendant and the class she represented be permitted to compete in soccer and other sports.

In *Leffel v. Wisconsin Intercollegiate Athletic Association* (1978), a change in the court's thinking was noted. The court ruled in favor of a class action suit permitting females membership on male baseball, tennis and swim teams. This decision was made even though a swim team for women existed.

In *O'Connor v. Board of Education of School District 23* (1982), 11-year-old Karen O'Connor, a proficient athlete and basketball player, was denied an opportunity to try out for the sixth grade competitive (male) basketball team. O'Connor had accumulated years of very successful experience in basketball, little league and soccer; she had excelled in all physical activities. Her complaint was principally an Equal Protection complaint; however, she did include Title IX in the action. Defendant's reason for maintaining the separate basketball teams was to maximize the participation of both sexes. O'Connor's claim was that she should be allowed to develop her skills to the maximum, and that development could be accomplished only through competition with boys.

The court found a compelling state interest in a need for separate teams in order to maximize opportunities for girls. The court balanced that concern with O'Connor's right to be challenged in play and ruled in favor of the school district.

In *Force v. Pierce City R-VI School* (1983), Nichole Force successfully gained entry to the eighth grade football squad as a result of a claim under the equal protection clause. The 13-year-old had played football in elementary school, and with her brothers. When her request to the Pierce City, Missouri School Board to play football was denied, she sought an injunction and a ruling. Her claim was that she was denied the opportunity to play football solely as a result of her sex, and therefore was entitled to a claim under the Fourteenth Amendment Equal Protection Clause.

Defendants' arguments were:

> four important governmental objections . . . (a) maximization of equal athletic educational opportunities for all students, regardless of gender; (b) maintenance of athletic educational programs which are as safe for participants as possible; (c) compliance with Title IX of the Education Amendments of 1972 and the regulations there under; and (d) compliance with the constitution and bylaws of MSHSAA. (1024)

In reference to the maximization of opportunities, the defendants argued that if females were allowed on the football team, males would take over the volleyball team because "males will outperform females in most athletic endeavors." (1025) The court found no evidence that the males at the junior high school were "waiting eagerly for volleyball to be desegregated." (1025) Further, it was not clear that had the boys been awaiting such an event they would have been able to take over, given the decisions in a number of cases.

The court agreed with the defendants, that safety was an important governmental objective. However, they echoed the statement in *Hoover*, wondering why no effort had been made to eliminate those males who could not play football safely.

Defendants' point on Title IX compliance was found to be faulty. The court asserted that there was "nothing whatsoever in Title IX or its implementing regulations which would mandate the defendants' actions . . . Title IX's regulations leave each school free to choose whether co-educational participation in a contact sport will be permitted." (1024-1025) The court noted that Title IX does not dictate that boys play on girls teams or that girls play on boys teams. It permits each agency the opportunity to design its own program.

In addressing the issue of compliance with the state athletic association constitution and bylaws, the court first established that the association actions could be considered as "state action" and then noted that the rule was discriminatory under the Fourteenth Amendment. It should be noted that *Clinton v. Nagy* (1974) and *Darrin v. Gould* (1975), both requests by girls to play football, reached the same conclusion.

A number of young girls have attempted to gain membership to Little League and community recreation programs. Ten-year-old Pamela Magill (*Magill v. Avonworth Baseball Conference*, 1975) sought injunctive relief to be permitted to participate with boys in the contact sport of Little League baseball. Despite the absence of an alternative program for girls, the court dismissed the case.

Success for the plaintiff was achieved in a similar situation, in *National Organization for Women v. Little League Baseball, Inc.* (1974). The Essex County's National Organization for Women filed a class action suit on behalf of all girls eight to 12 years of age who wanted to play Little League Baseball.

In another case, Pookie Fortin (*Fortin v. Darlington Little Leagues, Inc.*, 1975), received tremendous publicity as she gained entry to little league. Fortin was denied access by the lower court; however, the first circuit reversed the decision.

Males Seeking Membership on Female Teams

Courts have been split on decisions to allow men the opportunity to play on women's teams. A 1979 ruling in Rhode Island (*Gomes v. Rhode*

Island Interscholastic League) permitted a male to play on the volleyball team. However, in the same year, an Illinois Appellate Court (*Petrie v. Illinois High School Association*) rejected a similar request. Males also have been denied the opportunity to play on girls' tennis teams in New York (*Mularadelis v. Haldane Central School Board*, 1980) and on volleyball teams in Arizona (Clark v. Arizona Interscholastic Association, 1982).

The reasoning for denying males the opportunity to play on female teams was that a similar team existed for them. When a similar team did not exist for males, the situation was treated as one of affirmative action, or the provision of an opportunity for females to become equals competitively. The *Mularadelis* case put it this way: "Special recognition and favored treatment can constitutionally be afforded members of the female sex under the circumstances." (464) The court noted that, as women are moving into athletic programs, it and many other courts see a period of time when males may be denied the opportunity to play on female teams.

Attorney General v. Massachusetts Interscholastic Athletic Association (1979) was a unique request. The attorney general and others brought action against the state association for declaration that a rule that denied males membership on female teams, but permitted females membership an male teams (when comparable teams were not available to females), was invalid. The Supreme Court of Massachusetts declared the rule invalid.

An important facet of the court deliberation was the exploration of the idea that there may be alternatives to what is considered an appropriate athletics program. Although little time was devoted to identification of what the alternatives might be, it is one of a very few cases that even addressed the idea that there may be alternatives to present sports programs. (For further information on this topic see Clement, 1987).

Females Requesting Equal Financial Aid and Support for Separate Teams

Most cases of females requesting equal financial aid and support for separate teams have been filed under Title IX, rather than under the Fourteenth Amendment Equal Protection Clause. However, the following case is the first collegiate case filed under the Equal Protection Clause, and appears to be a landmark in the litigation for equity in athletics.

Haffer v. Temple University (1987) was a class action suit alleging unlawful sex discrimination in Temple University's athletic program. Plaintiffs were all women currently participating in school athletics and those who had been deterred from participating because of sex discrimination in the athletic program. Plaintiff's claims focused on three basic areas:

1. the extent to which Temple affords women students fewer "opportunities to compete" in intercollegiate athletics;
2. the alleged disparity in resources allocated to the men's and women's intercollegiate athletic programs; and
3. the alleged disparity in the allocation of financial aid to male and female students. (Slip Opinion)

The actions, the plaintiffs claimed, were in violation of the Fourteenth Amendment Equal Protection Clause and the Pennsylvania Equal Rights Amendment. Plaintiffs also claimed that the distribution of financial aid was in violation of Title IX of the Education Amendments of 1972, (20 U.S.C. §1681).

Originally, Temple's case was based on alleged violation of Title IX (*Haffer v. Temple University of the Commonwealth System of Higher Education*, 1982; affirmed, 1982). After the Supreme Court decision in *Grove City* (1984), Haffer removed all aspects of Title IX except for the athletic scholarship and financial aid requests and amended the complaint, adding federal and state constitutional claims.

Plaintiffs alleged that the women's athletic program at Temple was unequal in every conceivable way. The university undergraduate population was approximately half male, half female; however, athletic opportunities for women were less than one half of those available to men. (Four hundred forty men participated; only 200 women had berths on competitive teams.) The university argued that "there was no reason to believe that equal numbers of male and female college students possess the exceptional skills and interests required for Division One intercollegiate athletics." (Slip Opinion) Their argument was that a pool of qualified talented female athletes did not exist at Temple University. Plaintiffs response was that the number of men and women possessing skill and interest required for intercollegiate athletics was not independent of the money devoted to scholarships, publicity and recruiting.

Temple University spent $2,100 more per year per male athlete, than for a female athlete. In addition to the financial situation, testimony and depositions produced information showing Temple women possessing a higher average winning percentage and a higher mean cumulative grade point average than the men. Plaintiffs alleged discrepancies were numerous.

The court ruled for the defendant on the issues of training meals, tutoring, facilities and scheduling. They ruled for the plaintiff on all other issues. Among those issues were coaching time, financial aid and increased opportunities.

TITLE IX CASES

Prior to the implementation of Title IX, most complaints were filed on behalf of minors seeking membership in high school athletics or community leagues. Therefore, early precedent in sport and athletics was established at the youth and high school level. With the implementation of Title IX institutions of higher education, few who had sought relief in the courts, turned to the Office of Civil Rights. Though the first example involves teenage girls, Title IX appears to be far more important to college and university athletes than to elementary and secondary school athletes.

Following the implementation of Title IX, most complaints were brought under both Title IX and the Fourteenth Amendment Equal Protection Clause. *Yellow Springs Exempted Village School District v. Ohio High School Athletic Association* (1981) was unique in that a school district, rather than an individual, sought declaration that the rule on contact sports was unconstitutional and in violation of Title IX.

In *Yellow Springs*, the persons involved were middle school girls seeking membership on the basketball team. The Yellow Springs girls tried out and made the team. However, if their memberships on the team were retained, the school district would no longer have been able to compete in the state association. United States District Court for the Southern District of Ohio, Western, Division entered judgment for the plaintiff. The U.S. Court of Appeals Sixth Circuit reversed the lower court's decision, finding the high school association rule unconstitutional. The Court also granted an injunction enjoining the OHSAA from enforcing the rule.

A significant aspect of the case was the fact that the court found the actions of the high school league, a nongovernmental agency, to be state actions. The private agency was considered to be engaged in a state action because they were dictating terms to a state agency. Therefore, the league was not considered a private agency, and fell under Title IX. The court also was asked to rule on the constitutionality of Title IX, but refused to do so.

Questions have been raised as to the extent of the coverage of Title IX, such as: Are all aspects of state and federal institutions covered, or does the coverage include only those programs receiving money directly from the Federal government? In *Othen v. Ann Arbor School Board* (1982), the court ruled that athletics did not fall under Title IX, unless the program received direct Federal funding. A similar decision was awarded by the courts in *Bennett v. West Texas State University* (1981) and (1986).

As the term "program specific" gained popularity, publicity was gained by the *Grove City College v. Bell* (1983) decision. The issue was whether the Department of Education had authority to enforce Title IX against a college that received no direct funds from the Federal government, with the exception of Basic Educational Opportunity Grants. Grove City College was a private co-educational institution of higher education located in Pennsylvania.

In 1976, the college was asked to provide routine assurances of compliance with Title IX. Grove City College refused to provide the assurances, stating they did not receive federal money. The Department of Education initiated proceedings to terminate grants and loans to Grove City College students. Of the 2,200 students attending Grove City College, 140 were eligible for Basic Educational Opportunity Grants and 342 had obtained Guaranteed Student Loans. No other Federal or state financial assistance was provided. An administrative hearing resulted in a ruling that Grove City College was a recipient of federal financial assistance.

Grove City College, joined by four student recipients of grants and loans, sought relief in district court. They requested the court declare void the department of education order to terminate the grants and loans, enjoin the government from requiring them to file an assurance of compliance and declare that the regulation, as employed by the department, was beyond the parameters of Title IX. The district court stopped the department of education from terminating the grants. The department appealed to the Supreme Court. The Supreme Court granted certiorari.

The Supreme Court (*Grove City College v. Bell,* 1984) affirmed the circuit court decision, stating:

> The Assurance of Compliance regulation itself does not, on its face, impose institutionwide obligations. Recipients must provide assurance only that 'each education program or activity operated by . . . [them] and to which this part applies will be operated in compliance with this part. (1222)

One of the few times Title IX was used as the primary legal theory at the secondary level was *Lantz v. Ambach* (1985). Jacqueline Lantz, a 16-year-old high school junior, was denied the opportunity to play football. No team existed for women. She challenged a New York State Public High School Athletic Association rule stating that no mixed competition could occur in basketball, boxing, football, ice hockey, rugby and wrestling. Her challenge was that the rule violated Title IX and the Equal Protection Clause of the Fourteenth Amendment. With reference to Title IX, the court, influenced by Grove City, stated that "it is not clear that Title IX applies to this case. To violate Title IX, the sex discrimination must occur in the specific program which receives federal financial assistance." (665)

Lantz's success in enjoining the regulation and being awarded the opportunity to try out for the team was on the Fourteenth Amendment claim. As the court pointed out, her Fourteenth Amendment claim would be upheld where an "exceedingly persuasive justification showing at least that the classification serves important government objectives and that the discrimination means employed are substantially related to the achievement of those objectives." (665)

Probably the most comprehensive decision in school athletics is *Ridgeway v. Montana High School Association* (1986). Ridgeway was a class action suit brought on the behalf of all Montana high school girls alleging violation of Title IX, the Fourteenth Amendment and the state constitution, as a result of sex discrimination in athletics.

Plaintiffs' complaint was that a denial of full participation in athletics resulted in a denied opportunity to develop to their fullest educational potential. The girls claimed discrimination existed in the number of sports; seasons the sports were available; length of the seasons; scheduling of practice and games; access to facilities, equipment, coaching, trainers, transportation, school band and other forms of team support; uniforms; publicity and others. The court ordered a dismissal, incorporating a settlement agreement between the parties. By order of the dismissal without prejudice, the court approved the parties agreement and retained continuing jurisdiction to enforce the agreement.

A facilitator, answerable to the court, was appointed. Defendants were required to provide a plan for implementation of the settlement to the facilitator. The settlement applied to the entire state of Montana.

Details of the case are presented because of a strong possibility that similar complaints will be instituted in other states. The court's formula for equity also serves as an ideal risk management system (Chapter Thirteen will address risk management.) Montana's inequities in sport were listed as:

a. Greater number of sports sanctioned by MHSA and offered by the schools for boys than for girls;

b. Disparities in length and continuity of athletic seasons, providing more advantageous seasons for boys;

c. Greater press coverage for boys' athletic events than for girls' athletic events;

d. Disparities in the number, quality, and salaries of coaches for boys' and girls' athletic programs;

e. More favorable team support for boys' athletic programs than for girls', particularly in the areas of cheerleader and band appear-

ances, half-time performances, and booster clubs;
f. Disparities in the times and places for practices and events, pro-
    viding boys' sports with more "prime time" practices and greater
    access to superior facilities;
g. Disparate treatment in the schools' recognition boards, halls of
    fame, or trophy cases;
h. Disparities in provision of meals, laundry facilities, per diem
    allowances and overnight trips;
i. Greater access for boys' teams to superior equipment, supplies,
    and uniforms;
j. Disparities in the quality of officiating at girls' and boys' athletic
    events. (1572)

Under the settlement agreement, the office of public instruction was
required;

a. To provide a vehicle for any aggrieved party to pursue a griev-
    ance pursuant to OPI's standard grievance procedure;
b. To provide to the school districts in Montana technical assistance
    in self-evaluation and self-improvement in providing sex equity
    in athletics, subject to the limitations of state and federal funding
    resources, in the following particulars;
    (i)   To respond to questions on issues of equity and to provide
          interpretations of state and federal law;
    (ii) To distribute sex equity materials and handbooks and to
          keep school districts apprised of developments in the law;
    (iii) To provide various workshops intended to develop aware-
          ness of sex equity issues;
    (iv) To continue its in-house committee on equity to assure that
          all publications are free from sex bias and are in compliance
          with the law;
    (v)   To continue other specified state level activities including
          workshops, training, and provision of handbooks on equity
          and ·self-evaluation;
    (vi) To conduct certain activities at the national level, including
          hosting the 1984 National Conference on Equity, continuing
          to work with the Mountain West Desegregation Center, and
          keeping in contact with other state education agencies for
          information and materials pertaining to sex equity;
c. To distribute copies of the Settlement Agreement to any high
    school over which it has authority under Montana law;
d. To submit a plan for implementation of the Settlement Agree-

ment and thereafter to submit a written progress report. (1572-1573)

Schools were required:

   a.   To offer the same number of sports for both males and females during the school year, except where an explicit and deliberate effort has been made to increase interest in an additional sport for the sex of students having fewer sports, and a survey has been conducted and establishes insufficient interest to field a team in a new sport. In that event, the school district is required to continue its efforts to equalize sports offerings until such offerings are equalized;
   b.   To seek, endeavor to hire, and where available to hire qualified coaches for male and female athletic teams and to hire comparable numbers of coaches based upon the number of participants; further, to develop and utilize criteria for hiring and evaluating coaches and to take appropriate measures where inadequate coaching is found;
   c.   To pay equal salaries for equal work by coaches of female and male teams, based upon gender-neutral criteria;
   d.   To issue press releases and arrange for advertising giving equal emphasis to male and female athletic events, and to further encourage comparable coverage of male and female sports;
   e.   To provide on an equal basis to male and female athletes team support, such as pep assemblies, school announcements, rosters, programs, pep band, cheerleaders and drill team performances;
   f.   To schedule the times and places for practices and athletic events for male and female teams of the same and comparable sports on an equal basis, providing equal access to "prime time" practice and use of equally desirable facilities;
   g.   To provide laundry services, if at all, to males and females on an equal basis;
   h.   To afford comparable recognition to female and male sports in the form of recognition boards, halls of fame or trophy cases;
   i.   To provide the same per diem monetary allowance for male and female athletes for meals, and comparable accommodations and opportunities for overnight trips;
   j.   To provide uniforms, accessories, equipment and supplies of comparable quality and at comparable replacement rates to females and males on an equal basis;
   k.   To affirmatively encourage booster or fan clubs to devote comparable attention to the promotion and encouragement of fe-

male and male sports, and to refrain from assistance of discriminatory organizations;

l. To provide transportation to male and female teams on an equal basis;

m. To provide the services of an athletic trainer, if any, on an equal basis to male and female athletes;

n. To hire the best available qualified officials for both female and male extracurricular athletic events;

o. To participate with MHSA in improving recruitment opportunities for athletes playing a sport during a season which is outside the national norm for that sport;

p. To prepare a sex equity in athletics policy, to establish a grievance procedure, to designate a coordinator for such policies and procedure, and to disseminate this information to the student body, faculty and parents;

q. To give notice to the class of the Settlement Agreement by dissemination to students and parents and by retaining copies of the Agreement for the use of students and parents within the district;

r. For those school districts named as defendants, to submit a plan for implementation of the Settlement Agreement and thereafter to submit a written progress report. (1573-1574)

A similar case of equity in athletics is *Blair v. Washington State University* (1987). Though this case and its holding was brought under state law and has precedent for the state of Washington, numerous other states with similar statutes can use the case to provide guidance to their universities.

The suit was brought on behalf of all female athletes and coaches against Washington State University and its Board of Regents. Complaint alleged that Washington State women athletes' received inferior treatment in funding, fund raising efforts, publicity and promotions, scholarships, facilities, equipment, coaching, uniforms, practice clothing, awards and administrative staff and supplies. Women received approximately 23 percent of the funds allocated males.

The trial court concluded that the "University had acted or failed to act in the operation of the University's intercollegiate athletic program in a manner that resulted in discriminatory treatment of females." (1381) The court's detailed injunction required that the women's program receive 37.5 percent of the university's financial support during the 1982-1983 school year, and an increase of two percent each year until the support represented the undergraduate male-female enrollment percentages. Note, however that, one of the points in the injunction was that football was to be treated as a separate operation.

The plaintiff appealed the decision with reference to the football clause. The Supreme Court of Washington reversed the decision and stated the trial court abused its discretion in excluding football from the calculations for finances and participation opportunities. Washington's equal rights amendment had not mentioned football as a protected class.

The court did, however, state that money generated by a sport could be used exclusively for that specific sport's benefit. This ruling has tremendous significance for the methodology that will be essential to bookkeeping in athletics. Few athletic programs have cost ratio figures including depreciation of facilities, time spent by administrators and fund raisers. Inclusion of these figures would permit a comprehensive picture of the allocation of resources, including revenue generated. Results of such comprehensive budgeting could show that, despite revenue generated, certain activities operate at a loss.

EQUAL PROTECTION IN GRADE STANDARDS

Two cases that challenged the concept of a grade requirement for membership on athletic teams are *Baily v. Truby and Myles* (1984) and *Spring Branch Independent School District v. Stamos* (1985). *Bailey* was a consolidated case concerning the validity of grade requirement for participation in extracurricular activities, particularly intercollegiate sport. The action was a request from a local school district to the state board of education to withdraw a rule stating that all students wishing to compete in interscholastic athletics had to maintain a "C" average. There was also a request from a student for an injunction of the rule. The court affirmed the state's rule.

In *Spring Branch*, a provision of the Texas Education Code required a student to maintain a "70" average in all classes in order to take part in extracurricular activities. The trial court found the rule unconstitutional and stopped enforcement of the "No Pass-No Play" section of the Texas Code. On appeal, the Supreme Court of Texas reversed the trial court's holding, stating the "No Pass-No Play" rule did not violate the students' equal protection or due process constitutional rights.

DUE PROCESS CASES

Due process requires certain steps in providing individuals with the right to be heard and the right to defend their actions. When an individual could be suspended from an educational institution or denied a right to participate in competitive or recreational sport, a system needs to be devised to enable that person the opportunity to understand the denial and to present his or her side of the case. Age and level of maturity, as well as whether the opportunity is clearly a fundamental right influences not only the system for due process but the need to provide anything other than a minimal opportunity for due process.

Professionals disagree. The decisions of the courts are unclear as to what is adequate due process under given situations. Because of this inability to clearly articulate a consistent standard, it is recommended that an extensive due process system be used. The following court cases will assist the physical activity professional in arriving at that standard.

Behagen v. Intercollegiate Conference of Faculty Representatives (1972) serves to provide a standard of due process for suspensions in major college athletic competition. Following a brawl in a basketball game between Minnesota and Ohio State University, Behagen and others were suspended from the Minnesota team. Though no one contested the brawl had occurred, plaintiffs claimed their right to due process was violated. Plaintiffs requested an injunction from the court.

At the time, the Big Ten Conference was loosely structured, with little written guidance for use in resolving such an issue. As a result, both the conference and the university were working out the problems simultaneously. The university, after examining its own failure to provide adequate due process, decided to reinstate the athletes. The commissioner of the Big Ten Conference overruled the university and suspended the athletes. This suspension prompted the request mentioned above.

The court noted that the elements of a due process hearing in a situation like this should include:

1. Written notice of time and place of hearing at least two days in advance of the hearing.
2. Notice should contain the specific charges against the person and the grounds which, if proven, would justify imposing a penalty.
3. The hearing should enable the Director of Athletics to hear both sides of the story. This hearing would not require a full judicial hearing or the right to cross-examine witnesses.
4. Hearing should include the presentation of direct testimony in the form of statements of the facts by each party. All versions of the incident should be presented.
5. Plaintiffs should receive a list of all witnesses who will appear.
6. Plaintiffs should be allowed to hear all testimony.
7. Plaintiffs should be given a written report of the Directors' findings of fact, and if there is to be punishment the basis for such punishment.
8. The proceedings should be recorded, and the tapes made available to the plaintiffs.

9. Should plaintiffs wish, they may appeal the decision to the faculty representatives or through any other channels previously designated by a University. (608)

Five years later, the University of Minnesota was again faced with a due process issue; however, this time the NCAA would not permit the university adequate time for the internal hearings mentioned above to occur prior to enforcing the sanctions (*Regents of The University of Minnesota v. National Collegiate Athletic Association*, 1977). NCAA declared each of the three Minnesota players ineligible as a result of: selling complimentary season passes, having been entertained at a booster's cabin or using a WATS line for personal long distance calls. The players admitted to the violations.

Minnesota requested each student appear before the internal faculty representatives committee on athletics. The committee then ruled on each violation. For example, in the situation of the student selling his complimentary season pass, the committee agreed that "this clearly violates the principle that an amateur athlete should not profit from his or her athletic ability." (356) The committee went on to say that the student had admitted his fault, their findings suggest the practice was widespread and that a ruling of ineligibility would be a grossly unfair sanction. The NCAA argued that it had exclusive authority over a student's eligibility; therefore, the faculty committee decision would not be honored. One of the athletes requested an injunction from the district court.

The United States District Court for the District of Minnesota granted the players application for an injunction and the University of Minnesota permitted the athlete to return to the basketball team. NCAA appealed. The United States Court of Appeals, Eighth Circuit reversed the lower court decision, stating that Minnesota, in joining NCAA, had agreed to live by the Associations' constitution and bylaws. The results of this and other cases do, to some extent, support the idea that universities are not required to submit the dismissal of student athletes to due process. Such a decision does not appear to exist in any other area of the law. Professionals in collegiate athletics should monitor court decisions on dismissal and discuss their due process policies periodically with legal counsel.

The landmark due process decision in the schools was *Goss v. Lopez* (1975). Columbus, Ohio high school students had been suspended without a hearing from school for misconduct for 10 days. The students brought a class action suit against school officials, declaring the Ohio statute permitting such suspension was in violation of their due process rights under the Fourteenth Amendment. The district court held that the statute was unconstitutional and the students had been denied due process under the Fourteenth Amendment. The court outlined the following due process system which was described as a minimum requirement of notice and a hearing for use in this setting:

1. When a student's behavior exhibits any of the following, he or she can be removed immediately:
   a) Disrupts academic environment
   b) Endangers fellow students, teachers or other school officials
   c) Damages property
2. Notice of suspension proceedings must be sent to student's parents within 24 hours of the decision to conduct them.
3. Hearings are to be held within 72 hours of student's removal.
4. Hearings are to include statements in support of the charges and statements in defense of the charge. (735)

The school authorities appealed. The United States Supreme Court ruled that students suspended for short periods of time were entitled to a minimal due process, as stated above, under the Fourteenth Amendment.

SUMMARY

Elements of the Fourteenth Amendment most important to the professional in sport and physical activity are the Equal Protection Clause, Substantive Due Process and Procedural Due Process. An equal protection challenge must show that groups of people are being treated differently without adequate justification. Legal analysis involves balancing the interests of the state with the interests of the individual by employing a three tier classification of rational basis, intermediate review and strict scrutiny.

Fourteenth Amendment Due Process consists of two forms: substantive and procedural. Substantive Due Process is a system for reviewing the judgments of legislative branches. Procedural Due Process provides an opportunity for individuals to be heard. Procedural Due Process guarantees a person an opportunity to be informed of charges against them, a hearing, representation by counsel and a fair trial.

Title IX provides statutory authority for redress in discrimination similar to that found in the Equal Protection Clause. Examples of each of the elements of the Fourteenth Amendment and Title IX have been presented.

References

Attorney General v. Massachusetts Interscholastic Athletic Association, 393 N.E. 2d 284 (1979).
Bailey v. Truby and Myles, 321 S.E. 2d 302 (1984).

Bednar v. Nebraska School Activities Association, 531 F. 2d 922 (1976).
Behagen v. Intercollegiate Conference of Faculty Representatives, 346 F. Supp. 602 (1972).
Bennett v. West Texas State University, 525 F. Supp. 77 (N.D. Tex. 1981).
Bennett v. West Texas State University, 698 F. 2d 1215 (5th Cir. 1983), cert. denied 466 U.S. 903, 104 S. Ct. 1677, 80 L. Ed 2d 152 (1984).
Bennett v. West Texas State University, 799 F. 2d 155 (5th Cir. 1986).
Blair v. Washington State University, 740 P. 2d 1379 (Wash. 1987).
Brenden v. Independent School District, 342 F. Supp. 1224 (D. Minn. 1972) affirmed 477 F. 2d 1292 (8th Cir. 1973).
Cannon v. University of Chicago, 441 U.S. 677 (1979).
Carnes v. Tennessee Secondary School Athletic Association, 415 F. Supp. 569 (1976).
Clark v. Arizona Interscholastic Association, 695 F. 2d 1126 (1982).
Clement, Annie, (1987). Legal theory and sex discrimination in sport. In Marlene Adrian (Ed.), *Sports Women* (138-153) Basel, Switzerland: Karger Press.
Clinton v. Nagy, 411 F. Supp. 1396 (1974).
Craig v. Boren, 429 U.S. 190 (1976).
Darrin v. Gould, 85 Wash. 2d 859, 540 P. 2d 882 (1975).
Education Amendments of 1972, 901, 20 U.S.C. §1681 (1976).
Force v. Pierce City R-VI School, 570 F. Supp. 1020 (1983).
Fortin v. Darlington Little League, Inc., 376 F. Supp. 473 (D RI., 1974) rev'd 514 F. 2d 344 (1975).
Gilpin v. Kansas State High School Activities *Association*, 377 F. Supp. 1233 (1974).
Gomes v. Rhode Island Interscholastic League, 469 F. Supp. 659 (D.R.I.), vacated as moot, 604 F. 2d 733 (1979).
Goss v. Lopez, 95 S. Ct. 729, 419 U.S. 565, 42 L. Ed. 2d 725 (1975).
Grove City College v. Bell, 687 F. 2d 684 (3rd Cir., 1982), pet. for cert. granted, 103 S. Ct. 1181, 74 L. Ed. 2d (1983).
Grove City College v. Bell, 465 U.S. 555, 79 L. Ed. 2d 516, 104 S. Ct. 1211 (1984).
Gunther, Gerald. (1985). *Constitutional law, cases and materials.* (10th ed.) Mineola, NY: The Foundation Press, Inc.
Haas v. South Bend Community School Corp., 289 N.E. 2d 495 (1972).
Haffer v. Temple University of the Commonwealth System of Higher Education, 524 F. Supp. 531 (E.D. Pa. 1981), aff'd, 688 F. 2d 14 (3rd Cir. 1982).
Haffer v. Temple University, October 30, 1987, Slip Opinion.
Haverkamp v. Unified School District #380, Civil Action No. 86-2067-S, May 20, 1986, Slip Opinion.
Hollander v. Connecticut Interscholastic Athletic Conference, Inc., Civil No. 12-49-27 (Super. Ct., New Haven Co., Conn., March 29, 1971), appeal dismissed 295 A. 2d 671 (1972).
Hoover v. Meiklejohn, 430 F. 2d 164 (1977).
Lantz v. Ambach, 620 F. Supp. 663 (D.C.N.Y. 1985).
Leffel v. Wisconsin Intercollegiate Athletic Association, 444 F. Supp. 117 (E.D. Wisc. 1978).
Magill v. Avonworth Baseball Conference, 364 F. Supp. 1212 (W.D. Pa. 1973), 516 F. 2nd 1328 (1975).
Morris v. Michigan State Board of Education, 472 F. 2d 1207 (1973).
Mularadelis v. Haldane Central School Board, 427 N.Y. Supp. 2d 458 (1980).
National Organization for Women v. Little League Baseball, Inc., 127 N.J. Super. 522, 318 A. 2nd 33 (1974), 338 A. 2d 198 (1974).
North Haven v. Bell, 102 S. Ct. 1912, 72 L. Ed. 2d 299 (1982).
O'Connor v. Board of Education of School District 23, 545 F. Supp. 336 (1982).
O'Connor v. Board of Education of School District 23, 645 F. 2d 578 (1981).
Othen v. Ann Arbor School Board, 507 F. Supp. 1376 (E.D. Mich. 1981), affirmed on grounds not involving Title IX, 699 F. 2d 309 (1982).
Petrie v. Illinois High School Association, 75 Ill. App. 3d 980, 394 N.E. 2d 855 (1979).
Reed v. Nebraska Athletic Association, 341 F. Supp. 258 (D. Neb. 1972).
Regents of the University of Minnesota v. National Collegiate Athletic Association, 560 F. 2nd 352 (1977).
Ridgeway v. Montana High School Association, 633 F. Supp. 1546 (1986), 638 F. Supp. 326 (1986).
Rittacco v. Norwin School District, 361 F. Supp. 930 (W.D. Pa. 1973).
Roe v. Wade, 410 U.S. 113 (1973).
Sex discrimination in interscholastic high school athletes. Syracuse Law Review. 25, 535 (1974).
Spring Branch I.S.D. v. Stamos, 695 S.W. 2d 556 (1985).
Tribe, Laurence H. 1978. *American Constitutional Law.* Mineola, NY: The Foundation Press, Inc.
United States Constitution. Amend. XIV, §1.
Yellow Springs Exempted Village School District v. Ohio High School Athletic Association, 647 F. 2d 651 (1981).

11
Contracts

Professionals in sport and physical activity often are asked to sign contracts, to prepare contracts for others to sign and to negotiate agreements prepared by others. Contracts are used in employing officials, in making agreements with vendors and in obtaining facilities for competitive athletics. Also, nearly all full-time employees in the profession are asked to sign a yearly contract. Knowledge of contracts is essential to professionals.

A contract is usually described as a promise, or a set of promises, for breach of which the law gives a remedy, or for the performance of which the law recognizes as duty. Calamari and Perillo (1987), in the introduction to *The Law of Contracts* state that most definitions fail to point out that a "contract usually requires the assent [or agreement] of more than one person." (2) They also note a popular definition of contract as a "legally enforceable agreement." (2)

Contracts may be express or implied in fact. Express contracts mean that the nature of the agreement has been expressed in writing, or made orally. Contracts resulting from conduct, rather than oral or written agreement, are referred to as implied in fact contracts. Courts do not distinguish between express or implied in fact contracts; their role is to enforce any existing contract. In general, however, the existence of implied in fact contracts are sometimes difficult to prove, as are oral agreements. The Uniform Commercial Code and other state and Federal regulations require the agreement be placed in writing when it involves certain contents and certain sums of money.

AGREEMENTS

A bargaining agreement is an agreement between two parties in which at least one party has made a promise to the other, or any promise given in exchange for a consideration. Generally, an agreement is defined as an objective manifestation of mutual assent by two or more people to an understanding; however, a promise is an expression of intent that something will or will not happen. Elements of a bargaining agreement usually contain:

1. one or more promises and one or more parties to whom the promise has been made,
2. a manifestation of mutual assent by the parties,
3. a consideration and
4. a legally binding agreement.

These elements may be put in writing in a document called a contract.

In addition to an express contract and an implied in fact contract, a party also may be able to enforce a promise on the basis of the fact that he or she relied on the promise. Though a formal agreement is incomplete, courts will consider the fact that one of the parties relied on the agreement, particularly if the reliance has served to damage the party. In situations where a party has been unjustly enriched as a result of a void contract, the courts will expect the party to pay for the enrichment.

An agreement usually consists of an offer, acceptance by the party to whom it was offered and consideration. Consideration may be a sum of money, a promise to do or not to do something, or the fact that reliance exists. Agreements failing to contain these elements may be found void by the courts. Agreements inequitable in their construction, providing one party a far better arrangement than the other party, may be void.

BREACH OF CONTRACT

Breach of a contract is a failure to live up to one or more of the promises in a contract. This failure to perform is not legally excused. When a person breaches a contract, the non-breaching party may choose to take that party to court. The court will determine whether the agreement is valid. If found to be valid, the courts have a number of choices, including directing the parties to carry out the promise contained in the agreement. Specific performance is requesting that the promised act be initiated at once. The court also may assess monetary damages to the breaching party to restore the plaintiff to the position held prior to the agreement.

WRITTEN AGREEMENT

When the contract is in writing and the parties have assented to the writing as an expression of their agreement, the courts agree on a standard of interpretation. The standard is the ordinary meaning of the writing to the parties at the time and place of the initial agreement and under the circumstances of its construction. Employment contracts may be vague, containing only the major job responsibilities. On the other hand, contracts may be so explicit that they include details of work tasks, identification of holidays and free days, class size for teachers, poundage of lifting for industry, length of work day, system of transfer, sick pay and grievance procedures. Union contracts tend to include greater detail than other employment contracts.

Contracts negotiated by professional athletes usually are quite complex. Most professional teams have standard player contracts. Clauses, such as requiring a water bed be put in an athlete's hotel room during travel, are put into the contract to meet the needs of the athlete.

Occasionally, written contracts may incorporate policy handbooks and other official documents into the written statement. This means, for example, that a signature on the contract identifies that the signer will adhere to the policies and be aware of rules contained in the incorporated document.

In order to make a legal agreement, parties must be legally qualified to engage in a contract. One important element is that all parties to the agreement be 18 or more years of age. Should the agreement require qualifications, such as teacher or coaching certification or medical or legal licensure, the party requiring those credentials must have them to make the agreement binding.

Misunderstandings about employment contracts are frequent in agencies in which such contracts must be ratified by a board. This situation occurs often in state agencies. For example, when a coach is offered a contract, signs the contract and returns it to the school system, the coach usually assumes the agreement is complete. However, in order for the agreement to be complete, the returned contract has to be approved at the next board meeting.

There is a history of cases of such contracts not accepted by boards of education. When the prospective teacher has sued, the courts have maintained that the agreement signed by the teacher was not a valid contract until it was ratified by the school board. Unfortunately, most professionals discontinue seeking employment after signing a contract and usually permit the school district and/or university to announce their appointment even though it does not exist. Whether school districts under these circumstances have a right to announce the new employees status prior to board of education action is an interesting point not discussed in the literature on litigation.

Agreements in spas, racquet clubs, part-time coaching and some physical education settings tend to be contracts that clearly establish the independent contractor status of the employee. Use of the independent contractor agreement has evolved since 1980, and has not had adequate time to be litigated in the courts. (Review Chapter Eight for a discussion of independent contractors, and a system for analyzing such a contract.) Any agreement should be drawn or approved by legal counsel.

In general, school districts have a system for employing, dismissing and tenuring teachers. The system is written out in explicit detail and provided to all teacher candidates upon interview or acceptance of a position. This system includes the processes for evaluation, due process and appeal. In most districts, a second system has been established for employing extracurricular activity specialists. These systems tend to differ from district to district and, when not included in the bargaining contract, often differ in their implementation from the written format. Two consistent characteristics of these part-time contracts are: a one-year time frame with a new or renewal each year, and no requirement for due process unless the contract is to be terminated prior to the completion of the year.

CASES IN CONTRACT

Contract litigation in physical activity centers around coaching/teaching contracts at the secondary and collegiate level. Though employment agreements in other areas of physical activity have not been brought to the courts, all professionals should be aware of contract litigation.

Employment Agreements at School Level

Since 1980, a number of actions have been filed over a coach's right to his/her position as head coach. Must they receive due process? It appears, with the exception of West Virginia and Texas, a one-year non-renewable or renewable at will contract is the norm. Non-renewable means there is no expectation. If the coach wins every game, or if the teacher proves to be the finest on staff, the contract may or may not be renewed. Renewable at will means the contract will be renewed only if both the employer and employee agree a renewal is the best arrangement.

Bryan v. Alabama (1985) involved a high school teacher/coach who was relieved of his coaching duties. He was, however, retained as a tenured teacher. Bryan appealed the coaching decision to the Alabama State Tenure Commission. That commission dismissed the petition for lack of jurisdiction. It did not consider Bryan a tenured coach, or to have jurisdiction over him when the school board had treated him as a non-tenured coach. Bryan then appealed to the circuit court. The court ruled that the decision of the Alabama State Tenure Commission was consistent with Alabama law; "That there is no requirement that coaches be certified. Thus, Bryan's position as a coach is not entitled to the protection of the Tenure Act." (1055)

Bryan then appealed to the Court of Civil Appeals of Alabama. The court upheld the earlier decision, saying that a coach was not a teacher under the Alabama Tenure Law as it was currently constituted. Therefore, Bryan could not be tenured as a coach. Similar decisions also have occurred in Florida, Illinois, Minnesota, Nebraska, and South Dakota.

Although the West Virginia cases, *Smith v. Board of Education of County of Logan* (1985) and *Hosaflook v. Nestor* (1986), and Texas case *Grounds v. Tolar Independent School District* (1986) do not represent the pattern in coaching contract litigation, they do provide interesting insight into the issue. Smith first learned of his dismissal as head football coach in the local newspaper. When he questioned the dismissal, no explanation was given. Smith indicated to the court that he had never been evaluated, nor was ever informed he was not satisfactorially meeting his job responsibilities.

The court ruled that the West Virginia Code §18A-4-16 passed by the legislature in April, 1981 and made effective in July, 1981 indicated

> Nothing in the "separate contract" statute operates to deprive teacher - coaches of their procedural employment rights. The statute's intended purpose was to grant them additional protection by mandating that school boards could not assign teachers to coaching duties without their express consent, and more importantly, could not condition their teaching employment upon acceptance or continuation of coaching duties. (688)

The Supreme Court of Appeals of West Virginia reinstated Smith as Logan High School football coach, with back pay.

Hosaflook was a similar case. Head football coach and tenured teacher, Hosaflook was notified by letter, following completion of the football season, that he would no longer be coaching. He was informed that he would be given a hearing open to the public, or in executive session. The reasons for the transfer from the coaching/teaching position to the teaching position were outlined in detail. Hosaflook requested a closed hearing. Following the hearing, the board of education voted to support the superintendent's recommendation and remove Hosaflook from coaching.

Hosaflook appealed to the state superintendent. The state superintendent found that no written evaluation had been made, violating state board policy. Also, a requirement of written evaluation would have to be met prior to the termination of a coach under the West Virginia code. He ruled that Hosaflook should be reinstated because the "reasons given for non-renewal of the appellant's coaching contract were not adequately proved." (800) The Circuit Court of Upshur County however, reversed the superintendent's decision, saying the code of West Virginia was not applicable to a coaching position.

Finally, the Supreme Court of Appeals of West Virginia reversed the Circuit Court's decision, saying the West Virginia statute required football coaches to be evaluated. It also stated that the purpose of an evaluation was to help the employee improve their skills, thus benefiting the students. The court's holding was that the coach should be reinstated because the school district had failed to evaluate him or give him an opportunity to improve.

In the Texas case of *Grounds*, the plaintiff was a probationary teacher/head football coach. Gary Grounds was first employed by the district under a one-year contract as a teacher. The second year contract read as "Teacher/Coach Football (Head Football Coach)." (890) (At the time of the initiation of the second contract, the Tolar School District had not adopted a probationary policy for new employees.) During the second year of Grounds' employment, the district adopted a probationary evaluation policy for teachers employed less than two years. This policy was in accord with the Texas Education Code.

After completion of his second year of employment, Grounds was notified that his contract would not be renewed. He requested a hearing. The request was denied on the basis that he was a probationary employee; thus, he had no right to a hearing. Grounds then appealed to the state commissioner of education. "The Commissioner reversed the District's decision, finding that Grounds was not a probationary employee, and ordered re-employment in the 'same professional capacity' for the . . . school year." (890)

Grounds' new contract did not include coaching duties. He refused the contract because it did not include coaching, and brought an action against the school district. The district court ruled for the school district. The court of appeals affirmed. However, the Supreme Court of Texas reversed the decisions of the district court and the court of appeals, upholding the decision of the state commissioner of education. Grounds was to be re-employed in the same professional capacity, teacher and coach, as he had been employed in the previous year.

Another issue affecting coaches and teachers is the requirement, often quite subtle in contracts and agreements, that certified and qualified coaches are required to coach, even though they do not wish to be assigned such responsibilities. *Unified School District v. Swanson* (1986) presented such a situation. Charles Swanson, a history/driver education/physical education teacher, was also the basketball coach. He resigned his basketball coaching position. The superintendent made an effort to recruit a basketball coach but was unsuccessful. He then reassigned Swanson the basketball position. Swanson declined.

The school district brought a declaratory judgment requiring Swanson to coach, based upon a provision in the employees' association contract which "provided for assignment of supplemental duties when these duties could not be filled voluntarily." (527) The district court upheld the school district, finding Swanson's refusal to coach basketball insubordination and breach of contract.

The Court of Appeals of Kansas reversed the lower court decision, using the law obtained in *Swager v. Board of Education U.S.D. No. 412* (1984), and *Ottawa Education Association v. U.S.D. No. 290* (1983). The ruling was "that a teacher may not have his primary contract terminated for refusal to accept a supplemental contract. Provisions of a negotiated agreement which conflict with a statutory scheme are void and unenforceable." (528)

In *Babitzke v. Silverton Union High School* (1985), Tracy Babitzke, a teacher and coach, encountered the same type of problem when she resigned after six years as gymnastics coach. Her reason for resigning was that her tiny physical stature no longer permitted her to spot the increasingly advanced skills. Her initial request was for an assistant position. When that position was denied, she formally resigned the coaching aspects of the job. The district argued that "her gymnastic coaching was an indivisible part of her teaching contract, that when she resigned from gymnastics coaching she resigned from all of her duties." (95)

Babitzke's complaint, first heard by the school board, was dismissed. It was then taken to an employment fair dismissal appeal board, who reinstated Babitzke, saying she had not resigned her teaching position. The school appealed. The Court of Appeals of Oregon affirmed the fair dismissal appeal board decision, stating that:

> Her contract did not state, nor was it part of her contract because of any statute, district policy or rule, that if she resigned from any of her extra duty responsibilities it was a resignation from all of her duties. The district dismissed her without her consent and without following the procedures prescribed by law. (98)

Babitzke was reinstated as a permanent teacher and was no longer required to coach gymnastics.

Employment Agreements At the Collegiate Level

Coaching at the college level differs greatly from coaching at the scholastic level. Collegiate coaching contracts carry many financially valuable assets beyond the actual salary.

Rodgers v. Georgia Tech Athletic Association (1983) is an example of such a contract. "Pepper" Rogers, Georgia Tech's head football coach, sued the nonprofit association that governed the university's athletics for $496,000 after his contract was terminated following a losing season. Though Rodgers was fired, he maintained his monthly salary, pension and insurance benefits. The suit was for lost revenue from his television and radio shows, summer camps, free housing, club memberships, extra life insurance and speaking engagements.

The trial court upheld the university, saying salary, pension and medical was more than adequate. Rodgers appealed. Georgia Court of Appeals reversed the decision, breaking new ground in this area. Rodgers was allowed to maintain some "perquisites," a word coined in his contract. Those "perquisites" the association did not control also were eliminated. The ground breaking element of the case, was the fact that the court was willing to consider any of the extras as negotiable items.

SUMMARY

Agreements and written contracts are everyday occurrences in sport and physical activity. Professionals often are asked to sign, draft or negotiate such agreements and therefore should be familiar with the procedures.

A contract is a promise or set of promises for breach of which the law gives a remedy, or for the performance of which the law recognizes as duty. Contracts can be express or implied in fact. Courts will uphold contracts that are express or implied whether verbal or written. The role of the court is to enforce the agreement of the parties.

An agreement consists of an offer, acceptance by the party to whom it was offered and consideration. Breach of a contract is a failure to live up to one or more of the agreements or promises.

Most contract litigation in sport and physical activity occurs in schools and colleges. Coaches appear to be involved more often than others.

References

Babitzke v. Silverton Union High School, 695 P. 2d 93, 72 Or. App. 153 (1985).
Bryan v. Alabama, 472 S. 2d 1052, (1985).
Calamari, John D., and Joseph M. Perillo, 1987. *The Law of Contracts.* St. Paul, MN: West Publishing Company.
Grounds v. Tolar Independent School District, 707 S.W. 2d (Tex. 1986).
Hosaflook v. Nestor, 346 S.E. 2d 798 (W. Va. 1986).
Ottawa Education Association v. U.S.D. No. 290, 233 Kan. 865, 666 P. 2d 680 (1983).
Rodgers v. Georgia Tech Athletic Association, 166 G. App. 156, 303 S.E. 2d 467 (1983).
Smith v. Board of Education of County of Logan, 341 S.E. 2d 685 (West Va. 1985).
Swager v. Board of Education U.S.D. No. 412, 9 Kan. App. 2d 648, 688 P. 2d 270 (1984).
Unified School District v. Swanson, 717 P. 2d 526 (1986).

12
Handicapped Legislation

Though uniform standards for the education of handicapped children began to gain prominence in the 1960s, rights for handicapped persons weren't legislated until the 1970s. Prior to that time, many handicapped children were excluded from the schools because it was thought their presence would disrupt the learning environment. Two cases that set standards for federal legislature for the handicapped were *Pennsylvania Association for Retarded Children [PARC] v. Commonwealth of Pennsylvania* (1971) and *Mills v. Board of Education of the District of Columbia* (1972).

PARC was a class action suit brought by the Pennsylvania Association for Retarded Children and parents of 13 retarded children, on behalf of all retarded persons ages six through 21 in the state of Pennsylvania who were then excluded from programs of education in the public schools. The constitutionality of four state statutes depriving the mentally retarded of schooling was the focus of the challenge. They alleged the statutes violated the plaintiffs' due process and equal protection rights. (Note that this is a Fourteenth Amendment case; review Chapter Ten.) Defendants in the suit were the commonwealth of Pennsylvania, the secretary of welfare, the state board of education and 13 different school districts.

As a result of the hearings, the parties agreed to work out a consent agreement under the direction of two "masters" appointed by the court. In this case, the court did not rule for one party or the other but sent both parties back to the drawing board to create a workable plan. Courts have often used this approach in desegregation of school systems. Defendants were asked to formulate and present to the masters a plan to locate, evaluate and give notice to all members of the plaintiff class. When the details of the plan had been agreed to, the court approved and adopted the consent agreement. A summary of points contained in the consent agreement follows:

1. State law (in Pennsylvania) cannot postpone, terminate or in any way deny to any mentally retarded child access to a free public program of education.
2. Tuition for free public education cannot be denied to a mentally retarded child except on the same terms as may be applied to certain other exceptional children.
3. Homebound instruction cannot be denied to a mentally retarded child.
4. A free public education must be provided every mentally retarded child between the ages of six and 21.
5. When defendants provide preschool programs of education for children less than six years of age, access to free public programs of education appropriate to learning capacity must be provided for all mentally retarded children of the same age.
6. Notice and opportunity for a hearing must be provided the parents of all mentally retarded children prior to a change in educational status.
7. All mentally retarded children must be re-evaluated every two years, or annually, upon the parents' request. Notice and the opportunity for a hearing must accompany each re-evaluation.

Mills, another class action suit, was brought on behalf of all children of the District of Columbia, labeled as having behavioral problems, being mentally retarded, emotionally disturbed or hyperactive, who had been denied an education in the public schools. The problem cited in the case was:

failure of the District of Columbia to provide publicly supported education and training to the plaintiffs and other "exceptional" children . . . and the excluding, suspending, expelling, reassigning and transferring of "exceptional" children from regular public school classes without affording them due process of law. (868)

As a result of the decision, the court ordered that:

no child eligible for a publicly supported education in the District of Columbia public schools shall be excluded from a regular public school assignment by a rule, policy, or practice of the Board of Education of the District of Columbia or its agents unless such child is provided (a) adequate alternative educational services suited to the child's needs, which may include special education or tuition grants, and (b) a constitutionally adequate prior hearing and periodic review of the child's status, progress, and the adequacy of any educational alternative. (878)

SECTION 504 AND PUBLIC LAW 94-142

As a result of *PARC* and *Mills*, public awareness of the plight of the handicapped child grew. This awareness stimulated Congress to move rapidly in providing Federal legislation and funding to assist school districts in educating the handicapped. In 1973, Congress passed the rehabilitation act known as Section 504. Section 504 states:

No otherwise qualified handicapped individual in the United States, as defined in section 7(6), shall, solely by reason of his handicap, be excluded from the participation in, be denied the benefit of, or be subjected to discrimination under any program or activity receiving Federal financial assistance. (45 CFR 84)

In 1975, Congress passed public law 94-142, the Education of all Handicapped Children. Section three, part C states:

it is the purpose of this Act to assure that all handicapped children have available to them, within the time periods specified in section 612(2)(B), a free appropriate public education which emphasizes special education and related services designed to meet their unique needs, to assure that the rights of handicapped children and their parents or guardians are protected, to assist States and localities to provide for the education of all handicapped children, and to assess and assure the effectiveness of efforts to educate handicapped children. (20 U.S.C.A. 1401)

These statutes provide the Federal government's stand on the need to improve educational programs for the handicapped. Public law 94-142 identifies handicapped children as those who are hard of hearing, speech impaired, visually impaired, mentally retarded, emotionally disturbed, orthopedically impaired or suffering from some specific learning disability. Section 504 defines a handicapped person as anyone having a physical or medical impairment that creates a substantive limit on one or more major life activities. The activities include walking, seeing, hearing, breathing, learning, working and self-care. In addition to including all handicaps in P.L. 94-142, Section 504 includes persons addicted to the use of drugs or alcohol.

Aspects of public law 94-142 important to professionals in physical activity are:

1. All handicapped children between the ages of three and 21 shall have a free appropriate public education. Congress, in recognizing that education was the role of the state, noted that 94-142 applied to the ages established by each state for free public education.
2. In addition to free appropriate public education, handicapped children are to receive related services designed to meet their needs.
3. Handicapped children are to be placed in the least restrictive environment appropriate to their needs. This means that whenever possible they are to be mainstreamed or placed in a regular classroom. The goal is to provide the optimal environment to meet their specific learning needs.
4. An individualized education program (IEP) is to be designed for each child. The IEP is to be adhered to in the education of the child. It is to be re-evaluated annually.
5. Parents are permitted access to their children's records.
6. Parents are to be accorded due process procedures including: prior notice of proposed change in educational placement; opportunity for a hearing, including the right to be represented by council; right to present evidence and to confront and cross-examine witnesses; a transcript of the hearing and decision and an opportunity to appeal. The child has a right to remain in his current placement during the above process.

FREE APPROPRIATE PUBLIC EDUCATION

Considerable litigation has occurred in the last few years in an effort to clarify the meanings of two terms used in the ruling: free appropriate public education and related services. In *Board of Education v. Rowley* (1982), the Supreme Court issued its first decision on the question of what was "free appropriate public education".

Amy Rowley, an eight-year-old bright, hearing impaired first-grade student, was successfully mainstreamed in a regular kindergarten class. When her first grade IEP called for mainstreaming with only an electronic hearing device, Amy's parents requested that in addition to the requirements of the IEP she be provided with a full-time qualified sign-language interpreter. The school adopted only the recommendations of the IEP.

The parents requested a due process hearing. The independent examiner agreed with the administration that an interpreter was not necessary because "Amy was achieving educationally, academically and socially without such assistance." (3040) The New York Commissioner of Education affirmed the examiner's decision.

The Rowleys brought suit in the U.S. District Court for the Southern District of New York, (Rowley, 1980) claiming the district's refusal to provide a full-time interpreter violated Amy's right to a free appropriate public education. The District Court upheld the plaintiffs, saying that even though Amy was learning at an efficient pace, the provision of the interpreter would enable her to achieve her full maximum potential. The Court of Appeals affirmed the District Court's decision.

The United States Supreme Court (*Board of Education of Hendrick Hudson Central School District v. Rowley*, 1982) reversed the decisions of the lower courts, denying Amy the service of an interpreter. It said that a free appropriate public education was satisfied when "personalized instruction with sufficient support services to permit the child to benefit educationally" (3049) was provided.

Though the records provide little litigation on these issues in the area of physical activity, professionals should be alert not only to P.O. 94-142, but to laws within their states, affecting the handicapped. H. Rutherford Turnbull III, writing in a 1978 *Phi Delta Kappan*, suggests the following for consideration when working with the handicapped:

1. Zero reject — no handicapped child may be excluded from a free appropriate public education.
2. Nondiscriminatory evaluation — every handicapped child must be fairly assessed so that he may be properly placed and served in the public schools.
3. Appropriate education — every handicapped child must be given an education that is meaningful to him taking his handicaps into account.
4. Least restrictive placement — a handicapped child may not be segregated inappropriately from his non-handicapped schoolmates.
5. Procedural due process — each handicapped child has the right to protest a school's decisions about his education. (523)

Related Services

The definition of related services in the Rehabilitation Act of 1973 is:

transportation, and such developmental, corrective, and other support services, (including speech pathology and audiology, psychological services, physical and occupational therapy, recreation, and medical and counseling services, except that such medical services shall be for diagnostic and evaluative purposes only) as may be required to assist the handicapped child to benefit from special education. (20 U.S.C. §1401 (17) 1982)

O'Hara, in the 1986 *School Law Update*, mentions two cases in recreation; however, both of the requests were to provide transportation to recreational activities so as to increase the child's social environment. Though no case is currently available to demonstrate a child's need for recreation or a requirement that a specific form of recreation be provided, physical activity professionals should be aware of this legal obligation.

CASES IN HANDICAPPED SPORTS PARTICIPATION

There have been a number of instances in which qualified sports participants have been denied an opportunity to practice and compete on regulation teams and in regulation events because of their handicap. The reasons for the denials seem to include:

1. A paternalistic attitude toward the need for a safe environment for the handicapped person. Though the handicapped person (and when appropriate, the parents), wishes to compete, others seem to better know what is appropriate for the athlete.
2. The placement of members of the medical profession in a position in which they appear obliged to state that the handicapped individual could not be injured as a result of their participation in activity. Medical professionals are seldom asked to make such claims on behalf of the normal child.
3. A need felt, by the agency, to avoid assuming what appears to the agency to be an unnecessary risk in permitting the person to compete.
4. A feeling within the agency that permitting the person to compete could bring harm to the other participants. Note that in instances where large braces or other protective gear could harm another performer, a real problem exists and may serve as grounds for eliminating the handicapped performer.

The following cases provide examples of the courts' views on athletic participation by handicapped performers: two football situations involving males, one at the college level and one at the secondary level and a case of one female wishing to play the contact sport of basketball at the secondary level. The handicap in two situations is vision, hearing the third case.

John Colombo, a 15-year-old, was denied participation in football, lacrosse and soccer as a result of a hearing deficiency, in *Colombo v. Sewanhaka Central High School District No. 2* (1976). A routine medical examination diagnosed John as having no hearing in one ear and a 50 percent loss in the other ear. The hearing loss had existed since birth, and John was equipped with a hearing aid. The medical analysis was that John had a "permanent auditory blind" right side and a diminished sound perception on his left side, even with the use of the hearing aid, and that this inability to directionalize the source of sound leaves him at increased risk of bodily harm as compared with students with a full sensory perception." (519) Plaintiff contended that the psychological damage, the willingness of the parents to assume the liability and the student's previous athletic record offset the medical statement.

Conflicting views were presented to the court with reference to Colombo's safety in participation and the safety of other students participating with him. The court, in ruling for the school, mentioned other cases in which courts had been reluctant to interfere with the judgment of a doctor-advised directive. In this case, they supported the directive of the school physician and denied Colombo the opportunity to play football, lacrosse and soccer.

In *Kampmeier v. Harris* (1978), Margaret Kampmeier was able to convince the court that a medical directive was not the most important element in determining the rights of a budding athlete. Kampmeier, a junior high school student, was denied the right to play basketball when a medical examination showed she had defective vision in one eye as a result of a congenital cataract. Kampmeier was a good athlete and used protective eye gear to deal with the problem. The petition to the court included affidavits of two physicians who stated that Kampmeier was capable of participating in contact sports and that it would be "reasonably safe for her to do so while wearing protective gear." (745) The action was first brought against Nyquist in his capacity as commissioner of education (*Kampmeier v. Nyquist*, 1977), and later brought against Harris et al., as a member of the board of education of the Pittsford Central School District, 1978.

In *Wright v. Columbia University* (1981), Joseph Wright, an outstanding high school football player, was denied the opportunity to participate on Columbia University's football team as result of an eye impairment that had existed since birth. He succeeded in his claim under the rights of the handicapped under Section 504 of the Rehabilitation Act of 1973. In his request for a temporary restraining order to allow him to play, he noted that:

not withstanding his lack of vision in one eye, he was an outstanding high school running back; that given the opportunity, he is capable of playing on Columbia's team; that, aside from his handicap, he is "otherwise qualified" to participate in the program; and that his coaches concur with this assessment. Finally, plaintiff and his parents are apparently willing to release Columbia from any potential liability which it might incur by virtue of his participation in the football program. (791)

Columbia's arguments were based on its physician's statement that Wright should not play football. The court, in finding for the student, noted that Wright was in fact a college student capable of attaining a "B" average at Columbia, and could therefore be considered a mature adult. He also had received many scholastic and athletic awards at the secondary level. Therefore, the court stated, "the plaintiff is indeed an intelligent, motivated young man who is capable of making this decision which affects his health and well-being." (794)

Another case, *New York Roadrunners Club v. State Division of Human Rights* (1982) should be studied especially by those professionals involved in the management of events. The case involved the denial of the use of wheel chairs in the New York City Marathon. The state rights appeal board affirmed the state division of human rights, finding that the private club had engaged in unlawful discrimination by not permitting the wheel chair participants to compete. The Court of Appeals of New York upheld the New York City Marathon, a private organization, in denying the wheel chair athletes participation in the event.

Issues discussed by the court and appearing in the dissenting opinion included the responsibility of private versus public agencies to accommodate the public in general, the efficacy of rules to include the handicapped, the safety concern when including motorized vehicles in a road race, the fact that the race was run on public roads and the need to provide competitive athletic events for all persons.

While accommodations have been provided, most handicapped people in today's road races, persons embarking on new athletic ventures, may encounter some of these problems as the events are put into action. Again, the rights of all groups of people have to be examined and balanced, one against the other. For example, the problem of safety may be accommodated by the identification of lanes for certain participants or the issuance of a warning to all runners to be alert to participants in wheel chairs. Most runners are highly sensitive to avoiding the individual in front of them; such sensitivity would have to be focused toward avoiding the wheel chairs.

SUMMARY

Teachers and coaches of the handicapped are highly sensitive to their responsibilities for the physical and mental concerns of the student athletes. Teachers of the handicapped or instructors in a mainstreaming environment need to understand the extent of their liability, of the school districts' liability and of any immunity that might be provided to them as a result of adhering to 94-142.

Another concern is the teacher's rights and responsibilities when the teacher believes the handicapped student could bring harm to other members of the class. A balance of the handicapped person's right to participate in physical activity in relation to the right of the other students to an injury-free environment must be examined. The biggest problem will be to determine whether the potential injury is a real possibility. The teacher's decision and role in the matter must be a part of the risk management program (refer to Chapter Thirteen).

Professionals often fail to realize that a complaint charging them with a denial of a student's civil rights is just as difficult a legal matter as a claim to adjudicate liability for a tort, such as negligence.

PARC and Mills, the early cases involving the rights of handicapped children, prompted the government to create Public Law 94-142, the education of all handicapped children. Public Law 94-142, working in conjunction with Section 504 of the Rehabilitation Act of 1973, provides rights to all handicapped persons. These rights include:

a) a free appropriate education for all youth ages three to 21,
b) related services essential to an appropriate education,
c) opportunity to learn and work in a least restrictive environment,
d) an individualized program of education (IEP) and
e) privileges of fall due process as to issues of evaluation and placement.

References

Board of Education of the Hendrick Hudson Central School District v. Rowley, 102 S. Ct. 3034, 458 U.S. 176, 73 L. Ed. 2d 690 (1982).
Colombo v. Sewanhaka Central High School District No. 2, 383 N.Y. Supp. 2d 518 (1976).
Kampmeier v. Nyquist, 553 F. 2d 296 (1977).
Kampmeier v. Harris, 403 N.Y. Supp. 2d 638 (1978), 411 N.Y. Supp. 2d 744 (1978).
Mills v. Board of Education of the District of Columbia, 348 F. Supp. 866 (1972).
New York Roadrunners Club v. State Division of Human Rights, 55 N.Y. 2d 122, 432 N.E. 2d 780 (1982).
O'Hara, Julie Underwood. 1986. Special education related services under 94-142, School Law Update 1986. Washington D.C.
Pennsylvania Association for Retarded Children [PARC] v. Commonwealth of Pennsylvania, 334 F. Supp. 1257 (1971), 343 F. Supp. 279 (1972).

Public Law 94-142, The Education of Handicapped Children, 20 U.S.C.A. § 1400-1461.

Rehabilitation Act of 1973, 29 U.S.C. § 701.

Rehabilitation Act of 1973, 29 U.S.C. § 504 § 794. (Final regulations published at 42 Fed. Reg. 22676 (May 4, 1977) (Codified as 45 CFR 84).

Rowley v. Board of Education, of The Hendrick Hudson Central School District, Westchester County, 483 F. Supp. 528 (S.D.N.Y. 1980), 483 F. Supp. 536, aff'd, 632 F. 2d 945 (1980), rev'd, 102 S. Ct. 3034 (1982).

Turnbull, H. Rutherford III. 1978. The past and future impact of court decisions in special education. *Phi Delta Kappan*, 523.

Wright v. Columbia University, 520 F. Supp. 789 (1981).

13

Risk Management

Risk management is the identification, evaluation and control of loss to property, clients, employees and the public. A risk management program requires a systematic analysis of the entire working environment, with close analysis of exposure to loss and of potential legal liability. Such a program is essential for all professionals and administrators. Professionals expect administrators to be concerned with issues of safety and liability, often failing to notice that when they take over the responsibility for a group of people, they become administrators in the eyes of the law. This chapter identifies who may be sued; discusses a process for dealing with risks, involving a three-step approach of identification, evaluation and control of the risk; and recommends defense strategies to be used in the event of a suit.

Any professional may be sued. A suit is brought when an individual believes he or she has been wronged and decides to place liability for that wrong on another person or agency. Monetary damages are nearly always the goal in tort situations; civil rights cases seldom request large monetary settlements.

Tort, or personal injury litigation, is often the result of a serious injury in which the victim also has sustained considerable financial loss. The loss may be for past medical bills, lost earnings or the expense of rehabilitation. It also may include future or anticipated losses for those persons requiring permanent physical assistance and rehabilitation. For a catastrophic injury, the expenses may be very high.

In civil rights litigation, the victim is attempting to gain a right or to enjoin someone or some agency from violating personal rights. With the exception of attorney fees, few monetary exchanges are involved.

After an individual determines he or she has been harmed, an attorney will be selected who, in turn, will suggest that all persons involved in the incident become part of the suit. A professional is sued usually because someone wishes to hold another accountable for the injuries; rarely is one sued for poor instruction or coaching, sloppy equipment inspections or failure to supervise employees. Outrageous hazards and overt violations of civil rights exist in sport and physical activity settings, yet most people involved are seldom sued. Court records verify that outstanding professionals have been placed on the stand to defend their teaching, supervisory and administrative skills. Professionals should assume they could be sued, think about their behavior if they are sued and plan a defensive strategy that will provide them every chance possible to succeed in a court of law.

In an ideal setting, the agency, university, school or corporation assumes responsibility for the risk management program; unfortunately, such leadership does not always occur. All professionals should have a risk management program even if the agency with whom they are affiliated does not require such a program.

Those persons whose agencies engage in comprehensive risk management will want to carefully examine the program to be sure that it meets the needs of the physical activity environment. As experts in physical activity, we need to clearly identify an optimum enviroment and communicate to the professionals in risk assessment the potential for harm. Components of a risk management program are dictated by the requirements of a particular position and the environment in which the person works. No matter how small or how large the risk management system dictated by one's responsibilities and obligations, this chapter will help to guide the creation of the system.

This text has identified numerous illustrations of professional liability. As each of the major topics has been introduced, an overview of the law applicable to that area has been presented. Following the legal theory, hypothetical examples and real cases illustrating the use of the legal theory have been presented. Effort has been made to draw cases and examples of significance to professionals in the area of sport and physical activity. All of this information will be the source through which professionals will derive risk management programs or audits; systems tailored to meet the needs of their jobs. Some, especially administrators, will formulate a risk management system for use by an entire business.

IDENTIFICATION

The first step in creating or examining an existing risk management program is to identify all areas of exposure to risk. For example, in your examination of facilities, determine methods for checking facilities, such as the frequency of the checks, the identification of the individual responsible for the check and the process of reporting, correcting and repairing damaged equipment and facilities. The following is a sample guideline of the elements that need to be examined in creating the risk management system and the audit forms. No effort has been made to create a comprehensive system, nor has any effort been made to tailor the ideas to a specific agency or type of service. However, an effort has been made to attempt to demonstrate the vast extent of topics that professionals should consider in devising the system.

Organizing elements for topics which may be helpful in triggering ideas in sport and physical activity are the following:

- Facilities
- Equipment
- Assessment
- Content and Progression of Activity
- Officiating
- Supervision
- Waivers
- Emergency and Accident Procedure
- Securing Rights of Participants
- Fiscal and Contract

Facilities

1. A protocol for the routine checking of facilities should exist. Frequency of inspection as well as the name of the individual conducting the inspection should be included in the record.
2. A system of identification and follow-up for repair of facilities and equipment should be devised and used. All requests for repair should be recorded and dated. Also, one should implement a system for closing facilities in need of repair.
3. Facilities are to be maintained in an orderly fashion. Periodic inspection should assure the standard.
4. Outdoor facilities should be inspected for hazards, as well as cleanliness.
5. A record of all property owned by the agency should exist. In the case of loss by fire or vandalism, such a list will have to be produced in a short period of time. Such lists are requisite to collecting on nearly all insurance policies. Relying on the ability to recall such facts will nearly guarantee that some items will be forgotten.
6. When facilities are in the planning stages, all recommendations and standards on appropriate facilities should be reviewed. If recommended construction has been used, all sources of information should be retained, to use as a means of justifying the

planning in the event that the building is not satisfactory.

7. Facility designs that create a hazard should be identified and remedied. For example:
   a. swimming pools too shallow, or walls too close to the gymnasium play area;
   b. sharp edges, uneven floor boards, inadequate lighting and objects such as drinking fountains or bleachers that protrude into the play area; and
   c. failure to use skid resistant materials on wet floors.
8. Swimming pools are to meet local health standards. Bottoms of swimming pools should be clearly visible.
9. A careful inspection of outdoor traffic patterns should be conducted, paying attention to motor vehicles that could interfere as persons move from one facility to another.

Equipment

1. A master list of all equipment should exist.
2. All equipment, whether mounted in a facility or free standing, should be cleaned and inspected on a periodic basis. Signed inspection documents should be retained.
3. Requests for equipment repair should be in writing. Equipment needing repair should be taken out of use immediately.
4. Equipment should be maintained according to the manufacturer specifications. Care should be taken to identify those pieces of equipment with warranties that will be invalidated if the equipment is repaired by someone other than a designated professional. If the manufacturer does not provide specifications for repair, the equipment should be maintained according to practices within the industry.
5. Instructions and warnings from equipment manufacturers should be posted in a conspicuous place so all participants can see them. The professional should be aware of the manufacturers' and retailers' statements about the use of the equipment.
6. A safety system to provide emergency power in case of loss of lights should be available.
7. When specific equipment is essential to participation in a particular sport, such equipment must be used, or the participants should be banned from the activity.
8. All equipment used in competitive sports should meet the standard established by the sport.
9. Equipment used to provide safety should fit properly to assure the safety for which it was designed.

10. Statutes of the state with reference to facilities and equipment should be known and followed.

Assessment

1. An easy-to-use assessment inventory should be created for each client in an activity. An ideal way to create such an inventory for large groups is to devise a basic lesson for use in the first few class periods. If possible, videotape each of these lessons. The instructor then can create a check sheet to be used when viewing the video to ascertain the skill level of the group. While this system is not of the sophisticated level of an individual education program (IEP), it is a system that can be managed with larger groups.
2. Individualized skill assessment should be used in teaching and coaching to make decisions about the performer's ability to move to a more difficult skill.
3. Documents regarding assessment must be maintained.

Content and Progression of Activity

1. Instructional content should be selected with a knowledge of the client in mind. An instructor must be able to justify the physical demand placed on the performer.
2. Planning should be documented. Courses of study, curricular bulletins, lesson plans, learning sequences, dance routines and other planning material which could be presented to a court of law if requested, should be preserved.
3. When instruction is given to a client or to a student, it is important that others present during the instruction are able to either repeat the instruction or document that it was presented if asked to do so by a court of law.
4. Records should document major benchmarks in student progress. Information adequate to document the fact that a student is ready for an advanced risk-taking skill is essential to the teacher, coach or independent advisor.
5. Personal and corporate fitness specialists have computer printouts or check sheet systems which maintain a schedule of a participant's progress. These schedules document progress and readiness to move onto a more difficult skill. Such information should be retained.
6. The following specific elements should be considered in program planning:
   a. conditioning as a preparatory activity to full participation,

b. matching of performers according to height, weight and speed in body contact sports and

c. appropriate placement of mats and spotting techniques for gymnastics.

7. The methodologies employed for instruction must meet the test of peer scrutiny.

8. When specific equipment is essential for safe participation, such facts must be noted on teaching plans.

Officiating

1. All official games should be played according to official rules. Serving as an official, one has an obligation to control the play on the court or field within the framework of the rules. Failure to maintain such control could be considered negligence.

2. Officials should be required to officiate only. Individuals cannot adequately serve as official and teacher at the same time, nor can they serve as official and player at the same time. When a teacher must serve as an official, game rules are to be structured so the teacher can teach and continue to maintain a safe environment.

3. In official athletic competition, official rules should be used and obeyed. Officials should be under contract to conduct all official game play. Facilities and equipment should meet the requirements of the league.

Supervision

1. A code of behavior should be established.

2. All horse play must be eliminated.

3. Penalties need to be established that will punish those participants behaving in an unsafe manner, sufficient to deter them from continuing the behavior.

4. Control in the activity environment must be maintained at all times.

5. All medical records should be retained on file.

Waivers

A waiver is a legal document that can result in a clash between contract and tort law. Under contract law, persons can contract for most anything, including contracting away their rights. This is freedom to contract. Adults signing a waiver, provided they fully understand the ramifications of the risk, can contract away their rights.

Under contract law, a minor's rights cannot be contracted away by the minor or the minor's parents. Parents signing a waiver for their child to engage in an activity cannot contract away that child's right; therefore, waivers of minors are not treated as contracts. These waivers are used merely to alert parents to the risks involved in physical activity and to make it known to the parents that their offspring are engaged in a hazardous undertaking.

Tort law holds as a fundamental principle that a person is responsible for acts which bring injury to another. Under tort theory, waivers have been honored on some occasions, but not honored on others. In negligence situations, the courts have tended to uphold a waiver when the:

a. party signing the waiver fully understood what was being released and
b. party was not a minor.

Under no circumstances have the courts upheld a waiver absolving an agency or a person from recklessness, or wilful and wanton neglect.

1. Waivers provide an ideal method of alerting participants to the potential of catastrophic injury as well as to the serious risks involved in various physical activities. Waivers should be clear and easy to understand, specific to the activity and describe the situation in detail.
2. Waivers should clearly outline the participant's responsibility for the participant's own safety and for the safety of other performers.
3. Waivers should not only deal with the possibility of injury, they also should include:
   a) detail of safety required of the participant;
   b) how participant will be handled in an accident setting;
   c) civil rights of the athlete including drug testing, discipline, records and releases to the press and
   d) expectations of performer with reference to public appearance, practice and travel.
4. A waiver may incorporate specific documents, the contents of which are included in the waiver. Include the statement that the signer has read, understands and agrees to the total contents of the waiver.
5. All waivers should be carefully reviewed by legal counsel to be sure they accomplish the objectives desired.
6. When waivers are signed by adults for minors they must be ratified or resigned by the minor when the minor reaches the age of majority.

Emergency-Accident Procedure

1. Procedures should be carefully designed and available in writing to all persons who might have to use or participate in such a situation. The plan should include transportation as well as the identification of appropriate medical facilities.
2. At least one person who can administer immediate and temporary care must always be available. Internal and external assistance should be identified.
3. Visiting teams, which might have to use the system, need to be fully informed of the system, what it includes and how to access it.
4. Accident forms are to be designed so the story of the accident can be recorded as efficiently as possible. The goal is to be able to obtain an objective statement from:
   a. the victim, if possible;
   b. supervisor or teacher and
   c. two witnesses.
5. Accident reports should contain a statement of the first aid and emergency treatment provided, the activity in progress at the time of the accident, the specific location of the instructor and the proximity of other members in the activity environment. If equipment was involved it should be examined and secured for inspection by authorities.
6. Accident reports should be retained over the time frame recommended by legal counsel.

Securing Rights of Participants

1. Agencies must decide if lockers will be subject to search. If they may be searched at any time, this information has to be available to those contracting to use the lockers. Persons leasing lockers should be asked to sign a statement indicating their knowledge of the locker search agreement.
2. The Fourteenth Amendment Equal Protection Clause demands that all groups of people (i.e. race or sex) be treated equally. Systems explained in detail in the cases in Chapter Ten and in the Clement publications serve as a protocol for eliminating the risk of discrimination.

   An appropriate benchmark standard for sex descrimination in athletes, for example, would be to provide a program in which the number of competitive berths represents the population of the student body.
3. Materials presented on P.L. 94-142 in Chapter Eleven can be used to build the protocol for handicapped persons.

Personnel

1. Written procedures for advertising jobs and soliciting candidates must be designed, used and recorded.
2. Employee records should contain:
   a. identification of minimum as well as advanced qualifications for each employee with reference to responsibilities, i.e. water safety certification, or college degrees and
   b. contracts, references and observation reports.
3. Employers have ascertained that:
   a. agencies licensing or certifying employees adhere to acceptable professional standards,
   b. employees know and adhere to the duty of care recommended by their profession,
   c. professionals are knowledgeable about the latest research in their area and are using the information,
   d. employees know of injuries inherent in sports and physical activity and recognize the characteristics of participants who might be particularly vulnerable and
   e. professionals engaging in competitive athletics realize they could be held for an intentional tort as a result of coaching or teaching an obvious violation of game rules.

      An opponent does not consent to play in an environment in which plans have been made to intentionally violate the rules. This is not the type of act one could legitimately expect to encounter. For example, football injuries have allegedly been caused by the improper teaching of head and helmet techniques.
4. Employee evaluation, retention and termination policies should exist, be used and records kept, because:
   a. evaluations support the building of quality and
   b. a full due process system needs to be documented.
5. Employee and participant handbooks exist, and serve to fully inform.
6. A system for release of employee and client documents has been devised and is used. It identifies who, when and why each category of document can or should be released.

Fiscal and Contract

1. Administrators should know the sources and amounts of revenue and the risks involved if the revenue should cease. For example, they need to be aware of the level of income obtained from leas-

ing and the ramifications of a failure to find a tenant.

2. Past losses in equipment and facilities need to be assessed and figured into the plan.

3. In programs in which gate receipts or the staging of major events are essential to revenue generation, the risk of a riot or other hazard should be assessed.

4. When contracts are created in staging events liability should be spread among vendors. All contracts should be skillfully prepared to eliminate the situation of having a school or other agency become the sole source of liability.

5. Know state and local statutes and regulations with respect to fiscal and contract obligations.

6. Avoid signing hold harmless or indemnification agreements with manufacturers or retailers of athletic equipment. A hold harmless agreement is a contractual arrangement whereby one party assumes the liability inherent in a situation, thereby relieving the other party of responsibility (*Black's Law Dictionary*). Indemnification is securing another against loss or damage. Professionals need to be sure they have not assumed the liability for a product by contract. Should such a contract have been signed, the agency or the person signing is liable for injury, loss or damage incurred by anyone as a result of using the equipment.

7. Be cognizant of losses occurring in nearby similar agencies.

8. When transferring risks to others by contract, be sure:
   a. Transferees know what they are signing. If a part-time coach is asked to sign an independent contractor agreement, be sure the coach knows what is involved in being an independent contractor (review Chapter Eight).
   b. You request that independent contractors prove insurance coverage to protect the employer.
   c. Communication is very good. Failure to be assured of the other party's knowledge of the agreement could result in a court finding an independent contractor agreement void.

SYSTEM AUDIT

The system audit is a set of steps to be used by administrators in carrying out the risk management program:

1. Educate all members of the agency about the need for a risk management program:
   a. Create an awareness among employees as to the vulnerability of certain practices.
   b. Provide an understanding of the litigation process.

1) Know what happens in a law suit.
2) Become familiar with discovery and what it will mean to record keeping, accident reports, course outlines, activity sequences and curriculum guides.
3) Invite local counsel to visit with staff and inform them about oral depositions, and how they might be used. Counsel may also mention the role of expert witnesses.

2. Know the expected role of employees, and of counsel. Who will be represented by counsel? And, under what conditions will counsel be provided?
3. Know the types and coverage of both employee and personal insurance.
4. Be familiar with the status of governmental immunity and comparative liability in the state. Also, know that immunity differs among agencies.
5. Become aware of warnings (serious accidents, complaints or threats) that could result in exposure to risk.
6. Study the consequences of litigation, such as cost, psychic energy and drain on administration time.
7. Examine alternatives to litigation.
8. Explore methods of optimizing your agency's position if suit is filed.
9. Fully comprehend the duty or standard of care for the agency in general and for each specific position within the agency.

The risk management audit process will result in a document that may be subject to discovery by a court of law. With that in mind, effort should be made to avoid specific negative or problem statements.

EVALUATION

When the identification is complete, each item or area must be evaluated to ascertain the amount of risk that may exist. Certain ways of conducting business will be determined to have a low probability of incurring substantial liability; other methods will be identified as possessing a high level of vulnerability to liability. Also, some areas will have a low potential for an accident; but, should an accident occur, the activity may have a greater chance that the accident could result in death or serious injury. Vulnerability is assessed in terms of:

1. *Probability*:
   a. high probability of injury or harm or
   b. low probability of injury or harm.

2. *Severity*:
   a. serious injury or death or
   b. minor discomfort.
3. *Magnitude*:
   a. many people injured or harmed or
   b. few people injured or harmed.

Among activities considered vulnerable, decisions need to be made to either change the system and reduce the vulnerability, maintain the system or modify the system. A vulnerable system is maintained when experts determine the value of the activity for the participants outweighs the danger inherent in the activity. An example is the retention of the trampoline as an integral part of instruction in human movement, despite the fact that its use has been the subject of substantial litigation.

The trampoline and the diving board are among the best instruments for teaching kinesthetic acuity. Elimination of these teaching instruments is depriving future generations an understanding of one aspect of body control.

CONTROL

Control is the third essential in successful risk management programming. Liability can be controlled or reduced by:

- Avoiding or eliminating the program or activity
- Accepting the risk and agreeing to assume the responsibility
- Transferring the risk through either contract or insurance
- Changing activity to reduce potential injury

Avoiding or Eliminating the Program or Activity

If the program or activity provides no meaningful role in the total operation of the agency it should be eliminated. If the present system is not the best system for program delivery and also allows for considerable vulnerability, a better method should be devised. Most of the time the program or activity has a value to the agency. That value has to be balanced against the cost of insurance.

The threat of suit or the assessment of potential loss should never cause a professional to agree to an inferior method of program delivery. If a specific activity or piece of equipment is the best method available, that activity or equipment should continue in use.

Accepting the Risk and Agreeing to Assume the Responsibility

When a decision is made to retain the risk or maintain a program vulnerable to litigation, a defense strategy must be devised. The two most important components of the defense strategy are (1) a comprehensive safety or compliance check so the agency and other interested parties would realize every effort had been made to take all precautions, with reference to the risk and (2) an assessment of the cost of maintaining the risk or vulnerable program. For example, the use of equipment which could prove dangerous to the novice may be restricted to specific periods of the day, permitted only in small groups or accessed only by those who have passed a preliminary skill test.

Transferring the Risk Through Either Insurance or Contract

When a decision is made to maintain an area vulnerable to litigation, the defense strategy should include the cost of potential litigation. Insurance is an integral part of this risk management control. The dollar figures within any insurance policy should be based on an audit of potential vulnerability and a reasonable figure considering current court judgments in the area. In a thorough insurance program, the professional is covered for the unforeseen and the coverage is considered adequate by the professional, legal counsel and the insurance company.

The changes in today's insurance markets are creating a number of new approaches to insurance coverage. Coverage may be by a regular policy, self insurance, regular policy with a high deductible and the use of self insurance to cover the deductible or a risk management pool. A factor of extreme importance in insurance is the ability of the professional and the agency to identify others wishing to obtain similar coverage.

When an agency prides itself on quality, licensed and well-prepared staff, up-to-date equipment and low instructor-client ratios, they must be assured by the insurance carrier that others insured under the same risk pool maintain the same high standards. The insurance carrier must use risk figures derived from agencies similar in quality to yours in creating premium prices and liability potential.

For example, according to the results of case law, the well maintained, fully life guarded collegiate swim pool diving boards are not vulnerable to litigation like the backyard above-ground pools placed on a lot close enough to permit neighbors the opportunity to dive from their garage roofs. Though the activity is the same, the potential for injury is minimal in the first situation and is nearly guaranteed in the second. Insurance companies who filter out these differences and permit reasonable premiums to quality agencies, need to be sought out and used.

Self insurance means the agency does not seek out an insurance carrier, but places the sum of money it would pay for yearly coverage in an escrow account, to be used in case of a loss. Such a plan provides a major risk to the assets of the agency during the time the sum in escrow is low. However, if no claims are made and the escrow premiums begin to add up, not only has the agency acquired a fine self insurance program but a valuable asset. Agencies who have not had a major loss in 10 to 15 years may consider this risk approach to insurance.

Insurance policies with large deductibles combine the two options mentioned above. Agencies/schools are insured by a company for a very large loss; however, they have agreed to self insure for minor losses. Significant reduction in premiums is the reason an agency would seek out this plan. It also enables the agency to feel secure that its entire assets could not be wiped out by one substantial loss.

Risk management insurance pools are the grouping of many like agencies in a common pool under an insurance carrier. As this is a new trend many agencies similarly situated, requiring the same type of insurance against similar potential losses, are forming groups and going to insurance brokers to obtain coverage. (Guidelines with reference to selecting an insurance carrier also apply here.) Agency groups often have access to statistics with reference to injuries and claims collected that can be presented to a carrier for examination. Usually, such groups also will agree to participation in a risk management audit and ongoing program. This type of insurance may be the vehicle of the future for maintaining coverage of risk in sport and physical activity.

The risk also may be transferred by contract by using the independent contractor agreement described in Chapter Eight. This enables an agency to transfer liability to an instructor, a vendor of equipment or a landlord. All of these contracts and agreements should be drawn up, or at least checked by legal counsel. When the risk is transferred, the bottom line often is that a portion of the profit of the agency also is transferred. Agency profits and risk are two factors that go hand in hand. When risk is transferred, some profit will accompany that transfer.

Changing Activity to Reduce Potential Injury

An alternate program may meet all of the goals of the program considered vulnerable. When such a substitute is available, the prudent manager will accept the program. Agencies that have substituted soccer for football may have made such a change for this reason. At present, injury rates and the cost of safety gear in soccer are substantially lower than the rate and cost of football. Other aspects of the environment may be modified or changed, such as improving the record keeping process, instituting specific safety procedures, changing or improving supervision or training employees.

Review each of the methods of data gathering in the record area to be sure that such documents were created to assure the civil and contractual rights of the professionals and of the client/student.

Once a complaint is filed against professionals, the quality of their administration, teaching and supervision becomes an important factor. Though one cannot entirely avoid suit, adequate preparation and precaution can provide a defense strategy which will significantly increase potential for success in litigation.

A sound risk management program requires the professional to:

a. anticipate and identify potential for loss;
b. evaluate the magnitude of the exposure to loss in degree and frequency,
c. recommend dropping the activity, modifying or continuing activity;
d. identify methods for dealing with exposure to risk and
e. review the system periodically and reconstitute plans accordingly.

SUMMARY

1. Professionals should be cognizant of the fact that anyone may be sued. One's success in a court of law will rest largely upon whether the program meets the appropriate standard of care for the activity, the equipment and facilities were in proper condition, the instruction and supervision was adequate and conducted in an accepted sequence and that all of the above are well documented.
2. Professionals should be aware of their responsibilities and the authority that accompanies the responsibilities.
3. Professionals should know their role with reference to product liability. Manufacturer and retailer warnings should be posted in such a way that they cannot be missed.
4. All employees are to possess certificates and licenses routinely expected of persons in similar positions. Substitutes must also meet these requirements or be provided with additional supervision.
5. Know your program. Identify others with similar programs and maintain communication with persons working in similar pro-

grams and persons working in programs with vastly different approaches.

6. Know what is occurring in your program and as a result of periodic checks, be sure the program you envision is the reality in operation.

Plan throughly, check the execution of the plan, maintain comprehensive records and assume that if placed in a court of law, you will succeed.

References

Black, Henry Campbell. 1979. *Black's Law Dictionary.* (5th Ed.). St. Paul, MN: West Publishing Company.
Clement, Annie. 1987. A selected checklist of risk management concerns in recreational/sport/exercise programs. *Sport, park and recreation law reporter.* Canton, OH: Professional Report Corporation, Volume 1, No. 2, p. 32.
Clement, Annie. 1986. Preventative law: the risk management audit. *Future focus.* Columbus, Ohio: Ohio Association for Health, Physical Education and Recreation, 27. Fall. ed.

Appendix A*

Steven C. **LARSON**, a minor, by Percy Larson, his father and natural guardian, Percy Larson, Individually, and Phyllis Larson, Respondents,

v.

INDEPENDENT SCHOOL DISTRICT NO. 314, BRAHAM Minnesota, and

James Lamont, Defendants,

Lyle Lundquist, Appellant (49854),
and
Jack Peterson, Appellant (49271).
Nos. 49271, 49854.
Supreme Court of Minnesota.
Nov. 9, 1979.
Rehearing Denied Jan. 28, 1980.

Plaintiff brought action on behalf of minor, individually and as natural guardian of minor, against superintendent of school district, principal of high school, and physical education teacher for injuries received by minor in eighth grade physical education class at high school. The District Court, Isanti County, Thomas G. Forsberg, J., awarded to minor judgment against teacher and principal and found school district was jointly and severally liable in certain sum and entered directed verdict in favor of superintendent, and parties appealed and cross-appealed. The Supreme Court, Peterson, J., held that: (1) jury's finding that injury of student in physical education class was due in part to negligence of principal of school was not manifestly and palpably contrary to evidence as a whole; (2) superintendent was not sufficiently involved in actions or inactions to be found negligent; (3) judgment utilized by physical education instructor in determining how to spot and teach an advanced gymnastic exercise was not decision making entitled to protection under doctrine of discretionary immunity and, therefore, instructor was liable for his negligent spotting and teaching of the exercise; (4) principal who abdicated his responsibility for developing and administering teaching of physical education curriculum was not engaged in decision making at planning level and, therefore, his liability for negligent discharge of that responsibility was not precluded by doctrine of discretionary immunity; and (5) principal was not entitled to indemnity from school district and his liability was not limited to amount of insurance coverage the school district was requried to carry.

Affirmed.

Wahl, J., dissented in part and concurred in part with opinion.
Otis, J., dissented with opinion.

Lommen, Cole & Stageberg and John P. Lommen, Minneapolis, for Lundquist and School Dist. No. 314.
Gislason, Dosland, Malecki, Gilason & Halvorson, C. Allen Dosland, and Steven C. Isaacson, New Ulm, for Peterson.
Rider, Bennett, Egan & Arundel, David F. Fitzgerald, and Eric J. Magnuson, Minneapolis, Parker & Olsen and Robert S. Parker, Cambridge, for Larson.
Thomas E. Peterson, Minneapolis, for School Dist. No. 314.
Jardine, Logan & O'Brien and James J. Galman, St. Paul, for Lamont.
William B. Korstad, Roger Sahr, Minneapolis, G. William Smith, St. Paul, John D. Quinlivan, St. Cloud, Parker & Olsen, Cambridge, James J. Galman, St. Paul, Korstad, Lund, Soules, Erdall & McKendrick, Minneapolis, for Minnesota Assn. of Secondary School Principals.

Heard, considered, and decided by the court en banc.

PETERSON, Justice.

This action was brought on behalf of plaintiff Steven C. Larson, a minor, by plaintiff Percy Larson, individually and as natural guardian of Steven, against defendants Lyle H. Lundquist, Jack Peterson, and James Lamont, for injuries received by Steven on April 12, 1971, in an eighth grade physical education class at Braham Junior-Senior High School.[1] Trial was held in Isanti County District Court before Judge Thomas G. Forsberg, commencing on November 1, 1977. The trial court granted La-

---

[1] Defendants Jack Peterson and James Lamont moved for summary judgment, and the motions were granted on November 17, 1975, by Judge Carroll Larson of the Isanti County District Court. Judgment was entered on November 17, 1975, dismissing the actions against Peterson and Lamont. Plaintiffs Steven C. Larson and Percy Larson appealed to this court on November 24, 1975, and we held (*Larson v. Independent School Dist. No. 314*, 312 Minn. 583, 252 N.W.2d 128 [1977]) that summary judgment dismissing Peterson and Lamont be reversed and a new trial ordered, because Judge Larson did not have all of the pretrial depositions available to him at the time of his decision.

mont's motion for a directed verdict on November 28, 1977, on the ground that plaintiffs had not established a prima facie case of negligence against Lamont. On December 1, 1977, the jury returned a verdict finding Lundquist 90 percent negligent, Peterson 10 percent negligent, and Steven free from negligence.

The trial court awarded Steven, individually, judgment against Peterson and Lundquist, jointly and severally, in the sum of $1,013,639.75 together with his costs and disbursements and awarded Percy Larson $142,937.89 together with his costs and disbursements. The trial court further held that procurement of liability insurance in the sum of $50,000 by Independent School District No. 314 under Minn. St. 1971, c. 466, waived the school district's absolute defense of governmental immunity for torts committed by its employees to the extent of $50,000 and that the school district was thereby jointly and severally liable with Peterson and Lundquist in the sum of $50,000 to each plaintiff.[2]

Post-trial motions for judgment notwithstanding the verdict or for a new trial, made on behalf of Lundquist and Peterson, were denied by order of the trial court on June 20, 1978. Lundquist and Peterson appeal from the order and from the judgment entered in favor of plaintiffs on July 12, 1978. Plaintiffs cross-appeal the order for a directed verdict in favor of Lamont. We affirm.

On April 12, 1971, Steven was severely injured while performing a gymnastic exercise known as a "headspring over a rolled mat," a required activity in his eighth grade physical education class. As a result of landing on his head, and from the force of running and diving onto the rolled mat, Steven broke his neck. The injury resulted in quadraplegic paralysis.

At the time of the accident, Steven was a student at Braham Junior-Senior High School. He was participating in a compulsory physical education class being taught by Lundquist, a first-year teacher with a teaching certificate in physical education. Lundquist had commenced teaching physical education classes at the school on March 10, 1971, when the former physical education teacher, Mark Embretson, was required to report for military duty. The accident occurred nine class periods after Lundquist had replaced Embretson. Lamont was the superintendent of the school district, and Peterson was the principal of Braham Junior-Senior High School.

Plaintiffs' allegations of negligence against Lundquist were based upon arguments that Lundquist was teaching Steven's class the headspring before the class had participated in the necessary preliminary pro-

---

[2] In a footnote to their appellate brief, plaintiffs argue that the judgment of the trial court should be amended to hold the school district liable for the entire sum of the verdict. We disagree and hold that the trial court correctly applied the provisions of Minn. St. 1971, c 466.

gressions of less advanced gymnastic exercises, progressions designed in part for safety, and that Lundquist was improperly spotting the exercise at the time Steven was injured.[3] The evidence at trial demonstrated that the headspring is an advanced gymnastic exercise[4] and, in the words of one of plaintiffs' expert witnesses, is "a high danger skill." Lundquist does not on this appeal specifically contest the sufficiency of the evidence as it relates to his negligence.[5] Furthermore, there is sufficient evidence in the record that Lundquist was negligent in teaching the headspring at the time and that Steven's accident occurred because Lundquist was negligent in spotting the headspring.

Plaintiffs' contentions of negligence against Superintendent Lamont and Principal Peterson were that they had not properly developed, administered, and supervised the physical education curriculum; that they had not properly handled the transition from Embretson to Lundquist; and that they had not properly supervised Lundquist's physical education instruction.

As principal, Peterson had a duty to exercise reasonable care in supervising the development, planning, and administration of the physical education curriculum within the school; in supervising and evaluating the work of teachers within the school; and in maintaining conditions conducive to the safety and welfare of students during the school day.[6] In effect, the jury found that Peterson's actions as an administrator were unreasonable and that his failure to reasonably administer the curriculum and supervise the teaching of an inexperienced instructor created

---

[3] Two mats are used in performing a headspring over a rolled mat — one mat lies flat upon the floor, and the other mat is rolled and placed upon it. The standard technique for spotting the headspring, as indicated by the evidence, is for the spotter to straddle and sit upon the rolled mat or to crouch over it, using the weight of his body and legs to anchor the mat and using his hands to assist and provide protection to the person performing the headspring. The evidence demonstrated that a spotter was not straddling the rolled mat at the time of Steven's accident. Lyle H. Lundquist was standing near the rolled mat, spotting on the approach, and two student spotters, as instructed by Lundquist, were standing on the landing portion of the flat mat.

[4] The headspring consists of a number of basic skills, including a forward roll, a kip-up, a headstand with a forward roll, and a squat-to-stand with a run. Running to the mat makes the headspring a more complex maneuver, but is unnecessary. Lundquist included running to the mat in teaching the headspring to Steven's class.

[5] Lundquist does contend that he was deprived of a fair trial by errors of the trial court in the reception of evidence. Our examination of the record discloses that Lundquist's contention is without merit.

[6] The duties prescribed for a principal by manuals of the department of education and the school district included: (1) Administering the rules and regulations of the board of education and the rules of the state pertaining to education; (2) making recommendations to the superintendent regarding courses of study and changes in the curriculum; (3) developing, organizing, administering, and implementing the curricular activity program; (4) observing the work of teachers in classrooms and serving as a consultant for improving and revising the curriculum; (5) providing for the orientation of new teachers on school policies and classroom procedures; (6) holding staff meetings; (7) organizing the program of studies and preparing individual class schedules; and (8) maintaining conditions that would ensure the safety and welfare of pupils during the school day.

the opportunity for Steven's accident to occur. A review of the record demonstrates that the jury could make such a finding.[7]

[1] Other than to furnish Lundquist with a copy of Curriculum Bulletin No. 11, "A Guide for Instruction in Physical Education, Secondary Schools, Grades 7-12, Boys and Girls," published by the department of education,[8] Peterson did not actively participate in developing or administering the physical education curriculum. Responsibility for those matters was entirely in the hands of Lundquist, a first-year teacher with little prior experience in physical education,[9] even though it was his first occasion to plan a unit of physical education as a physical education instructor. Plaintiffs introduced expert testimony which indicated a need for closely supervising the planning of a unit of gymnastics when a young teacher with little experience was involved. Furthermore, Peterson did not give Lundquist minimal guidance, such as telling him to abide by the provisions of Curriculum Bulletin No. 11 or explaining use of the bulletin's provisions.[10]

During the transition from Embretson to Lundquist, Peterson never met with the two teachers to discuss the physical education curriculum. When Peterson was informed of the exact date in March 1971 upon which Embretson would be leaving, he told Lundquist to meet with Embretson and plan physical education classes for the remainder of the year for the entire junior-senior high school. Peterson gave no instructions to either Embretson or Lundquist regarding the transition plan to be formulated. Embretson and Lundquist met for approximately 30 minutes to discuss the transition. Their discussion about gymnastics was limited to whether a unit in gymnastics had been taught and the possibility of Lundquist's teaching such a unit that year. When Lundquist reported to Peterson, he told Peterson what subjects he was going to teach, but he did not discuss in detail what activities he was going to include or what method he was going to use to teach gymnastics, partly because Peterson

[7] This court will not disturb findings of fact by a jury unless they are manifestly and palpably contrary to the evidence as a whole. *Carpenter v. Mattison*, 300 Minn. 273, 219 N.W.2d 625 (1974); *Smith v. Hencir-Nichols, Inc.*, 276 Minn. 390, 150 N.W.2d 556 (1967).

[8] As more fully discussed later in this opinion, we believe the activities and courses of study prescribed in Curriculum Bulletin No. 11 were intended to be used as guidelines and did not establish mandatory affirmative duties for teachers, principals, or superintendents. However, because evidence at trial indicated that the bulletin was used by many Minnesota school districts as a standard for planning and teaching physical education, evidence of the manual's provisions was relevant for the jury's determination whether defendants breached the duty of care owed to Steven.

[9] Lundquist's only previous experience in physical education instruction had been as a student teacher and as a substitute physical education teacher at the school for a limited number of times during the year of Steven's accident.

[10] Testimony at trial indicated that introduction of the headspring by Lundquist to Steven's physical education class was not in accordance with the recommended scope and sequence of Curriculum Bulletin No. 11.

did not ask Lundquist detailed questions. No further meetings were held to discuss the transition.

Furthermore, testimony by one of plaintiffs' expert witnesses indicated that unit planning of physical education programs was important to ensure that proper progressions for the promotion of safety were followed and that such planning was to be in addition to daily lesson plans. Nevertheless, Embretson was not required to prepare a plan of activities for the entire school year, even though Peterson knew that Embretson might be leaving during the school year. Lundquist could not recall submitting, or Peterson's asking him to submit, a detailed written plan of what he was going to teach.

[2, 3] Because of Lundquist's inexperience, the jury could reasonably have believed that Peterson should have exercised closer supervision over planning and administering the physical education curriculum by specifically instructing Lundquist to refer to Curriculum Bulletin No. 11, by instructing an experienced physical education instructor like Embretson to closely plan the curriculum and submit a detailed report, or by requiring detailed written plans from Lundquist.[11] It could also have believed that Peterson should have more closely supervised the transition between Embretson and Lundquist by formulating definite goals and requiring detailed reports. The jury's finding that Peterson was negligent is supported by the evidence.[12]

The trial court directed a verdict in favor of Superintendent Lamont on the ground that plaintiffs did not establish a prima facie case of negligence against him. On appeal, plaintiffs contend that the jury question of Lamont's negligence was sufficiently presented at trial. They argue that Lamont had a specific duty to develop and administer the physical education curriculum in compliance with Curriculum Bulletin No. 11 and that the breach of that duty resulted in Lundquist's failure to teach in accordance with the bulletin, which was the cause of Steven's accident. We affirm the trial court's directed verdict.

[4] The crux of plaintiffs' position is that Curriculum Bulletin No. 11 established mandatory activities and courses of study which could not be

---

[11] Peterson argues he was not an expert in physical education and therefore was entitled to rely upon Lundquist's expertise. Peterson's argument disregards Lundquist's lack of experience. Furthermore, if Peterson believed he lacked the expertise necessary to oversee a physical education curriculum, he could have delegated that function to someone else.

[12] Peterson also contends that it was error for the trial court to qualify one of plaintiffs' witnesses as an expert and to admit testimony by him concerning the duties owed by a principal to a student. Peterson claims the witness had neither education in nor work experience as a school principal or superintendent. Peterson did not include this objection in the grounds he cited as a basis for requesting an order granting a new trial on all issues. Objections to evidentiary rulings which are not assigned as error in a motion for a new trial are not reviewable by this court on appeal from judgment. *Fritz v. Arnold Manufacturing Co.*, 305 Minn. 190, 232 N.W.2d 782 (1975). We therefore refuse to consider this argument.

departed from in a physical education curriculum. At the time of the accident, Minn. Reg. Edu 162(b) provided:

> "(b) Secondary school course. There shall be taught in every secondary school the prescribed course of study prepared and published by the commissioner of education in accordance with M.S. 121.11, Subd. 7 and M.S. 126.02, which is Curriculum Bulletin No. 11, 'A Guide for Instruction in Physical Education, Secondary School, Grades 7-12, Boys and Girls,' * * *"[13]

Plaintiffs contend this regulation demonstrates that Curriculum Bulletin No. 11 established mandatory affirmative duties for physical education instruction. We disagree.

The wording of Curriculum Bulletin No. 11 demonstrates that the bulletin was not intended to be viewed as a publication which established mandatory affirmative duties. For example, the preface to Curriculum Bulletin No. 11 provided:

> "While it is hoped that this guide will present a framework for developing the very best in physical education in today's modern and highly complex world as well as for providing a unified experience on a state-wide basis, it is in no way intended to restrict the initiative, creativity, and ingenuity on the part of the respective schools and their teaching staffs. Rather, it is the hope of the curriculum committee that the very nature of this guide will stimulate effort to evaluate the proposed program and thereby to adapt, modify, and strengthen the program wherever need exists."

Similarly, a chart in the bulletin which classified the level of difficulty of the headspring was entitled, "Recommended Scope and Sequence by Grades and Types of Activities." The bulletin also contained a section entitled, "Suggested Schedule of Physical Education Activities," which stated: "Each school is encouraged to develop its own program of activities, using as a guide the planned schedule of activities." In addition, the word "guide" was used in the title of the bulletin.

It is clear that the activities and courses of study prescribed by Curriculum Bulletin No. 11 were essentially recommendations intended to be used as guidelines in developing a physical education curriculum. The bulletin did not establish mandatory affirmative duties. While plaintiffs spend a great deal of time explaining the provisions of the bulletin and

[13] This regulation has since been changed and in its current form makes no reference to Curriculum Bulletin No. 11.

illustrating why they believe Lundquist did not teach according to the bulletin's provisions,[14] their efforts do not specifically address the issue of Lamont's negligence. There was neither a regulation nor a rule which made Lamont personally responsible for ensuring that the provisions of Curriculum Bulletin No. 11 were followed in the school's physical education curriculum.

Lamont had general supervisory and administrative authority over the school system and was ultimately responsible to the school board for the manner in which the school system was managed; however, the evidence at trial established that he was not required to personally develop a physical education curriculum and that the examples of negligence which plaintiff alleged occurred in the administration and supervision of the curriculum and in Lundquist's teaching and transition were responsibilities expressly and properly[15] delegated to Principal Peterson. Except for matters of budgeting and financing, Peterson was the delegated administrator of Braham Junior-Senior High School. The school district's policy manual required Peterson to develop, organize, and implement the school's curriculum, including physical education classes. It further made Peterson responsible for assigning duties to teachers, supervising classroom instruction, providing orientation for new teachers, and administering the requirements of the board of education.

[5] Superintendent Lamont was a level removed from these responsibilities. There is no showing in the record that Lamont had or should have had knowledge that Peterson had allowed an unsafe physical education curriculum to develop, that Peterson had improperly carried out the transition from Embretson to Lundquist, or that Peterson had failed to provide Lundquist with adequate supervision. There is no showing that Lamont was inadequately supervising Peterson's performance, or that Lamont had special knowledge of problems in the physical education curriculum or of Lundquist's teaching methods which would have put him on notice that the safety of students was being threatened.

Lamont was not sufficiently involved in the actions or inactions upon which plaintiffs based their cause of action. There was, therefore, insufficient evidence that a negligent act by Lamont caused Steven's accident. The trial court's directed verdict in favor of Lamont was proper.

[6, 7] Lundquist and Peterson also argue that any liability on their part for Steven's accident is precluded by the common-law doctrine of

---

[14] The physical education curriculum taught by Lundquist was improper, not necessarily because it deviated from Curriculum Bulletin No. 11, but because the weight of the evidence indicated that Steven's class had not been properly trained in the preliminaries necessary to safely perform the headspring, an advanced gymnastic exercise.

[15] Minn. Reg. Edu 5(b)(2) sets forth the general duties and responsibilities of the superintendent of a school district and expressly notes: "Delegation of certain duties to subordinates is assumed."

discretionary immunity. Under the doctrine of discretionary immunity, state officials and employees are not absolutely immune from suit but ordinarily may be held liable only in the performance of ministerial rather than discretionary duties. As we observed in *Susla v. State*, 311 Minn. 166, 175, 247 N.W. 2d 907, 912 (1976), "It is settled law in Minnesota that a public official charged by law with duties which call for the exercise of his judgment or discretion is not personally liable to an individual for damages unless he is guilty of a willful or malicious wrong." We have described a ministerial duty as follows:

> "* * * A ministerial duty is one in which nothing is left to discretion, a simple, definite duty arising under and because of stated conditions and imposed by law. The idea has been put in this language. 'Official duty is ministerial when it is absolute, certain and imperative, involving merely the execution of a specific duty arising from fixed and designated facts.' " (Citations omitted.) *Cook v. Trovatten*, 200 Minn. 221, 224, 274 N.W. 165, 167 (1937).

Classifying a person's acts as "discretionary" or "ministerial" is often difficult and, as recently noted in *Papenhausen v. Schoen*, 268 N.W.2d 565, 571 (Minn. 1978), such a distinction has been subject to enigmatic application and occasional breakdown. However, important guidance on the question of immunity in the present case can be found in *Williamson v. Cain*, 310 Minn. 59, 245 N.W.2d 242 (1976), and *Hansen v. City of St. Paul*, 298 Minn. 205, 214 N.W.2d 346 (1974).

We held in *Williamson* that state employees who caused damage to a neighboring structure while attempting to demolish an abandoned building were personally liable to the neighboring property owner, because they were performing a ministerial duty. We there reasoned:

> "* * * While the discretionary-ministerial distinction is a nebulous and difficult one because almost any act involves some measure of freedom of choice as well as some measure of perfunctory execution, the acts of the defendants here are clearly ministerial. Their job was simple and definite — to remove a house. While they undoubtedly had to make certain decisions in doing that job, the nature, quality, and complexity of their decision-making process does not entitle them to immunity from suit." 310 Minn. 61, 245 N.W.2d 244.

We held in *Hansen* that failure of St. Paul city officials to control vicious dogs, when they had knowledge that the identified and impoundable dogs prowled uncontrolled upon public sidewalks, did not involve a discretionary function and that the city therefore was not protected by the "discretionary acts" exception to municipal tort liability provided under Minn. St. 466-03, subd. 6. We noted that many jurisdictions, including Minnesota, found this kind of immunity to have greater applicability to decisions made on the executive or planning level of conduct than to decisions made on the operational level of conduct. 298 Minn. 211, 214 N.W.2d 350.

[8] The two cases illustrate that applicability of the doctrine of discretionary immunity is not dependent upon whether a person's duty requires some degree of judgment and discretion. The crucial focus is upon the nature of the act undertaken. Decisions intended to be protected by discretionary immunity are those made upon the planning level of conduct.

[9] Lundquist is not entitled to protection under the doctrine of discretionary immunity. The evidence established that he was negligent in spotting the headspring Steven was attempting to perform. While a person must use judgment in deciding how to spot a gymnastic exercise, the fact that he is using judgment does not establish that he is performing a discretionary duty. *Williamson v. Cain, supra.* Because of the special status school children have in the eyes of the law,[16] and because the headspring requires advanced gymnastic skills, the nature, quality, and complexity of the decisionmaking process used by Lundquist in deciding how to spot the headspring does not entitle him to immunity.

The manner in which Lundquist chose to spot the headspring did not involve a decision on the policy-making level. Once he decided to require Steven and others in his class to perform the headspring, it was Lundquist's responsibility to see that the headspring was safely taught and properly spotted. Lundquist's decision to spot the headspring in the manner he chose was a decision made on the operational level of conduct and clearly involved a ministerial duty.

Similarly, the improper teaching of the headspring essentially involved a ministerial function. In effect, the jury found that Steven's accident occurred, at least in part, because Lundquist attempted to teach Steven the headspring before he was able to safely perform the advanced gymnastic exercise. While it may be a policy-level decision whether a teacher will be required to teach gymnastics or the headspring over a rolled mat, the actual teaching is a ministerial function because it involves decisions made at the operational level of conduct. The headspring was improperly taught because Steven was required to attempt it before he had had an opportunity to learn the preliminary skills which would have

---

[16] "School children have a special status in the eyes of the law, and in view of the compulsory attendance statute deserve more than ordinary protection." *Spanel v. Mounds View School Dist No. 621,* 264 Minn. 279, 291, 118 N.W.2d 795, 802 (1962).

enabled him to safely perform the headspring. While Lundquist exercised judgment in deciding how to teach the headspring, the level of judgment he exercised was not intended to be covered under the doctrine of discretionary immunity.

[10] It is difficult to apply the doctrine of discretionary immunity to Peterson, because a principal is required to make many decisions at the policy-making level while administering a school; however, under the facts of the present case, it is clear that Peterson was not exercising discretionary judgment protected by the doctrine. The gravamen of plaintiffs' negligence case against Peterson was the argument that because of Lundquist's inexperience, Peterson should have more closely supervised the planning and administering of the physical education curriculum. Peterson's negligence was, therefore, not rooted in any policy judgment he made about teaching or developing the physical education curriculum. Peterson never made decisions about teaching and developing the physical education curriculum, and his failure to do so was the primary evidence of his negligence.

The evidence indicates that Peterson never considered the merits of the physical education curriculum or the manner in which Lundquist was going to teach it. Peterson was briefly told by Lundquist what subjects Lundquist was going to teach but details were neither volunteered by Lundquist nor requested by Peterson. Peterson never required Lundquist or Embretson to have a detailed meeting with him to specify the matters decided upon between them. Detailed, written reports on the curriculum were not requested by Peterson from either Embretson or Lundquist. Peterson made no effort to see how Curriculum Bulletin No. 11 was being used or, indeed, if it was being used.

The doctrine of discretionary immunity is intended to protect a public official or employee whose policy-making duties include choosing between various alternatives, even if one of the alternatives is to do nothing. Cf., *Silver v. City of Minneapolis*, 284 Minn. 266, 170 N.W.2d 206 (1969). In the present case, Peterson did not engage in a discretionary choice between alternatives; he made no decision about the curriculum. In effect, Peterson completely abdicated his responsibility for developing, administering, and teaching the physical education curriculum. Because Peterson never engaged in decision-making relevant to developing and administering the physical education curriculum, his negligence did not involve decision-making on the planning level of conduct.

[11] Discretionary immunity must be narrowly construed in light of the fact that it is an exception to the general rule of liability. Because of the special protection that the law affords school children, *Spanel v. Moundsview School Dist. No. 621*, 264 Minn. 279, 291, 118 N.W.2d 795, 802 (1962), failure by Peterson, in this case, to adequately supervise the plan-

ning and administering by Lundquist of the physical education curriculum cannot be considered decision-making that the doctrine of discretionary immunity is designed to protect. We therefore hold that Peterson's liability is not precluded by the doctrine of discretionary immunity.

Peterson also argues that his liability should be less than the amount determined by the trial court. He argues, and we reject, and (1) his liability is limited to the insurance coverage prescribed by Minn. St. 1971, § 466.04, and (2) that he is entitled to indemnity from the school district.

Minn. St. 1971, § 466.04, provided, in part, as follows:

> "Subdivision 1. Liability of any municipality on any claim within the scope of sections 466.01 to 466.15 shall not exceed
> a. $25,000 when the claim is one for death by wrongful act or omission and $50,000 to any claimant in any other case;
> b. $300,000 for any number of claims arising out of a single occurrence.
> No award for damages on any such claim shall include punitive damages.
> Subd. 2. The limitation imposed by this section on individual claimants includes damages claimed for loss of services or loss of support arising out of the same tort."

The above provisions and other provisions of Minn. St. 1971, c. 466, specifically dealt with municipal immunity and liability but did not specifically deal with liability and immunity of municipal officers or employees. Minn. St. 1978, § 466.04, subd. 1a, which was added to c. 466 by the legislature in 1976,[17] now grants the following limitations upon liability of officers and employees: "The liability of an officer or an employee of any municipality for a tort arising out of an alleged act or omission occurring in the performance of duty shall not exceed the limits set forth in subdivision 1, unless the officer or employee provides professional services and also is employed in his profession for compensation by a person or persons other than the municipality."[18]

---

[17] Laws 1976, c. 264 § 2.

[18] Minn. St. 1978, § 466.04, now provides: "Subdivision 1. Liability of any municipality on any claim within the scope of sections 466.01 to 466.15 shall not exceed

"(a) $100,000 when the claim is one for death by wrongful act or omission and $100,000 to any claimant in any other case; and

(b) $300,000 for any number of claims arising out of a single occurrence.

No award for damages on any such claim shall include punitive damages.

Subd. 1a. The liability of an officer or an employee of any municipality for a tort arising out of an alleged act or omission occurring in the performance of duty shall not exceed the limits set forth in subdivision 1, unless the officer or employee provides professional services and also is employed in his profession for compensation by a person or persons other than the municipality.

Subd. 1b. The total liability of the municipality on a claim against it and against its officers or em-

[12] Peterson states that there is no relevant legislative history relating to the 1976 amendment but contends that a fair reading of c. 466 demonstrates that the amendment was intended to cure an oversight in drafting and expresses more clearly the legislature's prior intention that where municipality liability insurance existed, the negligent acts of an employee were to be compensated for but only to the extent of the insurance coverage. Peterson argues that a governmental body can only act through its officers or employees and that the legislature always intended in c. 466 that an officer or employee be subjected to personal liability only to the extent the governing body was liable either by the statute or a higher amount of liability coverage. Peterson's argument is not persuasive.

[13] Adoption of an amendment by the legislature raises a presumption that it intended to make some change in existing law. *Western Union Telegraph Co. v. Spaeth*, 232 Minn. 128, 132, 44 N.W.2d 440, 442 (1950); *Fitzpatrick v. City of St. Paul*, 217 Minn. 59, 62, 13 N.W.2d 737, 738 (1944). Peterson did not produce sufficient evidence to rebut such a presumption. There was no specific mention of immunity or liability of a governing body's employees or officers in Minn. St. 1971, c. 466.[19] Peterson is, in effect, arguing that such language can nonetheless be inferred. We refuse to engage in such speculation.

Peterson also argues that he is entitled to indemnity from the school district because his actions were performed to fulfill his duties as principal and that any negligence on his part was passive in nature. He contends that where an agent is employed by another to do an act in the employer's behalf, it is the general rule that the law implies a promise of indemnity by the employer for damages that flow directly from the agent's acts.

[14,15] Peterson is not entitled to indemnity from the school district. His attempt to obtain indemnity is barred by governmental immunity conveyed to the school district under § 466.12, subd. 2. The limited waiver of immunity provided in § 466.12, subd. 3a, was the result of the legislature's desire that persons injured by the negligence of a school district's employee have recourse to the school district's insurance coverage. Pe-

ployees arising out of a single occurrence shall not exceed the limits set forth in subdivision 1.
    Subd. 2. The limitation imposed by this section on individual claimants includes damages claimed for loss of services or loss of support arising out of the same tort.
    Subd. 3. Where the amount awarded to or settled upon multiple claimants exceeds $300,000, any party may apply to any district court to apportion to each claimant his proper share of the total amount limited by subdivision 1 of this section. The share apportioned each claimant shall be in the proportion that the ratio of the award of settlement made to him bears to the aggregate awards and settlements for all claims arising out of the occurrence." (Italics supplied indicates addition to prior statute.)

[19] Additionally, it is arguable the legislature in Minn. St. 1971, c. 466, recognized officers and employees could be exposed to liability for which a municipality would be immune when it provided authorization for a municipality to indemnify an officer or employee. § 466.07, subd. 1. If a municipality's liability was coextensive with that of its officers or employees, there would be no need for indemnification.

terson does not come within the class to whom waiver of the school district's governmental immunity has been granted. His quest for indemnity is therefore barred by c. 466. Furthermore, Peterson was found personally negligent, and he may not seek indemnity from his employer, whose only liability to plaintiffs in this case is vicarious.[20]

Affirmed.

TODD, J., took no part in the consideration or decision of this case.

WAHL, Justice (dissenting in part, concurring in part).

I agree with the majority that the directed verdict in favor of the superintendent was proper, that the evidence supports the findings of fact that Lundquist was negligent, and that Lundquist's liability was not precluded by the doctrine of discretionary immunity. However, because the record indicates to me that Peterson's alleged negligence arose out of acts requiring judgment and discretion, I would hold that Peterson is protected from liability by the doctrine of discretionary immunity.[1]

Except for budgetary and financial matters, Peterson was primarily responsible for the running of the school. This job required him to make policy decisions of many types, decisions which required him to use skilled judgment and discretion. Peterson's recommendations to the school district to hire Lundquist, a certified and apparently satisfactory physical education instructor, was a matter of judgment. No less so was his decision to let Lundquist and the former instructor, Embretson, plan the program and the lessons. Curriculum Bulletin No. 11, which Peterson provided to the physical education department, expressly indicated it was the teacher's job to work out the details in accordance with its guidance. That delegation was also a discretionary act.

In *Susla v. State*, 311 Minn. 166, 247 N.W.2d 907 (1976), this court held that the duties of the commissioner of corrections and the warden of the State prison in supervising the prison industries program called for the exercise of judgment and discretion, and therefore the commissioner and the warden were immune from personal liability to an inmate injured by a machine in the prison factory. Peterson's duties supervising Lundquist involved no less discretion than those of the defendants in *Susla*.

[20] Unlike defendants Lundquist and Peterson, the school district was not found to be negligent in Steven's accident. The school district is only liable to plaintiffs under Minn. St. 1971, c. 466.

[1] The trial court did not hold Peterson entitled to discretionary immunity only because it believed this court had foreclosed that option in its earlier decision.

It is the majority view that Peterson's negligence was "not rooted in any policy judgment he made about teaching or developing the physical education curriculum," because Peterson had made no decision at all relevant to developing the curriculum. However, Peterson testified that he chose not to provide more specific direction to Lundquist or Embretson because the instructors were professionals with expertise in physical education, which he lacked.

This court in *Silver v. City of Minneapolis*, 284 Minn. 266, 170 N.W.2d 206 (1969), demonstrated that choosing to take no action can require as much an exercise of discretion as choosing one action over another. In *Silver*, citizens claimed that the city was negligent in failing to provide police and fire protection to their building after it had been requested. The court held that the proper deployment of police and fire protection in the face of impending riots, responding to certain requests but not to others, involved the exercise of the municipality's discretion.

Similarly, Peterson's decision not to request more detailed curriculum plans or to supervise Lundquist more closely was a discretionary decision made on the "planning level of conduct." Therefore, Peterson was immune from liability, and I would reverse on this issue.

Because I would hold Peterson immune from liability, I would not decide whether the jury's verdict of negligence against him should be upheld, whether his liability should be limited to the insurance coverage prescribed by Minn. St. 1971, § 466.04, or whether he is entitled to indemnity from the school district.

OTIS, Justice (dissenting).

In order to assess the conduct of Jack Peterson, it must be kept in mind that he was principal of the entire school, not just of the physical education department. He was required to supervise the development, planning, and administration of the school curriculum, to supervise and evaluate all of the teachers, and generally to maintain conditions conducive to the safety and welfare of all of the students throughout the school day.

The record indicates that Peterson acted responsibly during the transition from Embretson to Lundquist. Both of those teachers were qualified and certified as competent to plan and teach a physical education curriculum. On the other hand, Peterson was not. He required Lundquist to meet with Embretson before Lundquist took over the class and had him report back regarding their discussions. Peterson's performance as a general school administrator is not challenged. He gave both Embretson and Lundquist the Board of Education physical education guide book. He left the details to the experts — the teachers, as an efficient administrator should.

Peterson required and received weekly lesson plans from all of his teachers, including Lundquist. Both before and after the accident, he periodically observed Lundquist's physical education classes.

It is unclear to me what more a principal can be expected to do, particularly when he is not trained or experienced in every course taught in school. If plaintiff had proved that Peterson had some expertise in physical education techniques and that he had notice that his teacher was not conducting tumbling exercises safely, it may well be a jury could find him negligent for not correcting the situation. Such is not the case, however.

Several courts which have considered this issue have refused to hold a school principal liable. In *Luce v. Board of Education of Johnson City,* 2 A.D.2d 502, 157 N.Y.S.2d 123 (1956) the principal was not liable for negligent supervision when an elementary child was injured during a physical education class. The court said:

> "* * * Her duties, too, were administrative, supervisory, and general in nature. She was responsible for the assignment of class rooms, for discipline in the school, and administrative supervision over the teachers in the school. It does not appear that she had any authority, let alone duty, to personally supervise or to direct the nature of activities or limit the participation of any pupil in a physical education class. The physical education department was a separate arm of the Board of Education, operating in all of the schools. Mrs. Denton, the physical education teacher in immediate charge here, was an agent of the physical education department. It is a matter of common knowledge that in modern times the educational and competency requirements of such a teacher are high. Of necessity the detailed activities of each class and of each student therein must be left to such supervising teacher. As observed in *Thompson v. Board of Education,* 280 N.Y. 92, 96, 19 N.E.2d 796, 797: 'Appellant [a principal] could not personally attend to each class at the same time, nor was any such duty imposed upon him.' * * * It does not appear that the principal had the power or authority to direct the detailed conduct of a physical education class, or to substitute her judgment for that of [the teacher]." Id. at 506, 157 N.Y.S.2d at 127.

The *Luce* case was followed and quoted with approval by the Oregon Supreme Court in *Vendrell v. School District No. 26C Malheur County,* 226 Or. 263, 360 P.2d 282 (1961). In that case a student was injured while playing football. The court held that the principal had no duty to supervise "the detailed activities involved in the conduct of the athletic program." Id. at 270, 360 P.2d at 286. Two recent Kentucky cases have also refused to hold the principal liable without a clearer showing of a breach of duty. *Wesley v. Page*, 514 S.W.2d 697 (Ky. 1974); *Cox v. Barnes*, 469 S.W.2d 61 (Ky. 1971).

The impact and effect of the majority's decision may shift much of the responsibility for the safety and welfare of the students from the personnel best suited to handle such problems to an administrator who is not an expert in every area of teaching and cannot be in all places at all times. It would compel principals out of an abundance of caution to impose restrictions and restraints on subordinate teachers which might very well be inappropriate and wholly inconsistent with sound teaching practices. Except in the rare case where the principal is negligent in selecting a teacher or fails to respond to actual notice of a potential hazard I would limit the liability of the principal and impose it where it belongs — on the negligent teacher and on the school board which is vicariously responsible under principles of respondeat superior.

ORDER DENYING PETITON FOR REHEARING

Appellant, defendant principal Jack Peterson, petioning for rehearing, expresses grave concern that the effect of our decision denying the defense of discretionary immunity is "to subject administrators of public schools to liability for almost any conceivable mishap that might happen in the vast number of areas of the school."

[16] This concern is unfounded. Nothing in our opinion should be read to mean that school principals are never protected by the principle of discretionary immunity. The decision in this case is confined to its unique facts and on the narrow ground that, rather than exercising discretion, the appellant principal abdicated his responsibility by not acting at all. We have rejected the contention that he did not abdicate his responsibility and that "instead he delegated it to the experts as any good administrator should do."

The young physical education teacher, in whose gymnastics class the plaintiff pupil was injured, was new to the teaching profession, and he had never been called upon to prepare and implement a lesson plan as a full-time physical education instructor. The teacher was new, too, to plaintiff's class and had no knowledge of what the class had been taught in the past, important to a determination of whether this young pupil was prepared for the obviously hazardous exercise that resulted in paralyzing injury.

It should be noted that evidence from which the jury could find that defendant principal was negligent came from teaching professionals: a former principal, later a superintendent; a university professor of physical education curriculum; and a high school gymnastics coach and director of physical education. It was their testimony that gymnastics is an activity which can be more dangerous than other units of physical education and therefore requires carefully planned instruction; that a new teacher requires more careful supervision in the planning of his curriculum than an experienced teacher; and that a school principal should ensure that there is consultation with the new teacher as to what the class had learned and what it would be learning in the future. A principal, as a responsible school administrator, must exercise reasonable care in the discharge of such specific administrative responsibilities. These functions may not, without more, be entirely delegated by the responsible supervisor to others.

This most regrettable case for both the principal and the pupil prompted careful consideration at the outset and now on the petition for rehearing. Except as the petition makes apparent a misconception as to the scope of our holding, however, it raises no points not fully considered in our main opinion.

The petition accordingly must be and is denied.

GLOSSARY

Adjudication — A judicial action leading to a judgment.

Administrative Law — Rules, regulations and directives issued by the executive branch of government.

Allegation — Statement in pleadings setting forth what the party expects to prove.

Answer — The defendant's written response to the complaint.

Appeal — An application to a higher court to correct or modify the judgment of a lower court.

Appellant — The party that takes an appeal from one court to another. Sometimes called a petitioner.

Appellee — The party against whom an appeal is taken. Often called a respondent.

Assumption of Risk — An affirmative defense in a negligence action; a person who voluntarily exposes himself to a known and obvious danger may not recover for the injury.

Battery — The unprivileged intentional touching of another.

Breach of Contract — Failure, without legal excuse, to perform the obligations and terms of a contract.

Burden of Proof — The duty of proving or disproving facts disputed at trial.

Case Law — Judicial precedent created by court decisions; court or judge made laws.

Cause of Action — A legal right of redress against another, including the right to sue and the right to recover in court.

Certiorari — The name of a writ issued by a superior court such as the Supreme Court, directing a lower court to send up records and proceedings in a case.

Civil Action — A lawsuit instituted to protect a private right, as contrasted with a criminal action that protects the rights of a state.

Claim for Relief — A short statement in the complaint requesting a remedy.

Common Law — The law developed from decisions in American and English courts, not an action of the legislature.

Comparative Negligence — The relative degree of negligence on the part of the plaintiff and defendant, with damages awarded on a basis proportionate to each person's carelessness.

Compensatory Damages — Money awarded equivalent to the actual value of damages or injury.

Complaint — The initial pleading in a civil action filed by the plaintiff. Also called a petition.

Concurrent Jurisdiction — Two courts having the same authority, or joint responsibility.

Contributory Negligence — Conduct on the part of the plaintiff falling below the level required for the plaintiff's personal protection. It must contribute to the plaintiff's injury.

Crime — An act that is a violation of law punishable by the state or nation.

Declaratory Relief — A judgment that declares the rights of the parties or expresses the opinion of the court on a question of law, without ordering any action to be taken.

Decree — Order of the court of equity announcing the legal consequences of the facts found.

Defamation — Anything published or publicly spoken causing injury to person's good name, reputation or character.

Defendant — The party against whom the lawsuit is brought.

Demurrer — A pleading of defendant admitting to the plaintiff's allegation of facts, but asserting the plaintiff's claim fails to state a cause of action.

Deposition — A written record of verbal testimony in the form of questions and answers made before a public officer for use in a lawsuit.

Directed Verdict — A determination made at the direction of the judge in cases where there has been insufficient evidence to meet a party's burden of proof.

Discovery — The process by which opposing parties obtain information in preparation for trial.

Diversity of Citizenship — A case between two parties, each residing or doing business in a different state, or a case between a citizen of the U.S. and an alien.

Duty — A legal obligation.

Federal Question — A case involving an interpretation and application of the United States Constitution, Acts of Congress or treaties.

Foreseeability — An occurrence which a reasonable and prudent person would perceive and anticipate under existing conditions.

Governmental Function — Various activities of a political entity carried out for the protection and benefit of the general public.

Immunity — Freedom from suit.

Indemnify — To compensate one for a loss or to reimburse one for expenses incurred.

Injunction — A court order requiring a person to act or refrain from acting in a certain manner.

In Loco Parentis — Acting as a parent with respect to the care and supervision of a child.

Invitee — A person who goes upon the land or premises of another by express or implied invitation.

Judgment N.O.V. (Non Obestante Veredicto) — A judgment entered by the court for legal reasons that is contrary to verdict rendered by the jury.

Jurisdiction — The authority of the court to hear and decide a lawsuit.

Laches — A doctrine preventing parties from recovering a judgment due to their delay in bringing the lawsuit.

Liability — A legal responsibility, duty or obligation.

Libel — A written defamation of one's character or reputation.

Licensee — A term for a social guest.

Malfeasance — In negligence law it refers to the commission of an illegal act.

Misdeameanor — A lesser crime, punishable by a fine or imprisonment in a city or county jail for less than one year.

Misfeasance — The improper doing of an otherwise proper act; a negligent act.

Moot — An unsettled court decision that is settled by the happening of an event outside the court jurisdiction.

Negligence — Conduct falling below the standard of care required of a reasonable and prudent person in relation to the protection of others.

Nonsuit — Judgment against a plaintiff who is unable to prove a case or neglects to proceed to trial of a case after it has been put in issue.

Plaintiff — Person who brings an action.

Pleadings — Formal paper filed in a court action including plaintiff's complaint and defendant's answer. It shows what is alleged by the plaintiff and admitted or denied by the defendant.

Precedent — A decision considered as an example or authority for an identical or similar case arising under a similar question of law.

Prima Facie Case — A case in which the evidence is so strong that the adverse party can overthrow the evidence only by sufficient rebutting evidence.

Proximate Cause — Something which produces a result, without which, the result could not have occurred.

Ratification — Confirmation of a transaction.

Remand — The action of an appellate court sending a case back to a trial court for further action.

Respondeat Superior — A legal rule that holds an employer liable for the negligent acts and actions of employees.

Respondent — A party against whom a motion is filed in an appellate court.

Sovereign Immunity — A rule of law that a nation, state, or local unit of government cannot be sued without its consent.

Stare Decisis — A court doctrine recognizing the value of prior decisions (precedent) and requiring that courts follow the decision in resolving similar disputes.

Statute of Limitations — Statutes of the federal and state governments setting a maximum time period for the filing of lawsuits.

Statutory Law — Federal and state statutes, executive orders and city ordinances.

Summary Judgment — A decision of a court on the merits of a lawsuit when the pleadings and other documents reveal there is no genuine issue as to any material facts, and the party who sought the judgment is entitled to it as a matter of law.

Tort — Civil wrongs (as opposed to criminal), not arising from a breach of a contract.

Tortfessor — One who commits a tort. Also called a wrongdoer.

Ultra Vires Act — An action of a person which is outside the scope of authority granted by law.

Vicarious Liability — Substituted or indirect responsibility for someone else's actions arising out of a legal responsibility (see respondent superior).

Waiver — An intentional release of a known legal right.

Writ — A written court order or a judicial process.

Index of Cases

Anderson v. Heron Eng. Co. Inc., 86
Attorney General v. Massachusetts Interscholastic Athletic Association, 142

Babitzke v. Silverton Union High School, 161
Baily v. Truby and Myles, 150
Bearman v. University of Notre Dame, 66–67
Bednar v. Nebraska School Activities Association, 138
Behagen v. Intercollegiate Conference of Faculty Representatives, 151
Bellman v. San Francisco High School District, 40
Benitez v. City of New York, 48–49
Bennett v. West Texas State University, 144
Berg v. Merrick, 44–45
Berman v. Philadelphia Board of Education, 49
Bishop v. Colaw, 111
Blair v. Washington State University, 149–150
Board of Education of Hendrick Hudson Central School District v. Rowley, 166–167
Borek v. Schmelcher, 69–70
Bourque v. Duplechin, 65–66
Boyd v. Board of Directors of the McGehee School District, 109–110
Brahatcek v. Millard School District #17, 53
Brenden v. Independent School District, 137–138
Bryan v. Alabama, 158–159

Cannon v. University of Chicago, 136
Carnes v. Tennessee Secondary School Athletic Association, 138
Catania v. The University of Nebraska, 53
Chase v. Shasta Lake Union School District, 56
Clark v. Arizona Interscholastic Association, 141
Clark v. Furch, 43
Clark v. Goshen Sunday Morning Softball League, 36
Clinton v. Nagy, 141
Coleman v. Western Michigan University, 99, 101
Collins v. The Bossier Parish School Board, 54
Colombo v. Sewanhaka Central High School District No. 2, 169
Connick v. Myers, 116–117
Craig v. Boren, 133
Curtis v. Ohio State University, 58–59
Curtis Publishing Co. v. Butts, 93–94

D.R.C. v. State of Alaska, 125
Darrin v. Gould, 139, 141
Dibortolo v. Metropolitan School District of Washington Township, 42
Dillon v. Keatington Racquetball Club, 48
Dixon v. Outboard Marine Corp, 79
Dostert v. Berthold Public School District, 112

Doyle v. Mt. Healthy City School District Board of Education, 115–116, 117
Durkee v. Cooper of Canada Ltd., 80–81

Ehehalt v. Livingston Board of Education, 102

First Overseas Investment Corp. v. Cotton, 59
Flournoy v. McComas, 52
Force v. Pierce City R–VI School, 140–141
Ford v. Bonner County School, 101
Fortin v. Darlington Little League, Inc., 141
Frank v. Orleans Parish School Board, 74–75
Freeman v. Flake, 110

Garrett v. Nissen Corp, 81
Gatti v. World Wide Health Studio of Lake Charles, 59
Gentile v. McGregor Mfg. Co., 80
Gerrity v. Beatty, 49–50
Gertz v. Robert Welch, Inc., 93
Gilpin v. Kansas State High School Activities Association, 138
Givhan v. Western Line Consolidated School District, 116
Gomes v. Rhode Island Interscholastic League, 141–142
Goss v. Lopez, 152
Green v. Orleans Parish School Board, 43–44
Griggas v. Clauson, 64
Grounds v. Tolar Independent School District, 159, 160
Grove City College v. Bell, 144–145

Haas v. South Bend Community School Corp, 138
Hackbart v. Cincinnati Bengals, Inc., 69, 71, 73
Haffer v. Temple University, 142–143
Haffer v. Temple University of the Commonwealth of Higher Education, 143
Hanson v. Kynast, 69–70
Hauter v. Zogarts, 83
Hensley v. Muskin Corp, 79
Hogenson v. Williams, 67
Hollander v. Connecticut Interscholastic Athletic Conference Inc., 137
Hoover v. Meiklejohn, 139–141
Hornyak v. The Pomfret School, 55
Hosaflook v. Nestor, 159–160

Ingraham v. Wright, 74–75

Jackson v. Board of Education, 56

Kabella v. Bouschelle, 65
Kampmeier v. Harris, 169

Kampmeier v. Nyquist, 169
Keyishian v. Board of Regents of University of the State of New York, 113–114
Knapp v. Whitaker, 117
Kobylanski v. Chicago Board of Education, 45
Kuhlmeier v. Hazelwood School District, 118–119

Landers v. School District No. 203, O'Fallon, 46
Lantz v. Ambach, 145–146
Larson v. Independent School District No. 314, Braham, 22–25, 42
Leffel v. Wisconsin Intercollegiate Athletic Association, 140
LeVant v. N.C.A.A., 119
Light et al. v. Ohio University, 58
Long v. Zopp, 111
Lovitt v. Concord School District, 52
Lowman v. Davies, 113
Lueck v. City of Janesville, 41
Lunday v. Vogelmann, 52

Magill v. Avonworth Baseball Conference, 141
Manning v. Grimsley, 66
Marcum v. Dahl, 117
Markowitz v. Arizona Parks Board, 59–60
McKinley v. Slenderella, 47
Mills v. Board of Education of the District of Columbia, 163, 164–165, 171
Montague v. School Board of Thornton Fractional Township North High School District 215, 45–46
Morris v. Michigan State Board of Education, 138
Mularedelis v. Haldane Central School Board, 142

Nabozny v. Barnhill, 69–70, 71, 75
National Organization for Women v. Little League Baseball, Inc., 141
New Jersey v. T.L.O., 120–122
New York Roadrunners Club v. State Division of Human Rights, 170
New York Times Co. v. Sullivan, 92, 114
North Haven v. Bell, 136

O'Connor v. Board of Education of School District 23, 140
O'Dell v. School District of Independence, 46
Oswald v. Township High School District, 69–71
Othen v. Ann Arbor School Board, 144
Ottawa Education Association v. U.S.D. No. 290, 161

Patchogue-Medford Congress of Teachers v. Board of Education, 126
Pedersen v. Joliet Park District, 56
Pell v. Victor J. Andrew High School and A.M.F., Inc., 86–87
Pennsylvania Association for Retarded Children v. Commonwealth of Pennsylvania, 163–164, 165, 171

Petrie v. Illinois High School Association, 142
Pickering v. Board of Education, 114, 115, 117

Rawlings Sporting Goods Co. Inc. v. Daniels, 80
Reed v. Nebraska Athletic Association, 137
Regents of the University of Minnesota v. National Collegiate Athletic Association, 152
Rensing v. Indiana State University Board, 99–101
Ridgeway v. Montana High School Association, 146
Rittacco v. Norwin School District, 138–139
Rodgers v. Georgia Tech Athletic Association, 162
Roe v. Wade, 134
Ross v. Consumers Power Co., 17
Rowley v. Board of Education of the Hendrick Hudson Central School District, Westchester County, 167
Rutter v. Northeastern Beaver County School District, 35–37, 75

Schnepf v. Andrews, 47
Segerman v. Jones, 44–45
Shoemaker v. Handel, 126
Siau v. Rapids Parish School Board, 52–53
Smith v. Board of Education of County of Logan, 159
Smith v. Vernon Parish School Board, 43
Spring Branch Independent School District v. Stamos, 150
State ex. rel. T.L.O., 121
Swager v. Board of Education U.S.D. No. 412, 161
Swanson v. Wabash College, 51–52

Taylor v. Oakland Scavenger Company, 52
Tiemann v. Independent School District #740, 55–56
Tijerina v. Evans, 55
Tinker v. Des Moines School District, 107–108, 110
Tomjanovich v. California Sports Inc., 68

Ulandis v. Kline, 133
Unified School District v. Swanson, 160–161

Verhel v. Independent School District No. 709, 50

Warthen v. Southeast Oklahoma State University, 101–102
Webb v. McCullough, 122–125
Webber v. Yeo, 16
Williams v. Eaton, 108–109
Wright v. Columbia University, 169–70

Yellow Springs Exempted Village School District v. Ohio High School Athletic Association, 144

Zamora v. Pomeroy, 122

Index

Agreements, 156–57; 160, 162; bargaining agreements, 155–156; employment agreements, 158–162. See also Contracts
Appenzeller, Herb, 3
Assault, 63, 67, 75
Assumption of risk, 27, 31, 33–36, 38, 49, 73, 75, 81, 87

Battery, 63, 64–67, 75
Breach of warranty, 77, 81–83, 86, 89
Buckley Amendment, 118

Case analysis, 21–22, 26
Calamari, John D., 155
Comparative negligence, 23, 27, 31–32, 36, 38
Connors, Eugene T., 3
Consent, 33, 34, 36, 73–74, 75
Contracts, 33, 155, 157, 160, 161, 162, 178, 181, 182, 185; breach of, 156; express, 155; implied in fact, 155. See also Agreements
Contributory negligence, 27, 31–32, 38, 49, 53, 81
Courts of Appeals, 11–12

Damages; in defamation, 93; in fraud, in deceit and misrepresentation, 73; in product liability, 89, 90; in torts, 37
Deceit, 71–72, 75; damages in, 73
Defamation, 91–94, 102, 114; damages in, 93; defamation torts, 119
District Courts, 12
Drug testing, 119–120, 125–128. See also First Amendment, Fourth Amendment
Due process, 106, 150–152, 158, 163; procedural, 131, 134–135, 153; substantive, 131, 134, 153

Educational malpractice, 39–45, 46, 53, 61
Employer-employee relationships, 94, 100, 101, 102; independent contractor, 95–98, 102, 158, 182; master-servant, 95, 96, 97–98, 101; principal agent, 96, 97; respondent superior, doctrine of, 94; vicarious liability, 91, 94–95, 102
Equal protection, 131, 132, 163; Fourteenth Amendment Equal Protection Clause, 132–134, 135, 137, 138, 140, 142–145, 153, 180; in grade standards, 150

False imprisonment, 63, 67–68, 75
Federal Courts, 11–13
Federal Tort Claims Act, 15
Feinberg Law, 113–114
First Amendment, 92–93, 105, 106–107, 109–111, 114–120, 128. See also Freedom of speech, freedom of press

Fourteenth Amendment, 105, 106, 109, 111, 117, 122, 123, 131–132, 134–136, 146, 152, 153, 163. See also Equal protection
Fourth Amendment, 105, 120–123, 125, 128. See also Drug testing, search and seizure
Fraud, 71–72, 75
Freedom of press, 118–119, 128
Freedom of speech, 92, 106–107, 109–110, 113, 116, 117; and symbolic protest, 107–110; for teachers and coaches, 113–118. See also First Amendment

Gross negligence, 27, 31, 33, 38

Handicapped, 163, 171, 180; access to education, 164–168, 171; sports participation, 168–170

Immunity, 14, 46; discretionary, 16–17; governmental, 15, 16, 23, 52, 183; ministerial, 16–17; sovereign, 15; immunity statutes, 15–17, 18
In loco parentis, 67, 124
Invitee, 57, 61

Keeton, Robert, 33

Legal duty of care, 27–30, 56–58
Licensee, 57, 61

Misrepresentation, 71–72

Narol, Mel, 93
Necessity, 73, 74, 75
Negligence, 6, 29, 37–39, 52, 61, 65, 68, 73, 77, 89, 91, 171; degrees of, 27, 30–31, 38; elements of, 27; in product liability, 78–81; standards of, 45

O'Hara, Julie Underwood, 168

Perillo, Joseph M., 155
Privileged force, 67, 74–75
Product liability, 6, 77–80, 87–89, 187

Reckless misconduct, 63, 68–70, 73, 75, 94
Risk, 4–5, 28–29, 61, 85–88; risk management, 146, 171, 173–174, 174–187

Search and seizure, 120–124, 126, 128. See also Fourth Amendment
Self-defense, 73, 74, 75
Sex discrimination, 131, 136, 142, 145, 146, 180. See also Title IX of the Education Amendment of 1972
State Courts, 13–14

State Courts of Appeals, 13-14
State Supreme Courts, 13-14
State Trial Courts, 13-14
Strict liability, 6, 77, 80, 81, 84-87, 89-91, 94, 102
Supreme Court, 11-13

Title IX of the Education Amendment of 1972, 131,
    135-136, 143, 144-146, 153
Tort, 14, 173; defamation tort, 119; intentional
    tort, 6, 15, 16, 63-71, 75; tort law, 178-179
Tribe, Laurence H., 133
Turnbull, H. Rutherford, III, 167

Wade, John W., 87
Warranty; express, 81-82; implied, 82-83; of
    merchantability, 81, 89
Wilful, wanton, and reckless misconduct, 27, 31,
    33, 36, 38, 45
Wittenberg, Jeffrey D., 78
Worker's compensation, 91, 99-102